Janne Chr. Schulz und Sven Hermann (Hrsg.)

Hochleistungsrechnen in Baden-Württemberg —
Ausgewählte Aktivitäten im bwGRiD 2012

Beiträge zu Anwenderprojekten und
Infrastruktur im bwGRiD im Jahr 2012

AF239018

Hochleistungsrechnen in Baden-Württemberg — Ausgewählte Aktivitäten im bwGRiD 2012

Beiträge zu Anwenderprojekten
und Infrastruktur im bwGRiD 2012

von
Janne Chr. Schulz
Sven Hermann (Hrsg.)

Impressum

 Scientific
Publishing

Karlsruher Institut für Technologie (KIT)
KIT Scientific Publishing
Straße am Forum 2
D-76131 Karlsruhe

KIT Scientific Publishing is a registered trademark of Karlsruhe
Institute of Technology. Reprint using the book cover is not allowed.

www.ksp.kit.edu

Print on Demand 2014

ISBN 978-3-7315-0196-1
DOI 10.5445/KSP/1000039516

Vorwort

Das bwGRiD, eine einzigartige Kooperation zwischen den Hochschulen des Landes Baden-Württemberg, blickt inzwischen auf eine vierjährige Erfolgsgeschichte zurück. Das Projekt startete im Jahr 2008 an acht Universitäten des Landes Baden-Württemberg, um Wissenschaftlern aller Disziplinenen Ressourcen im Bereich des High Performance Computings effizient und hochverfügbar zur Verfügung zu stellen. Im Vordergrund steht der Aufbau einer dezentralen Grid-Infrastruktur, bei der homogene Parallelrechner-Cluster transparent zu einem Grid-Verbund gekoppelt werden. Das Projekt soll die Machbarkeit und den Nutzen von Grid-Konzepten für die Wissenschaft nachweisen und bisherige Organisations- und Sicherheitsproblematiken überwinden. Die Grid-Struktur ermöglicht eine Spezialisierung der einzelnen Rechenzentren im Anwendungs- und Hardwarebereich, sowie die Entwicklung neuer Cluster- und Softwarewerkzeuge. Das bwGRiD wurde darüberhinaus Bestandteil der bundesweiten D-Grid-Initative.

Das Bundesministerium für Bildung und Forschung (BMBF) und das Ministerium für Wissenschaft, Forschung und Kunst in Stuttgart haben zur Realisierung insgesamt über 5 Mio. Euro bereitgestellt, die sowohl in den Aufbau der Hardware-Infrastruktur als auch in die Betreuung des Grids fliessen. In Bezug auf die Form der Zusammenarbeit der Hochschulrechenzentren und im Vergleich zu ähnlichen Strukturen in anderen Bundesländern ist diese Infrastruktur einzigartig. Die bwGRiD-Nutzer finden seit Mitte 2010 an allen acht bwGRiD Cluster-Standorten eine Einheitsumgebung vor, die es ihnen ermöglicht, mit ihren Anwendungen problemlos von einem Standort zu einem anderen zu wechseln, ohne das die Programme neu konfiguriert oder eingerichtet werden müssen. Auf diese Weise werden die großen Rechenressourcen optimal genutzt.

Das bwGRiD bietet seinen Nutzern mit täglich insgesamt über 340 Tausend CPUh eine große Rechenkapazität an, die weit über das an einem Universitätsrechenzentrum üblicherweise verfügbare Maß hinaus geht. Zudem entstand durch Profilbildung bei der Auswahl der unterstützten Software eine landesweite Kooperation bei der Nutzerunterstützung.

Durch eine Erweiterung des Projektes im vergangenen Jahr mit den sogenannten "ergänzenden Maßnahmen" für den Zeitraum von Juli 2011 bis Ende Juni 2013 sollen die Weichen für die Zukunft des bwGRiDs gestellt werden: Die standortunabhängige Nutzung soll weiter verbessert, der Zugriff weiter erleichtert und der Kreis der Nutzer sowie die zugehörige Betreuung ausgeweitet werden. Die "ergänzenden Maßnahmen" bieten gleichzeitig die Grundlage für zukünftige HPC-Entwicklungen im Lande.

Das Projekt kann als eine Antwort auf die Erkenntnis verstanden werden, dass die heutigen Anforderungen in der Wissenschaft, sowohl bezogen auf die angeforderte Rechenkapazität, die Flexibilität der Bereitstellung oder die Vielfalt der untersuchten Problemstellungen und hierfür eingesetzten Software, als auch die breite Nutzerunterstützung und die standortübergreifende Benutzerverwaltung, nicht mehr von einem einzelnen Universitätsrechenzentrum gelöst werden können. Tendenzen im kommerziellen Umfeld wie das Cloud-Computing und die Konzentration bestimmter Standardservices zeigen, dass nur durch Konzentration und Spezialisierung die notwendigen Kapazitäten für ein breites Angebot geschaffen werden können.

Durch die nun über vierjährige Zusammenarbeit der Rechenzentren im Lande hat sich eine neue Kooperationskultur herausgebildet, die sich in anderen gemeinsamen Projekten manifestiert. Das Projekt bwIDM beschäftigt sich mit den Grundlagen eines landesweiten Identity Managements, welches nicht nur für die heutigen bwGRiD-Strukturen sondern auch für andere gemeinsame Landesdienste und zukünftige HPC-Projekte eine zentrale Rolle spielt. Mit dem Projekt bwFLA werden Überlegungen und Konzepte für einen langfristigen Zugriff auf digitale Daten und Umgebungen, wie sie auch im Forschungsdatenmanagement benötigt werden, entwickelt und realisiert. Nicht zuletzt manifestiert sich das bwGRiD und die etablierte Kooperation der Rechenzentren in den Konzepten für die nächste Generation des High Performance Computings im Lande indem die Erfahrungen des bwGRiD Projektes genutzt und auf Basis der erfolgreich kooperierenden Arbeitsgruppen neue Ansätze verfolgt werden.

Der 8. bwGRiD/BFG Workshop in Freiburg bot die Chance, einen breiten Überblick sowohl zum technischen und organisatorischen Stand des Projektes zu verschaffen, Anwender und Administratoren gleichsam zu Wort kommen zu lassen und den Austausch zwischen den Anwender–Communities zu fördern. Zudem erlaubte der Workshop nach vier Jahren Projektlaufzeit ein Zwischenfazit des Erreichten zu ziehen und mögliche zukünftige Entwicklungen zu diskutieren. Mit diesem Hintergedanken erfolgte die Auswahl der eingeladenen und aus einem Call-for-Papers hervorgegangenen Beiträge, die den Peer-Review Prozess erfolgreich überstanden haben. Aus diesen Beiträgen konnte ein breites Programm zusammengestellt werden, welches in der Keynote auf die Vorgeschichte des bwGRiDs einging, eine Reihe spannender Anwendungen des HPC vorstellte und verschiedene administrative Fragestellungen diskutierte.

Die Veranstalter möchten sich bei den Autoren für die eingereichten Beiträge, bei dem Programmkommitee für die Auswahl und bei den Organisatoren für die Durchführung des Workshops ganz herzlich bedanken. Nicht alle eingereichten Beiträge konnten für das Vortragsprogramm oder den hier vorliegenden Sammelband wegen des begrenzten Zeit- oder Platzumfangs vorgesehen werden. Der vorliegende Band verfolgt einen dreiteiligen Aufbau.

Der erste Teil ist der Geschichte und dem aktuellen Status des bwGRiDs gewidmet. Dazu kommen einerseits das Ministerium durch ein Geleitwort und andererseits einer der Väter des Projekts zur "Geburt des bwGRiD" zu Wort. Der gemeinsame Beitrag von Mitarbeitern des bwGRiDs mit einer Bestandsaufnahme rundet den ersten Teil ab.

Im zweiten Teil kommen die bwGRiD-Anwender zu Wort, die beeindruckende Projekte aus den unterschiedlichsten Disziplinen präsentieren. Die Autoren Karsten Fischer et al. präsentieren Ergebnisse aus der geomechanischen Forschung während die Autoren Vincent Heuveline et al. Methoden für die Berechnung von Flüssigkeiten im 3D-Raum untersuchen. Einen aktuellen Einblick in die Forschung und in die Anwendung von Computer-Clustern im Bereich der Linguistik bietet der Beitrag von Ulrike Schneider

und die Autoren Jan P. Meier-Kolthoff et al. stellen einen Ansatz zur effizienten Verarbeitung von Genomdaten auf dem bwGRiD vor.
Der dritte, mit "Administration" überschriebene Teil, ist eher technisch orientiert und befasst sich mit verschiedenen Aspekten des HPC-Betriebs, die von Fragen des effektiven Deployments bis hin zu Herausforderungen bei der richtigen Wahl der Netzwerkschnittstellen und Dateisysteme liegen.

Abschließend kann festgehalten werden, dass das bwGRiD zu einem wertvollen, nützlichen und unverzichtbaren Werkzeug für viele Forscherinnen und Forscher geworden ist, wie die Vielfalt der in diesem Sammelband vorliegenden Beiträge und wie der dreitägige bwGRiD/BFG Workshop in Freiburg zeigen.

Sven Herrman und Gerhard Schneider
Freiburg, den 25. Mai 2012

Inhaltsverzeichnis

Vorwort   I

WOLFGANG PETERS
Vom "Verschmierten Rechenzentrum" zur "Private Cloud"   1

PETER CASTELLAZ
IT-Infrastruktur in einem dynamischen Umfeld - Geleitwort zum Workshop   7

MAREK DYNOWSKI, MICHAEL JANCZYK, TOBIAS KIENZLE, MATTHIAS
LANDWEHR, REINHARD MAYER, ADRIAN REBER, NICO STRUCKMANN,
SABINE RICHLING, JANNE CHR. SCHULZ, SVEN HERMANN
Das bwGRiD heute – Eine erfolgreiche föderative HPC-Forschungsumgebung   17

Anwenderprojekte

KARSTEN FISCHER, ANDREAS HENK
Geomechanical Reservoir Modeling - a geological application of high performance computing   41

VINCENT HEUVELINE, EVE KETELAER, STAFFAN RONNAS, MAREIKE
SCHMIDTOBREICK, MARTIN WLOTZKA
Scalability Study of HiFlow^3 based on a Fluid Flow Channel Benchmark .   53

ULRIKE SCHNEIDER
CART Trees and Random Forests in Linguistics   67

JAN P. MEIER-KOLTHOFF, ALEXANDER F. AUCH, HANS-PETER KLENK, MARKUS GÖKER
GBDP on the grid: a genome-based approach for species delimitation adjusted for an automated and highly parallel processing of large data sets . . 83

Infrastruktur

ISGANDAR VALIZADA, KLAUS RECHERT, DIRK VON SUCHODOLETZ
Emulation-as-a-Service – Requirements and Design of Scalable Emulation Services for Digital Preservation 103

DIRK VON SUCHODOLETZ
Infiniband for Highspeed IP Networking 117

DIRK VON SUCHODOLETZ, ONUR CELEBIOGLU, GARIMA KOCHHAR
Benefits and Limitations of Highspeed Machine Interconnects 135

RICHARD ZAHORANSKY, SAHER SEMAAN
bwIDM: Anbindung nicht-webbasierter IT-Infrastrukturen an eine SAML/ Shibboleth-Föderation 161

CHRISTIAN MOSCH, BASTIAN BOEGEL, HELMUT LANG
Das bwGRiD Wissenschaftsportal 177

SEBASTIAN SCHMELZER, DIRK VON SUCHODOLETZ, MICHAEL JANCZYK, GERHARD SCHNEIDER
Flexible Cluster Node Provisioning in a Distributed Environment 203

KONRAD MEIER, SEBASTIAN SCHMELZER, DIRK VON SUCHODOLETZ
Evaluation of Network Bonding Performance in Client/Server Scenarios . . 221

Vom „Verschmierten Rechenzentrum" zur „Private Cloud"

Wolfgang Peters

Ministerium für Wissenschaft, Forschung und
Kunst Baden-Württemberg (a.D.)

Motivation – wissenschaftliches Rechnen in Deutschland

Bereits der EDV-Gesamtplan III von 1989 postulierte als eine der Forderungen an die IT in Forschung und Lehre die Steigerung des Technologietransfers zwischen Hochschulen und Wirtschaft zur Verbesserung der volkswirtschaftlichen Leistungsfähigkeit. Konsequenterweise stand dies besonders beim Einsatz der Höchstleistungsrechner immer im Blickpunkt und war 1996 eine Motivation zur Gründung der hww, der Höchstleistungsrechnerbetriebsgesellschaft für Wissenschaft und Wirtschaft. Die Betriebsgesellschaft wandelt sich aktuell zu einer Vermarktungsgesellschaft, was den Charakter des Technologietransfers eher noch betont. Dabei geht es weniger um das große Geldverdienen (die Kosten für das Land reduzieren sich gerade mal im einstelligen Prozentbereich) als vielmehr darum, in unserer Wirtschaft möglichst frühzeitig die neuesten Computertechnologien einzusetzen und damit zu deren Konkurrenzfähigkeit beizutragen. Eine ähnliche Vorstellung: Damals bei der Planung zu BW-Grid war es meine Absicht, durch die IT die Wissenschaft im Land voranzubringen, zumal durch die regionale Aufstellung der Cluster eine Affinität zur der jeweiligen Wirtschaftsregion gegeben war.

Ich war und bin überzeugt davon, dass zum Beispiel die Simulation technischer, naturwissenschaftlicher oder auch biologischer Vorgänge auf Rechnern enorme Vorteile gegenüber dem wissenschaftlichen Experiment haben kann. Anfang des neuen Jahrtausends habe ich diese Überzeugung in meinem Ministerium gegen die sich verbreitende Skepsis gegenüber neuen Höchstleistungsrechner bzw. einen Investitionsbedarf von damals ca. 35 Millionen Euro alle fünf Jahre vertreten. Grundsätzlich ist es zwar richtig, dass Computerleistung ca. alle fünf Jahre um den Faktor zehn billiger wird. Die Frage ist nur, ob die wissenschaftlichen Fragestellungen bis dahin nicht bereits von anderen auf der Welt gelöst wurden. Für den Wissenschaftsstandort Baden-Württemberg war und ist die Investition in die leistungsfähigsten Rechner daher unverzichtbar. Andererseits hilft auch die neueste Hardware nicht viel, wenn der Nutzer sein wissenschaftliches Modell erst fertig hat, wenn der Rechner bereits wieder veraltet ist. Neben der Investition in Hardware war es daher auch notwendig, die Nutzerinnen und Nutzer bzw. deren Projekte fit für den Rechner zu machen. Eine zentrale Rolle in diesem Kontext sollte BW-Grid einnehmen.

Das BW-Grid oder vom „Verschmierten Rechenzentrum" zur „Private Cloud"

BW-Grid1 war der Versuch, die Rechenzentren der Universitäten in Baden-Württemberg zur Zusammenarbeit zu verpflichten. Durch Arbeitsteilung bzw. weniger Doppelarbeit sollten sie in die Lage versetzt werden, insgesamt den Beratungs- und Benutzerservice gegenüber den wissenschaftlichen Nutzerinnen und Nutzern zu verbessern. Es war in gewissem Sinne ein trojanisches Pferd zum Wohle von Forschung und Lehre in Baden-Württemberg. Möchte man die Geschichte von BW-Grid verstehen, muss man eine ganze Reihe von Jahren zurückgehen.

BELWUE

Vor ziemlich genau 25 Jahren, am 1. Juni 1987, wurde das Baden Extended Lan Wuerttemberg (BELWUE) ins Leben gerufen. An diesem Tag hatte die Landesregierung beschlossen, Mittel für das neuartige Netz zur Verfügung zu stellen. BELWUE – auch „schöne Aussicht" – war nicht nur eine Buchstabenkreation von Paul Christ und eine technische Meisterleistung, sondern auch ein politisches Glanzstück. Es gelang nämlich, BELWUE gegen den OSI-Standard, für den sich das Bundesforschungsministerium mit dem

DFN stark gemacht hatte, und gegen den Quasi-Standard von IBM-SNA, den die Landesregierung für das Landessystemkonzept gewählt hatte, zu etablieren. Aus heutiger Sicht ist dies kaum noch nachvollziehbar, denn niemand würde auf die Idee kommen, etwas anderes als das IP-Protokoll für ein solches Netz zu verwenden. Auch die damalige Übertragungsleistung von 64 Kbit/s erscheint heute kurios. Ende der Achtziger aber war das das Maximum des technisch Machbaren, ebenso wie das finanzielle Volumen von umgerechnet ca. 2 Millionen Euro pro Jahr. Der Leiter eines großen Uni-Rechenzentrums in Niedersachsen hielt 64 Kbit/s zur damaligen Zeit sogar für die Obergrenze dessen, was die Universitäten jemals benötigen würden. Ende 1988 waren alle neun Universitäten an BELWUE angeschlossen, was Hans-Günter Schirdewahn zu folgendem Ausspruch veranlasste: „Mit BELWUE haben wir die Voraussetzungen für ein verschmiertes Universitätsrechenzentrum in Baden-Württemberg geschaffen." Die Idee eines verteilten Rechenzentrums existierte also schon damals, vor 25 Jahren. Allerdings mit einer etwas anderen Zielrichtung, verständlich, wenn man sich die Rechnerlandschaft der damaligen Zeit anschaut.

Die Rechnerlandschaft Ende der Achtziger

Mein Desktop-PC – Marke Eigenbau – hat eine Leistung von knapp 10.000 MIPS, einen Hauptspeicher von acht Gigabytes und zusammen rund 1.000 Gigabytes Festplattenspeicher. Die Leistung aller Universalrechnersysteme der neun Universitäten betrug Ende der Achtziger 112 (in Worten: einhundertzwölf) MIPS und 180 GByte Festplattenspeicher. Selbst die CRAY2, die wegen ihres großen Hauptspeichers berühmt war, hatte gerade mal ein Viertel meines Speicherausbaus. Mein PC hätte zur damaligen Zeit also locker das ganze Land versorgen können. Er hat mich deutlich unter 1.000 Euro gekostet; die Investitionssumme der damaligen Universalrechner im Land betrug knapp 80 Millionen DM oder 40 Millionen Euro. Die älteste in Betrieb befindliche Anlage war 1988 die Univac 1108 in Freiburg, mit elf Betriebsjahren ein wahrer Methusalem. Der Nachfolger, eine IBM 3090 mit einem Kaufpreis von knapp 5 Millionen Euro war bereits installiert. Zu diesem Zeitpunkt waren fünf der neun Rechenzentren VM-Installationen, nur die kleinen Unis hatten noch Exoten, wie das BS2000 in Mannheim oder das VME (ICL) in Hohenheim. Trotzdem hätte zumindest der Rechnerumzug von Heidelberg nach Stuttgart Anfang der Neunziger vermieden werden können - falls das mit dem verschmierten Rechenzentrum geklappt hätte. Aber auch so sind die blauen Riesen ausgestorben.

Ziel des „verschmierten" Rechenzentrums war es, einen Lastverbund aufzubauen sowie einen Funktionsverbund dahingehend zu etablieren, den Betriebssystemwechsel für den Nutzer leichter verkraftbar zu machen.

Die Rechnerlandschaft hat sich natürlich in den letzten Jahren deutlich gewandelt. Gleich geblieben ist allerdings der Aufwand zur Beschaffung: Bis heute machen sich in neuen Rechenzentren alle paar Jahre ein paar Spezialisten auf den aufwändigen und steinigen Weg, eine europäische Ausschreibung für einen neuen Rechner zu formulieren. Hierbei muss zunächst der künftige Bedarf beim Nutzer abgefragt werden, den dieser – wie ein Blick in die Umfrageergebnisse gezeigt hat – meist selbst kaum abschätzen konnte und kann.

Arbeitskreis der Leiter der Universitätsrechenzentren in Baden-Württemberg

Ohne den Arbeitskreis der Leiter der Universitätsrechenzentren in Baden-Württemberg (ALWR) hätte es BW-Grid – wie viele andere Projekte – vermutlich nie gegeben. Die Rechenzentrumsleiter waren für mich das wichtigste Forum, Ideen zu präsentieren, zu diskutieren, zu verfeinern, sie ggf. zu verwerfen oder umzusetzen. Mit dem Konzept der Universitäten Stuttgart und Ulm für ein gemeinsames UNIX-Cluster zur allgemeinen IT-Versorgung der wissenschaftlichen Nutzer in Stuttgart und Ulm konnten wir einen ersten Durchbruch in Richtung „verschmiertes Rechenzentrum" schaffen und damit sicherlich einen Vorläufer von BW-Grid. Sehr positiv war zudem, dass der Aufwand für die Ausschreibungen an dieser Stelle halbiert werden konnte. Das Projekt BW-Grid konnte ebenfalls umgesetzt werden, auch wenn einige RZ-Leiter zunächst sehr skeptisch waren und in der Endphase der Projektkonkretisierung die Diskussion teilweise hektisch geführt wurde. Letzteres war allerdings eher dem Zeitdruck geschuldet, den die vom Kollegen Resch plötzlich aufgetane Geldquelle – Restmittel aus dem D-Grid-Fördermitteltopf des BMBFT – mit sich brachte. Wir hätten BW-

Grid, wie zunächst geplant, auch ausschließlich aus Landesmitteln finanzieren können, aber dann wäre es für andere Projekte wie z. B. das Landes-Storage-Programm, die Subvention des BW-PC oder die Begleitprojekte zu BW-Grid eng geworden.

Bruch in der Versorgungspyramide

Vor vielen Jahren prägte die DFG-Kommission für IT-Infrastruktur (DFG-KfR) den Begriff der Versorgungspyramide: Auf der unteren Ebene stehen die Institutsrechner, darüber die entsprechend leistungsfähigeren Universalrechner der Rechenzentren. Reicht die Leistungsfähigkeit dieser Rechner nicht mehr aus, stehen als nächstes die vom Wissenschaftsrat so genannten Hochleistungsrechner bereit – in Baden-Württemberg der Landeshöchstleistungsrechner – und auf der höchsten Stufe die eigentlichen Höchstleistungsrechner (laut Wissenschaftsrat Rechner mit einem Kaufpreis über 35 Millionen DM – soweit ich weiß, wurde dies nie in Euro umgerechnet). In jüngster Zeit ist diese Pyramide noch um den PETA-Scale-Rechner im Gauß-Center for Supercomputing erweitert worden, den schnellsten Computer in Deutschland.

Zwischen den lokalen Rechenzentrumsrechnern und den Hoch- oder Höchstleistungsrechnern bestand (und besteht nach meiner Beobachtung leider immer noch) ein Bruch. Die durch die Versorgungspyramide suggerierte Durchgängigkeit von einem Level auf den nächsten existiert nämlich nicht wirklich. Immerhin findet der Nutzer auf jeder Ebene mittlerweile als Betriebssystem ein UNIX-Derivat, aber damit hören die Gemeinsamkeiten bereits auf. Meine Vorstellung ist, dass der Nutzer seine Modelle auf einem BW-Grid-Cluster entwirft und testet und dann ohne Systembruch, ohne neue Nutzer-ID, ohne Umprogrammierung etc. sein Projekt auf dem nächst leistungsfähigeren Rechner zum Ablauf bringen kann. Das setzt voraus, dass neben einem einheitlichen Betriebskonzept eine einheitliche Nutzerverwaltung, ein durchgängiges Sicherheitskonzept sowie ein landesweiter (ortsunabhängiger) Fileservice vorhanden sind. Dies sollte zumindest mittelfristig nicht nur auf den BW-Grid-Clustern, sondern in gleicher Weise nach oben auf den Landes- bzw. Bundeshöchstleistungsrechnern verfügbar werden. Und wenn wir dies alles über eine einzige Web-Portalschnittstelle anbieten und gleichzeitig die wissenschaftlichen Nutzer individuell unterstützen können, dann müsste dies meiner Meinung nach zwangsläufig zu einer Effizienzsteigerung in der Wissenschaft führen.

Nachklapp oder die Zukunft des verschmierten Rechenzentrums

Bereits in den 1990er Jahren hat Professor Rühle prophezeit, dass irgendwann einmal Compute-Power wie Strom aus der Steckdose kommen wird. Ich habe das Gefühl, dass mit den Cloud-Modellen von Amazon u. a. der Zeitpunkt nicht mehr weit weg ist. BW-Grid II wird exakt hiermit konkurrieren. Und auch wenn es niemand hören möchte: Es wird eine Private Cloud sein. Wenn wir (vielleicht noch mehr als bisher) unsere Personalkapazitäten bündeln und uns nicht vor Ort verzetteln, werden wir die kommerzielle Konkurrenz nicht fürchten müssen. Der Schlüssel zum Erfolg werden hierbei die Durchgängigkeit der Hardwarelösung, die Verfügbarkeit möglichst vieler Softwarepakete, die einfache Gestaltung des Zugangs sowie die individuelle Nutzerberatung sein. Die großen technischen Softwarepakete kosten bereits heute um den Faktor 10 mehr als die reine CPU-Power. Wenige Cent für eine Stunde CPU-Zeit in einer Cloud werden sich die großen Institute locker leisten können; sie werden es aber nicht tun, solange der Service der eigenen Rechenzentren stimmt. Dabei ist durchaus überlegenswert, auch solche kommerziellen Cloud-Lösungen mit im Web-Portal des BW-Grid anzubieten.

IT-Infrastruktur in einem dynamischen Umfeld – Geleitwort zum Workshop

Peter Castellaz

Ministerium für Wissenschaft, Forschung und
Kunst Baden-Württemberg

Die Wissenschaft hat in den letzten beiden Dekaden erhebliche Umbrüche hinsichtlich ihrer Arbeitsweise erlebt. Arbeitsmethoden und Arbeitsmittel waren einem teils dramatischen Wandel unterworfen. Neue, IT-gestützte Arbeitswerkzeuge haben mittlerweile in allen Wissenschaftsdisziplinen Einzug gehalten. Der Zugriff auf Forschungsdaten und die Fähigkeit, diese zeitnah zu analysieren, hat eine immense Bedeutung erhalten und die Art und Weise, wie geforscht und gelehrt wird, nachhaltig verändert.

In diesem Umfeld kommt der IT-Infrastruktur in den Hochschulen eine entscheidende Bedeutung als Basisinfrastruktur für die Wissenschaft zu. Der Wissenschaftler an seinem Arbeitsplatz steckt üblicherweise den (Strom-) Netzstecker in die Steckdose und den (Daten-) Netzstecker in die Ethernet-Buchse und erwartet, dass alles weitere reibungslos funktioniert. Und dies muss er auch erwarten dürfen – zumindest wenn die Hochschulen ihrem Anspruch auf Exzellenz in der Wissenschaft gerecht werden wollen. Die hinter dieser Ethernet-Buchse ablaufenden Workflows und Prozesse sind mittlerweile so komplex geworden, dass nur noch leistungsfähige, dienstleistungsorientierte Rechenzentren in Kooperation mit den wissenschaftlichen Bibliotheken die dafür notwendigen Dienste erbringen können. Die Rechenzentren sind dabei strategische Partner für Forschung und Lehre und bilden mit den Bibliotheken zunehmend gut koordinierte Informationszentren.

Neben Experiment und Theorie ist die dritte Säule der Wissenschaft Modellierung und Simulation oder neudeutsch Computational Science and Engineering (CSE), die in allen Phasen des wissenschaftlichen Arbeitsprozesses bis hin zur Publikation der Ergebnisse und der langfristigen Sicherung der Nachnutzung von Daten und Ergebnissen auf eine leistungsfähige IT- und Informationsinfrastruktur angewiesen ist. Insbesondere Computational Science and Engineering gewinnt für eine zunehmende Zahl von Wissenschaftsbereichen an Bedeutung, wie dies auch im jüngst veröffentlichten Positionspapier des Wissenschaftsrates zum Hoch- und Höchstleistungsrechnen festgestellt wird.

Dabei ist ein interessanter Widerspruch zwischen Bedeutung und Sichtbarkeit entstanden. Die Herausforderungen wachsen stetig – hier seien nur die Schlagworte Virtuelle Forschungsumgebungen, Forschungsdatenmanagement und datengetriebene Forschung erwähnt. Das Veränderungstempo gerade bei IT in der Wissenschaft wird künftig tendenziell eher zunehmen. Dies wird die Bedeutung und die Komplexität der notwendigen IT-Dienstleistungen erhöhen, zugleich aber hohe Anforderungen an eine für den Nutzer transparente, einfache Nutzbarkeit stellen. Die Kosten für IT-Infrastruktur und Informationsinfrastruktur werden sich also tendenziell erhöhen.

Gleichzeitig ist zu beobachten, dass die Leistungen der Rechenzentren und Bibliotheken in diesem Umfeld bei weitem nicht so deutlich wahrgenommen werden, wie sie es verdienen. Die Folge: Budgets in den Hochschulen (und, es sei zugegeben, auch im Wissenschaftsministerium) stagnieren oder werden gekürzt. Ein Grund dafür mag sein, dass „an der Basis" möglicherweise nur eine geringe Bereitschaft besteht, für eine funktionierende Basisinfrastruktur Geld bereitzustellen – sie ist notwendig, aber nicht „sexy" genug. Ich halte dies zwar für einen strategischen Fehler, denn dadurch entstehen immer wieder kostspielige Reibungsverluste in den Hochschulen, muss aber fairerweise zugeben, dass angesichts knapper Kassen in den nächsten Jahren steigende Budgets kaum durchsetzbar sein werden.

Doch nicht nur die Anforderungen von innen wachsen, auch von außen stehen die Rechenzentren zunehmend unter Druck und müssen um ihre „Kunden", die Wissenschaftler, kämpfen. In der Folge der Internetrevolution und der Web 2.0–Aktivitäten sind eine Reihe von technischen Möglichkeiten entstanden, die derzeit im Hype um „die Cloud" gipfeln und für Wissenschaftler eine erhebliche Anziehungskraft entfalten. Ein aktuelles Beispiel kann dies illustrieren: Gelockt durch zunächst kostenlosen Speicherplatz haben viele Wissenschaftler den Weg zu „Dropbox-artigen" Angeboten gefunden. Der Charme solcher Lösungen liegt in der Kombination aus Online-Speicher und Synchronisierungstool und deren einfacher Handhabung auf allen Endgeräten, also insbesondere auch auf den mobilen Endgeräten wie Tablets und Smartphones. Zwei an sich getrennte Dienste, geschickt kombiniert, erzeugen einen sehr attraktiven Mehrwert. Mancher Wissenschaftler mag sich kurz die Frage stellen „Warum kann mein Unirechenzentrum das nicht?", bevor er flugs zur kommerziellen Konkurrenz „abwandert". Dies ist nur ein Beispiel für die strategische Bedrohung für den Stellenwert und die künftige Rolle der Rechenzentren, der sich diese unbedingt stellen müssen. Das Thema Virtualisierung ist bereits in den Hochschulen angekommen, die Zukunft liegt jedoch in noch viel weiter reichenden Konzepten wie Compute Clouds, Storage Clouds und Service Clouds – geschickt kombiniert zu Community Clouds, die die spezifischen Bedürfnisse von Gruppen von Wissenschaftlern adressieren und erfüllen. Eine diensteorientierte Sichtweise wird hier notwendig sein, um die Herausforderungen der Zukunft angemessen bewältigen zu können. Wichtige Aspekte werden die bruchfreie Anbindung von mobilen Endgeräten sowie die Kombination von Compute-Diensten, Speicherdiensten und Netzdiensten sein. Kein Rechenzentrum kann alle diese Herausforderungen alleine meistern.

Ein Ausweg aus dieser Lage ist Kooperation. Bereits seit vielen Jahren kooperieren Rechenzentren der Hochschulen erfolgreich miteinander. Die Landesrektorenkonferenz der Universitäten hat Weitblick bewiesen, als sie 1981 den Arbeitskreis der Leiter der Wissenschaftlichen Rechenzentren der Universitäten, kurz ALWR, als ständiges LRK-Gremium einrichtete. Der Fachreferent im Wissenschaftsministerium genießt ständiges Gastrecht in diesem Gremium, was den unmittelbaren Dialog über strategische Fragen zwischen Rechenzentren und Ministerium erleichtert. Dadurch können neue Entwicklungen schnell analysiert, aufgegriffen und in konsistentes Förderhandeln des Landes umgesetzt werden. Diese Abstimmung ermöglicht es auch, sich rasch über arbeitsteiliges, gemeinsames Vorgehen bei wichtigen Fragen der Weiterentwicklung der IT-Infrastruktur in den Universitäten zu verständigen. Ich darf an dieser Stelle sagen, dass ich es als Privileg empfinde, mit diesem Kreis zusammenzuarbeiten. Auch die Rechenzentrumsleiter der Hochschulen für angewandte Wissenschaften haben einen Arbeitskreis, in dem über gemeinsame Aufgaben und Anliegen diskutiert wird.

Auch auf Arbeitsebene finden vielfältige Kooperationen zwischen den Rechenzentren statt, ein wichtiges Beispiel ist der bwGRiD-Verbund. Hier wurde bereits früh eine Kooperationsstruktur geschaffen, die es ermöglicht hat, Infrastrukturbeschaffungen mit der arbeitsteiligen Entwicklung von Diensten für das ganze Land zu koppeln.

bwGRiD: Herausforderungen und zukünftige Entwicklung

Eine intensive Kooperation ist gerade im Bereich des Computational Science and Engineering (CSE) unabdingbar. Der Wissenschaftsrat hat in seinem Positionspapier festgestellt, dass CSE sich immer stärker auch als eigenständiges Forschungs– und Fachgebiet etabliert, er spricht in diesem Zusammenhang sogar von einem Paradigmenwechsel. Wissenschaftsbereiche mit stark datengetriebener Forschung verschränken Datenanalyse und Theoriebildung immer enger miteinander. Simulationsmodelle werden in immer mehr Wissenschaftsbereichen immer wichtiger und erschließen sich neue Anwendungsfelder. Insbesondere in den Natur- und Ingenieurwissenschaften basieren Forschungs– und Entwicklungsergebnisse immer stärker auf Modellierung, Simulation und Optimierung; dies wurde auch vom ALWR in seinem Positionspapier zur IT-Infrastruktur in den Universitäten aus dem Jahr 2010 so gesehen. Simulationen und aufwändige Forschungsexperimente erzeugen extrem große Datenbestände, die entsprechende Umgebungen für die Analyse, Aufbereitung und Weiterverarbeitung der Daten benötigen. Dies hat Rückwirkungen auf die benötigte Infrastruktur.

Auch volkswirtschaftlich gesehen ist es unbestritten, das CSE und High Performance Computing (HPC) als Schlüsseltechnologien anzusehen sind, die ein wesentlicher Faktor für die Zukunftsfähigkeit der deutschen Wissenschaft sind. Auch die Wirschaft setzt zunehmend Simulationsmethoden ein zur Verbesserung von Produkten und Dienstleistungen. Die Verfügbarkeit von HPC-Infrastrukturen ist deshalb für die Wettbewerbsfähigkeit Deutschlands unverzichtbar, dies gilt für Baden-Württemberg als stark technologie- und exportorientiertes Bundesland in besonderem Maße und hat sich in der HPC-Landesstrategie entsprechend niedergeschlagen.

Von der Nutzung her unterscheidet der Wissenschaftsrat drei Arten der Nutzung von HPC-Ressourcen: Unter Capability Computing wird das Rechnen einzelner komplexer Probleme oder Modelle verstanden, die in der Regel gut parallelisierbar sind. Hierfür werden Rechnersysteme der obersten Leistungsklasse benötigt. Als Capacity Computing wird das gleichzeitige Rechnen vieler Probleme, Modelle oder Modellparameter bezeichnet. Hierfür werden leistungsfähige Rechnersysteme mit hohem Durchsatz benötigt. Das Real-Time Computing schließlich zeichnet sich durch Interaktivität aus und spielt z. B. im Bereich von Visualisierungen eine zunehmende Rolle. Hierfür wird spezielle Hard- und Software benötigt, die die hohen Anforderungen an Echtzeitanwendungen bedienen kann.

Der Wissenschaftsrat kommt in seinem Positionspapier zu einigen sehr wichtigen Schlussfolgerungen und Empfehlungen. So stellt er ausdrücklich fest, dass sich die aus verschiedenen Rechenleistungsstufen bestehende sogenannte Versorgungspyramide bewährt hat. Auf den einzelnen Rechenleistungsstufen solle es jeweils mehrere, sich in Rechnerarchitektur und Methodenkompetenz gegenseitig ergänzende Zentren geben. Rechenkapazität und Methodenkompetenz sollen gleichwertig stark entwickelt und bei steigendem Bedarf ausgebaut werden. Die Ressourcen sollen durch HPC-Kompetenzzentren bereit gestellt werden, die sich durch eine enge Integration von leistungsfähigen Rechnerinfrastrukturen, Methodenkompetenz, Anwenderberatung sowie universitäre Forschung und Lehre auszeichnen.

Die unterschiedlichen Leistungsklassen erfüllen dabei unterschiedlich geartete Versorgungsaufträge. Der sogenannte Tier 3 umfasst die Bereitstellung von Rechenleistung für Einzelwissenschaftlerinnen, Forschergruppen und Institute in den Hochschulen und wird typischerweise durch Rechencluster in Instituten und Rechenzentren an Hochschulen realisiert. Zentren des Tier 2 wie z.B. das Steinbuch Center for Computing des KIT übernehmen regionale bzw. fachspezifische Aufgaben, sie sind in der Gauß-Allianz organisiert. Die Zentren der Tiers 0 und 1, in Deutschland repräsentiert durch die drei Zentren des Gauss Centre for Supercomputing in Stuttgart, München und Jülich, decken die obersten Leistungsklassen auf nationaler bzw. europäischer Ebene ab.

Dem Tier 3 kommt eine wichtige Rolle zu bei der Aus- und Weiterbildung des wissenschaftlichen Nachwuchses und beim Transfer von Wissen in die Wirtschaft, da diese sukzessive an das Potenzial der leistungsstarken Rechnersysteme herangeführt werden können. Dies macht auch auf der Ebene des Tier 3 die Etablierung bzw. Stärkung von HPC-Kompetenzzentren sinnvoll, da diese für ihren jeweiligen Schwerpunkt als „HPC-Enabler" in die entsprechenden Scientific Communities hineinwirken.

HPC-Kompetenzzentren bündeln leistungsfähige Rechnerinfrastrukturen und Methodenkompetenz am selben Ort („Racks and Brains"), arbeiten intensiv mit Anwendungswissenschaftlerinnen und -wissenschaftlern in geographischer Nähe zusammen und sorgen für eine enge Anbindung benachbarter Universitäten oder außeruniversitärer Forschungseinrichtungen.

Wenn man diese Gedanken konsequent weiterentwickelt und mit den aktuellen Entwicklungen in Richtung Community Clouds und Compute Clouds kombiniert, so gelangt man in logischer Konsequenz zum Umsetzungskonzept der Universitäten in Baden-Württemberg für das Hochleistungsrechnen, das die Basis zur Weiterentwicklung des bwGRid-Verbundes bildet. Es wurde vom ALWR in Kooperation mit Anwendern und Methodenwissenschaftlern erarbeitet.

Dieses Konzept sieht insgesamt fünf Rechnercluster im Land vor, die als Tier 3 Systeme (bezogen auf den Betriebsstandort) in Baden-Württemberg zentralisiert und landesweit genutzt werden, entweder für ausgewiesene Fachwissenschaften im Falle der vier bwForCluster oder als Grundversorgungssystem im Falle des bwUniCluster. Das bwGRid wird von einer Rechenplattform zu einer Kooperations- und Kommunikationsplattform weiterentwickelt und fungiert gleichzeitig als organisatorischer Verbund für die Entwicklung von landesweiten, föderativ erbrachten Diensten („bwServices"). Die Neuordnung setzt auf Ausdifferenzierung der Rechenressourcen, sich ergänzende Strukturen und den Aufbau von Kompetenzzentren.

Die seit 1. Juli 2012 laufenden Landesprojekte „Föderatives Identitätsmanagement in Baden-Württemberg" (bwIDM), „Erweiterung der Large Scale Data Facility zur Datenspeicherung für die baden-württembergischen Hochschulen" (bwLSDF) und „bwGRiD – Ergänzende Maßnahmen" (bwGRiD-EM) flankieren diese Fortentwicklung der Kooperation der Universitätsrechenzentren. Sie setzen dabei auch auf den erfolgreichen Vorarbeiten des bwGRiD-Verbundes im Rahmen der Landesprojekte bwGRiD-System und bwGRiD-Portal auf, aber auch auf erfolgreichen Kooperationsprojekten wie dem CUSS-Cluster der Universitäten Stuttgart und Ulm, der im bwUniCluster aufgehen wird.

Mit dem Umsetzungskonzept und den Landesprojekten wird die am 15. Juni 2010 von der Landesregierung beschlossene Investitionsplanung für das Hoch- und Höchstleistungsrechnen für den Zeitraum bis 2016 ergänzt und durch flankierende Umsetzungsmaßnahmen abgesichert. Die Ebene Tier 3 wird damit vollwertig in die HPC-Landesstrategie integriert, die von Tier 0 bis Tier 3 alle Ebenen des High Performance Computing umfasst. Ein föderatives Betriebs- und Nutzerunterstützungskonzept, das auf den Erfahrungen im bwGRiD-Verbund aufbaut, wird eine verbesserte anwendungsdomänenbezogene Unterstützung der Nutzer ermöglichen. Dabei fungieren die Projektpartner des bwGRiD-Verbundes auch als lokale Know-how-Träger, die einen für den lokalen Nutzer transparenten Zugang zu den im Land verteilten HPC-Ressourcen der verschiedenen Tiers unterstützen. Gleichzeitig werden HPC-Kompetenzzentren im Sinne eines „HPC-Enabling" geschaffen, die Community-spezifisch Methodenkompetenz, Anwender und Nutzerunterstützung zusammenführen. Der stärkere Anwenderbezug zeigt sich bereits bei der aktiven Einbeziehung der (Forschungs–) Anwender in die Antragstellung für die bwForCluster. Der Tier 3 fungiert damit als Einstiegsebene für das größere Gebiet des Computational Science and Engineering, die sowohl Aus- und Weiterbildung als auch Technologie- und Wissenstransfer in die Wirtschaft noch besser unterstützen kann. Die Einbindung in die HPC-Landesstrategie führt durch eine stärkere Koordination von Beschaffungen, Betrieb und Anwenderunterstützung auch zu einer verbesserten Durchlässigkeit zu den Tiers 2 und 0/1 für den Nutzer. Dabei muss im Rahmen der Umsetzung auch das Thema Softwarelizenzen adressiert werden; für wichtige Softwarepakete bietet es sich z. B. an, Landeslizenzen abzuschließen.

Gleichzeitig muss im Rahmen des Gesamtsystems auf der Ebene des Tier 3 ein fairer Ausgleich von Lasten und Pflichten stattfinden, die sich aus Anschaffung, Betrieb und Nutzerunterstützung ergeben. Die hierzu notwendigen Absprachen werden im ALWR im Einvernehmen mit dem Wissenschaftsministerium ausgearbeitet.

Nicht zuletzt bildet der konsequent erfolgende Ausbau des Landeshochschulnetzes BelWue eine notwendige „physikalische" Grundlage für die Kooperationsvorhaben der Rechenzentren.

Ausblick

Die zu beobachtende Konvergenz der Informationstechnologien legt kooperative Versorgungsmodelle nahe. Auch ökonomisch ist es sinnvoll, die an den Universitäten vorhandenen Spezialisierungen zu bündeln und in föderativen Konzepten zum Einsatz zu bringen. Dies vermeidet unnötige Redundanzen und ermöglicht es, in einem komplexer werdenden Umfeld mit den begrenzten Ressourcen vorhandene Dienste zu verbessern und neue Dienste zu entwickeln und anzubieten.

Mit dem bwGRiD-Verbund als Basis für Community-spezifische Dienste und Anwendungen soll in Zukunft eine breitere Palette von Diensten und Anwendungen erschlossen werden. Eine stärkere Koordination auf der strategischen Ebene durch den ALWR und eine intensivere Koordination auf der technischen Ebene erlaubt es, die Stärken der einzelnen Rechenzentren in gemeinsamen Konzepten für verbesserte und neue Dienste (bwServices) landesweit zum Einsatz zu bringen.

Neben dem Hoch- und Höchstleistungsrechnen gibt es eine ganze Reihe von Themen, die gemeinsam in föderativen, aufeinander abgestimmten Konzepten angegangen werden müssen, so z.B. im Bereich Datenmanagement und Speicher. Diese Konzepte müssen in aller Regel auch mit nationalen und europäischen Entwicklungen und Konzepten harmonisiert werden, so beispielsweise beim Management großer wissenschaftlicher Datenmengen oder dem Thema (Langzeit-) Archivierung. Auch hier sind die Universitäten auf einem guten Weg, ihre Führungsrolle im Hochschulsystem verantwortungsbewusst wahrzunehmen.

Durch die sehr erfolgreichen Vorarbeiten der Rechenzentren im Land, unter anderem durch den bwGRiD-Verbund, und durch die etablierten Kooperationsbeziehungen im ALWR sind die Rechenzentren gut aufgestellt, um den Herausforderungen der Zukunft mit Mut und Entschlossenheit zu begegnen. Das Umsetzungskonzept der Universitäten des Landes für das Hochleistungsrechnen ist ein ausgezeichnetes Beispiel für die Zukunftsfähigkeit der Rechenzentren. Die Beiträge in diesem Konferenzband zeigen das große Engagement und die hohe Fachkompetenz, mit dem die Mitarbeiterinnen und Mitarbeiter der Rechenzentren an der Gestaltung dieser Zukunft arbeiten.

Das bwGRiD heute – Eine erfolgreiche föderative HPC-Forschungsumgebung

Marek Dynowski,[*] Michael Janczyk,[†] Tobias Kienzle,[‡]
Matthias Landwehr,[§] Reinhard Mayer,[¶] Adrian Reber,[‖]
Nico Struckmann,[**] Sabine Richling,[††] Janne Chr. Schulz,[‡‡]
Sven Hermann[§§]

Universität Tübingen

Zusammenfassung: Bedingt durch die zunehmende Bedeutung des „High Performance Computings "(HPC) für immer größere Teile der wissenschaftlichen Forschung wurde in der Vergangenheit ein Ausbau der bisher an den Universitäten vorhandenen Ressourcen erforderlich. Zur Deckung des zusätzlichen Bedarfs initiierten 2007 acht Universitäten aus Baden-Württemberg das bwGRiD Projekt mit dem Ziel, HPC-Systeme lokal auf Ebene der Rechenzentren für die wissenschaftliche Forschung im Land zur Verfügung zu stellen. Die Kosten für die Hardware des Projektes wurden vom Bundesministerium für Bildung und Forschung im Rahmen der D-Grid Initiative übernommen, die Finanzierung der Personalstellen erfolgte durch das Ministerium für Wissenschaft, Forschung und Kunst (MWK) Baden-Württemberg. Im Rahmen des Projektes wurden ursprünglich acht HPC-Cluster, bestehend aus identischer Hardware, angeschafft. Diese werden transparent in einem Clusterverbund an sieben Universitätsstandorten im Bundesland betrieben und stehen Mitgliedern des D-Grid Verbundes und Angehörigen der Hochschulen aus Baden-

---

[*] marek.dynowski@uni-tuebingen.de
[†] michael.janczyk@rz.uni-freiburg.de
[‡] kienzle@uni-mannheim.de
[§] matthias.landwehr@uni-konstanz.de
[¶] r.mayer@urz.uni-heidelberg.de
[‖] adrian.reber@hs-esslingen.de
[**] struckmann@hlrs.de
[††] richling@urz.uni-heidelberg.de
[‡‡] janne.schulz@rz.uni-freiburg.de
[§§] hermann@sicos-bw.de

Württemberg unentgeltlich zur Verfügung. Im Jahr 2010 beteiligte sich dann die Hochschule Esslingen mit einem eigenen Cluster an dem erfolgreichen Projekt. Zu dem Erfolg trug unter anderem der Verzicht auf Zugangsbeschränkungen oder Antragstellungen zur Nutzung der bwGRiD-Ressourcen bei. Dadurch wird auch Anwendern aus nicht-klassischen HPC-Disziplinen der Einstieg in das wissenschaftliche Hochleistungsrechnen sowie die Durchführung interdisziplinärer Projekte ermöglicht. Nicht zuletzt durch solche Maßnahmen hat sich das bwGRiD in den letzten fünf Jahren zu einem unverzichtbaren Werkzeug in weiten Teilen der Wissenschaft in Baden-Württemberg und darüber hinaus entwickelt. Überdies können die im Umgang mit diesen HPC-System gewonnenen Erfahrungen und Kenntnisse in die zukünftige Projektplanung einfließen und als Grundlage für Projekte auf größeren Hochleistungsrechnern dienen. In diesem Artikel werden die bisher erreichten Ziele und die dafür erforderlichen Maßnahmen aufgezeigt.

1 Einleitung

Der in den letzten Jahren gestiegene Bedarf an "High Performance Computing"-Ressourcen (HPC) in der Wissenschaft führte zur Planung und Umsetzung neuer Konzepte im Bereich der Daten- und Compute-Cloud. Aus diesen Überlegungen heraus entstand das bwGRiD-Konzept, welches einen dezentralen Betrieb mehrerer HPC-Cluster in einem Clusterverbund vorsieht. Hierzu sollen die über das gesamte Bundesland verteilten Ressourcen mithilfe des Landeshochschulnetzes BelWü[1] vernetzt und nach einem einheitlichen Betriebsmodell betrieben werden. Das Projekt ist Teil der D-Grid-Initiative der Bundesregierung und wird mit zusätzlicher finanzieller Unterstützung für Personalmittel vom Ministerium für Wissenschaft, Forschung und Kunst (MWK) in Baden-Württemberg gefördert. Ursprünglich nahmen die Universitäten Freiburg, Heidelberg, Karlsruhe, Konstanz, Mannheim, Tübingen und Ulm und das „High Performance Computing Center Stuttgart" (HLRS) in Stuttgart an dem Projekt teil. Anfangs übernahm das HLRS die Projektkoordination, die dann im Januar 2010 auf das KIT überging. Die zu Beginn des Projektes gemeinsam beschaffte Hardware bestand aus Komponenten des gleichen Typs, welche in unterschiedlichem Maße auf die jeweiligen Standorte verteilt wurden. Die beiden Cluster in Mannheim und Heidelberg sind seit 2009 über Infiniband-Glasfaser

---

[1] Baden-Württembergs extended LAN: Das Netz der wissenschaftlichen Einrichtungen in Baden- Württemberg, `http://www.belwue.de` [aufgerufen: 31.04.2012]

kopplung miteinander verbunden und werden seitdem als ein einziger Cluster mit gemeinsamer Nutzerverwaltung und gemeinsamen Batch-System betrieben. Im April 2010 beteiligte sich die Hochschule Esslingen mit einem eigenen lokalen HPC-Cluster, bestehend aus 180 Rechenknoten, am bwGRiD-Projekt. Zurzeit besteht das bwGRiD somit aus sieben Compute-Clustern, die an acht Standorten in Baden-Württemberg betrieben werden. Zum bwGRiD gehört auch ein zentrales Storage-System in Karlsruhe, das im Jahr 2009 aus Mitteln des MWK beschafft wurde. Das System stellt den bwGRiD-Nutzern einen Speicherplatz von insgesamt 128 TByte mit Backup und 256 TByte ohne Backup zur Verfügung. Die einzelnen Standorte sind mit einer Geschwindigkeit von 10 Gbit/s Lichtwellenleiter über das BelWü-Netzwerk vernetzt.

2 Projektentwicklung

Grundvoraussetzung für den transparenten Betrieb eines Clusterverbundes ist eine für die Anwender einheitliche Arbeitsumgebung an allen Standorten. Nur so kann diesen eine maximale Flexibilität bezüglich der Standortwahl für die Berechnung ihrer Jobs garantiert werden. Daher sind die Erarbeitung, Umsetzung und Beibehaltung gemeinsamer Betriebsstandards wesentliche Aufgaben des Betriebs des bwGRiD-Clusterverbunds. Ziel dieser Anstrengungen ist es, dem Anwender den Wechsel eines Cluster ohne vorheriges Anpassen seiner Skripte zu ermöglichen.

Einen wichtigen Punkt stellt in diesem Zusammenhang die am jeweiligen Standort verfügbare Software dar, welche den bwGRiD-Administratoren von den jeweils verantwortlichen Standorten als Modul zentral zur Verfügung gestellt wird. Die entsprechenden Software-Module können von Anwendern anhand des „Environment Modules Tools"[2] geladen werden, wodurch eine programm– und versionsspezifische Benutzerumgebung erzeugt wird. Um die Interoperabilität zwischen den Standorten zu gewährleisten, müssen die Namen der Softwaremodule und jeweiligen Benutzerumgebungen an den unterschiedlichen Clustern identisch sein. Dies wird dadurch sichergestellt, dass jeweils nur ein Standort für eine bestimmte Software

---

[2] Projektwebseite: `http://modules.sourceforge.net/` [aufgerufen: 18.05.2012]

zuständig ist. Trotz erheblicher Anstrengungen, gemeinsam verpflichtende Standards für die Erstellung und Namensgebung von Softwaremodulen zu entwickeln und umzusetzen, kam es jedoch in diesem Bereich in der Vergangenheit immer wieder zu Inkonsistenzen bzw. doppelten Arbeiten, da mehrere Standorte unabhängig voneinander an demselben Softwaremodul gearbeitet haben. Infolgedessen wurde gemeinsam die Einführung sogenannter „ITP-Requests" beschlossen. Hierbei handelt es sich um eine standardisierte E-Mail mit Informationen zu der jeweiligen Software. Vor der Erstellung oder Pflege eines Softwaremoduls wird diese an die bwGRiD-interne E-Mail-Liste gesendet, so dass sich Standorte melden können, die eventuell bereits mit der Software Erfahrungen haben. Die im Frühjahr des Jahres 2012 beschlossene Maßnahme führte bereits nach kurzer Zeit zu einer Verbesserung der internen Koordination der Wartung und Pflege der Softwarebestände.

Weiterhin konnte die Anwenderfreundlichkeit und Softwareadministration durch die Entwicklung eines Software-Browsers erheblich verbessert werden. Mit dem in Webseiten integrierbaren Tool kann der täglich aktualisierte Softwarestand auf allen Clustern des Verbundes abgefragt werden. Zusätzlich ist für die Administratoren ein Softwaretool zur Verfügung gestellt worden, das die Vollständigkeit der an einem Standort installierten Software(-versionen) überprüft. Die Entwicklung und Bereitstellung dieser Tools verbesserte die transparente Nutzung der Cluster erheblich und vereinfacht deren Administration. Trotz aller bisherigen Entwicklungen besteht bei der transparenten Bereitstellung von Software für den Clusterverbund noch Potenzial für Innovationen, sodass entsprechende Konzepte im Rahmen des Arbeitspaketes 4.3 unter Leitung von Konstanz entwickelt und umgesetzt werden sollen.

Die im bwGRiD mittlerweile auf fast allen Standorten installierten und verwendeten „Workspace Tools" vereinfachen den Nutzern das standortunabhängige Datenmanagement, da so temporärer Speicherplatz auf einer identischen Abstraktionsebene auf den lokalen Lustre- Dateisystemen zur Verfügung gestellt werden kann. Aufgrund der Vorteile der Workspaces wurde deren Nutzung im bwGRiD-Portal für die zeitlich begrenzte Speicherung von großen Datenmengen implementiert.

3 Ergänzende Maßnahmen

Im Verlauf des bwGRiD-Projektes wurden verschiedene Anforderungen für das Anbieten eines effizienten HPC-Dienstes für ein breites Spektrum wissenschaftlicher Anwender formuliert, die mit den zur Verfügung stehenden Ressourcen nicht zu erfüllen waren. Für die Ausarbeitung entsprechender Konzepte und deren Umsetzung waren zusätzliche Personal- und Sachmittel erforderlich. Daraufhin wurden die einzelnen Punkte zu einem Vollantrag zusammengefasst und dieser mit der Bezeichnung „bwGRiD – Ergänzende Maßnahmen" beim Ministerium für Wissenschaft, Forschung und Kunst eingereicht. Die Maßnahmen wurden Juli 2010 vom MWK genehmigt. Sie stellen die Weichen für die Zukunft des bwGRiD und auch für zukünftige Projekte im Bereich des HPC. Insbesondere der Zugriff auf die Ressourcen und deren Nutzung sollen erleichtert, die Interoperabilität weiter erhöht sowie der Kreis der Nutzer und die dazugehörige Betreuung ausgeweitet werden. Im folgenden Abschnitt werden die einzelnen Arbeitspakte und vorläufigen Ergebnisse vorgestellt. Das Arbeitspaket 5 („Portalabhängige Entwicklungen") wird ausführlich einem eigenen Artikel in diesem Konferenzband behandelt und ist daher nicht aufgeführt.

3.1 Arbeitspaket 1 – Authentifizierung und Autorisierung mittels föderativer Mechanismen

Bisher basiert die Authentifizierung der Grid-Anwender im bwGRiD auf X.509-Zertifikaten. Bevor ein entsprechender Zugang für einen Benutzer eingerichtet werden kann, muss dieser ein Grid-Nutzer-Zertifikat beantragen. Dieser Vorgang ist ein komplexer, mehrstufiger und daher fehleranfälliger Prozess, der für viele Nutzer eine hohe Zugangshürde darstellt. Zwar werden hierfür über vielfältige Medien Schritt-für-Schritt Anleitungen angeboten, jedoch ist die Durchführung auch für den Nutzer mit erheblichem Zeitaufwand verbunden. Im Rahmen der ergänzenden Maßnahmen soll deshalb ein neues und einfacheres Authentifizierungsverfahren für die Grid-Nutzung des bwGRiDs eingerichtet werden, mit dem sich die Angehörigen der Universitäten in Baden-Württemberg an allen Gridstandorten mit ihren lokalen Universitäts-Accounts einloggen können. Da es landesweit in Baden-Württemberg keine einheitliche Authentifizierungsinfrastruktur gibt, wird von dem bwIDM Projekt[3] eine föderierte Lösung auf Basis von Shibboleth[4] entwickelt und implementiert. Diese soll nicht nur vom bwGRiD-Projekt, sondern auch von anderen Landesdiensten wie beispielsweise dem IBS[5] eingesetzt werden. Voraussetzung für den Einsatz von Shibboleth im bwGRiD ist eine vollständige Unterstützung der zurzeit eingesetzten Zugangsmöglichkeiten. Stellenweise sind hierbei umfangreiche Änderungen im Bereich Shibboleth notwendig. Im folgenden werden die drei Möglichkeiten des Nutzerzugangs zu den bwGRiD Ressourcen vorgestellt.

Zugriff auf das bwGRiD Wissenschaftsportal   Das bwGRiD–Wissenschaftsportal ist eine Webapplikation, auf die mit Hilfe eines Browsers zugegriffen wird. Da Shibboleth ursprünglich für webbasierte Dienste entwickelt wurde, kann die Technologie ohne großen Aufwand in das Wissenschaftsportal integriert werden.

Konsolenbasierter Login   Wesentlich größer sind die Anstrengungen, die Shibboleth-Infrastruktur mit den bislang bei den konsolenbasierten Logins verwendeten Authentifizierungsmechanismen zu verbinden. Die Integration findet über die Erweiterung ECP^6 von Shibboleth statt. Dazu wurden von dem bwIDM-Projekt Werkzeuge (PAM und NSS Module) entwickelt, mit denen auf den Grid-Knoten eine Authentifizierung gegen Shibboleth möglich wird. Die Adaption der für die bwGRiD-Infrastruktur entwickelten Module wurde durchgeführt und in einer Testumgebung erfolgreich getestet.

---

[3] bwIDM: Übergreifendes   Identitätsmanagement,   `http://www.bw-grid.de/` `bwservices/bwidm/` [aufgerufen: 18.05.2012]

[4] Projektwebseite: `http://shibboleth.net/` [aufgerufen: 18.05.2012]

[5] IBS: Projekt ingegriertes Bibliothekssystem Baden–Württemberg, Link: `https://wiki.` `bsz-bw.de/lib/exe/fetch.php?media=l-team:ibs:flyer_adis_2012_04.pdf` [aufgerufen: 18.05.2012]

[6] ECP: Enhanced Client or Proxy, `https://wiki.shibboleth.net/confluence/` `display/SHIB2/ECP` [aufgerufen: 17.05.2012]

Portal-basierter Login via SSH auf die Grid-Knoten Da das Portal als Webapplikation als relativ leicht angreifbar angesehen wird, verbietet es sich, dem Portal einfach ein passwortfreies Login auf die Grid-Knoten für jeden User einzurichten. Gesucht ist eine Lösung, bei der sich das Portal nur als derjenige User einloggen kann, der auch am Portal angemeldet ist. Dafür braucht man ein Feature, das man mit „Credential Delegation" beschreiben kann, was aber von der Shibboleth-Architektur nicht unterstützt wird. Wir sehen daher zwei Möglichkeiten, eine solche Funktionalität zu realisieren:

1. Die Credential Delegation kann mit dem Shibboleth-Plugin *uPortal* erreicht werden. Dieses Modul müsste aber auf den Shibboleth-IdPs an allen Standorten installiert und gewartet werden.

2. Eine andere Möglichkeit ist eine Eigenentwicklung. Bei dieser Variante müssten keine zusätzlichen Plugins auf den Shibboleth-Servern installiert werden, es genügen kleinere Konfigurationen. Es wird ein Session-Passwort als Shibboleth-Attribut von dem Shibboleth-IdP an das Portal weitergegeben. Mit diesem Session-Passwort kann sich dann das Portal auf die Grid-Knoten einloggen. Die Session-Passwörter werden nur verschlüsselt übertragen, so kurz wie möglich gespeichert und soweit möglich als Hash-Wert statt als Klartext gehalten. Diese Lösung ist in einer Testumgebung bereits erfolgreich getestet worden.

Derzeit werden die Vor- und Nachteile beider Lösungsansätze erörtert. Eine endgültige Entscheidung wurde noch nicht getroffen.

3.2 Arbeitspaket 2 – bwGRiD User und Operations Support

Zurzeit ist der (Nutzer-)Support für die bwGRiD-Ressourcen lokal an den jeweiligen Standorten organisiert. Da hierbei unterschiedliche Systeme und Infrastrukturen verwendet werden, müssen sich Nutzer bei standortspezifischen Supportanfragen erst über die jeweiligen Möglichkeiten informieren, was die Nutzerfreundlichkeit erheblich einschränkt. Auch kann es bei fachbereichspezifischen oder gridweiten Supportanfragen unter Umständen zu Verzögerungen oder Kommunikationsproblemen kommen, da die korrekte Weiterleitung dem jeweiligen lokalen Ansprechpartnern obliegt. Zur Vermeidung der zuvor beschrieben Probleme soll im Rahmen dieses Arbeitspaketes die Entwicklung eines bwGRiD-weiten First-Line- sowie Operations-Supports erfolgen. Dieser soll in enger Zusammenarbeit mit den bereits bestehenden NGI-DE-Support-Gruppen und unter Nutzung des NGI-DE-Support-Portals aufgebaut werden. Zukünftig dient das bwGRiD-First-Line-Support-Team als zentrale Anlaufstelle für alle Nutzerprobleme im bwGRiD. Hierzu sollen Expertengruppen im bwGRiD-Kontext gebildet werden, die eng mit dem Supportteam zusammenarbeiten. Angestrebt wird eine Vernetzung der bereits bestehenden lokalen Servicedesks an den jeweiligen Standorten mit dem NGI-DE-Helpdesk. Durch die zusätzliche Supportschicht im Rahmen des NGI-DE-Portals wird die Bearbeitung von Incidents durch Mitarbeiter der bwGRiD-Standorte für alle Nutzer des bw-GRiD transparenter, ohne dass diese Kenntnis der am jeweiligen Standort lokal vorhandenen Supportstrukturen benötigen. Aus den gelösten Incidents entsteht außerdem mit der Zeit eine Wissensdatenbank für das bw-GRiD, die wiederum vom First-Line-Support genutzt werden kann.

Ein zweiter Aufgabenbereich umfasst die Überwachung der vorhandenen Infrastruktur und der produktiven Dienste im bwGRiD, um im Problemfall ein entsprechendes Ticket zu öffnen und die Behebung des Problems zu verfolgen bzw. zu begleiten und abzuschließen. Ziel ist die Bereitstellung von Werkzeugen für eine einheitliche Überwachung aller bwGRiD-Standorte, so dass Ausfälle und Wartungen für den Nutzer klar erkennbar werden. Aufgrund des ähnlichen Setups der Standorte sollen Monitoring-Werkzeuge und bisher eingesetzte Prozesse zum Sammeln von Informationen zu einer Standardlösung zusammengefasst werden, welche dann allen bwGRiD-Standorten für die Überwachung der Systeme zur Verfügung gestellt werden kann. Die Umsetzung des Arbeitspakets geschieht in enger Zusammenarbeit mit dem NGI-DE-Operations-Team und wird vom Standort Karlsruhe koordiniert.

3.3 Arbeitspaket 3.1 – Cluster-übergreifendes Scheduling

Ziel des Pakets ist die Optimierung der Auslastung freier Ressourcen zu erreichen und zudem eine standortunabhängige Nutzung der Hardware im bwGRiD zu ermöglichen sowie die Zugangsmechanismen für die Nutzer weiter zu vereinfachen. Dafür ist der Aufbau eines intelligenten Schedulings über die Cluster aller Standorte unumgänglich. Dazu werden unter anderem Scheduling-Policies benötigt, um die lokalen Scheduling-Systeme sinnvoll zu einem globalen System miteinander zu verbinden, welches die Heterogenität der Ressourcen an den einzelnen Standorten in Bezug auf die Hardwarekonfiguration und verfügbaren Software-Module sowie -Lizenzen berücksichtigt.

Um Scheduling-Policies für eine Job-Migration zwischen Standorten und die Anbindung an erste Werkzeuge aus Arbeitspaket 3.2 zwischen Stuttgart und Karlsruhe zu realisieren, wird zunächst die Job-Migration zwischen verschiedenen MOAB Instanzen umgesetzt, jedoch zunächst lokal begrenzt an einem Standort. Für das Umsetzen der Job-Migration zwischen verschiedenen MOAB Instanzen wurden zunächst zwei virtuelle Testcluster aufgesetzt, welche im nächsten Schritt mit dem realen Stuttgarter Cluster zu einem Schedulingsystem verbunden werden. Im Rahmen der Konfiguration der Testumgebung sind verschiedene Probleme aufgetreten. So hat sich herausgestellt, dass für die Grid-Funktionalität, die MOAB bietet, auch eine entsprechende Lizenz-Datei vorhanden sein muss. Auf Anfrage wurde vom Software-Hersteller Adaptive Computing für die beiden virtuellen Test-Cluster auch eine entsprechende, aber zeitlich begrenzte Lizenz zur Verfügung gestellt. Ein weiterer wichtiger Punkt für die automatische Migration ist die Voraussetzung, dass für jeden Benutzer auf allen Knoten ein passwortfreier SSH- oder GSI-SSH-Zugang vorhanden sein muss, damit auch die für einen Job benötigten Dateien übertragen und die Ergebnisse abgefragt werden können. Desweiteren funktionierte der automatische Datentransfer der Scheduling-Software MOAB nicht wie gewünscht. Zunächst lag die Ursache in der verwendeten Version von MOAB, welche in dieser Hinsicht noch fehlerhaft war. Ein Update der Testumgebung von MOAB Version 6.1.2 auf die Version 6.1.4 hat die Probleme aber nur zum Teil gelöst. Größere Dateien konnten noch immer nicht automatisch migriert werden. Durch detaillierte Analysen der von MOAB für den Dateitransfer verwendeten Perl-Skripte konnte die Ursache ermittelt und behoben werden. Darüber hinaus wurden die Skripte für den Dateitransfer so erweitert, dass auch ganze Verzeichnisse und reguläre Ausdrücken verwendet werden können. Dies ist sinnvoll, da nicht immer absehbar ist, wie die Benennung der erzeugten Ergebnis-Dateien lauten wird oder wie groß die Anzahl der Dateien nach Abschluss der Berechnungen sein wird.

Aktuell wird daran gearbeitet, die an den Standorten verfügbare Software beim Scheduling mit zu berücksichtigen. Da MOAB von Haus aus nur in begrenztem Umfang dafür Möglichkeiten bietet, die für unser Einsatzszenerio aufgrund der großen Anzahl nicht geeignet sind, muss dies durch eine eigene Implementierung realisiert werden. Hierfür sind die Anbindung an die „Authentication and Authorization Infrastructure" (AAI) aus Arbeitspaket 1 und die Optimierung der Scheduling-Policies auf Basis ermittelter Daten zwingende Voraussetzungen. Im nächsten Schritt wird das reale Stuttgarter Cluster in die Testumgebung eingebunden. Auch entsprechende Policies für das Scheduling zwischen der virtuellen Umgebung und dem realen Cluster werden ermittelt. Darauf folgend wird der Standort Karlsruhe eingebunden. Bei stabilem Betrieb werden danach die restlichen Cluster der bwGRiD-Standorte mit einbezogen und die Scheduling-Policies iterativ optimiert. Einen offenen Punkt stellt die Dateiübertragung dar: Die zum Zeitpunkt des Login vom Benutzer verwendeten temporären GSISSH Proxy Zertifikate sind häufig nicht mehr gültig bis die Ressourcen für eine Berechnung zur Verfügung stehen oder um die Ergebnisse danach abzuholen. Ein Lösungsansatz wäre hierfür beim ersten Login eines Benutzers im Hintergrund SSH-Schlüssel für den Datentransfer zu generieren und diese landesweit zu verteilen. Da dies aus sicherheitstechnischer Sicht nicht die optimale Lösung darstellt, muss hier geprüft werden inwiefern zur Lösung des Problems Shibboleth verwendet werden könnte. Zuletzt muss die Netzwerkauslastung der Standorte, die starken Schwankungen unterliegt, beim Scheduling mit einbezogen werden. Dazu sind belastbare, regelmäßig aktualisierte Messwerte nötig, die im Scheduling angemessen berücksichtigt werden müssen.

3.4 Arbeitspaket 3.2 – Werkzeuge zum Datenmanagement

Für die Speicherung von Daten stehen im bwGRiD lokale Speichersysteme an den jeweiligen Standorten oder der zentrale Speicher in Karlsruhe zur

Verfügung, wobei letzterer aufgrund der starken Nutzung die Kapazitätsgrenze bald erreichen wird.

Es gibt im bwGRiD derzeit keine Möglichkeit von einem Standort auf die Daten des anderen direkt zuzugreifen. Der Nutzer muss bisher ein Datentransfer manuell durchführen. Mechanismen zum automatischen Datentransfer können die manuelle Organisation der Daten reduzieren und den Anwendern das Datenmanagement erheblich erleichtern. Daher werden in diesem Arbeitspaket bereits bestehende Tools zur Vereinfachung des Datentransfers und der Datenhaltung evaluiert und für den Einsatz innerhalb des bwGRiDs angepasst. Ferner wird in Kooperation mit dem Arbeitspaket „clusterübergreifendes Scheduling" (Arbeitspaket 3.1) ein Datenkonzept für ein automatisiertes Datenmanagement des Schedulers entwickelt.

Die Grundlage für die Datentransfers zwischen den bwGRiD Standorten bildet das BelWü-Netzwerk, das seit Januar 2012 alle Standorte mit einer Geschwindigkeit von 10 Gbit/s Lichtwellenleiter verbindet. Die Performanz der Verbindung zwischen den Standorten ist entscheidend für das clusterübergreifende Scheduling und das damit verbundene Datenmanagement. Da die bwGRiD-Cluster Heidelberg und Mannheim über eine Infiniband-Glasfaserkopplung miteinander verbunden sind und als ein Cluster betrieben werden, ergeben sich acht Endpunkte, zwischen denen Daten transferiert werden müssen: Mannheim (Mannheim / Heidelberg), Karlsruhe (KIT/SCC), Karlsruhe Speicher, Stuttgart (HLRS), Esslingen, Tübingen, Ulm und Freiburg. Für den Datentransfer stellt bisher jeder Standort im bwGRiD das Globus Toolkit bereit. Das darin enthaltene Werkzeug GridFTP bietet sich daher an, um Daten zwischen den Frontendknoten der einzelnen Clustern zu kopieren. Zur Überwachung des Netzwerkes und zur Ermittlung der erreichbaren Bandbreiten werden im Rahmen des Arbeitspaketes regelmäßige Netzwerktests durchgeführt und die Ergebnisse in Form von kurzen Reports an alle Standorte kommuniziert. Hierfür werden die Daten grafisch[7] aufbereitet (Abbildung 1) und zusätzlich in Tabellenform zur Verfügung gestellt. Durch die Netzwerktests konnten bereits Netzwerkprobleme entdeckt und gezielt gelöst werden, sodass nun alle Standorte mit der

---

[7] GraphViz: Graph Visualization ist ein Open Source Projekt zur Visualisierung von Graphen (Netzwerk) von AT&T Research.

maximalen Bandbreite kommunizieren können. Die kontinuierliche Steigerung des Netzwerkdurchsatzes ist aus Abbildung 1 A – C ersichtlich. Zwar konnte die jeweilige Performanz der einzelnen Standorte aneinander angepasst werden, jedoch bestehen in diesem Bereich immer noch Unterschiede, die primär auf das LAN der Standorte inklusive Firewall und die Konfiguration der Endpunkte zurückzuführen sind.

Zunächst wurden ausschließlich die TCP-Verbindungen mit Iperf[8] getestet. Jede Verbindung wurde mehrfach für zehn Sekunden überprüft und die Anzahl der parallelen TCP-Verbindungen variiert. Um den täglichen Betrieb möglichst nicht zu behindern, wurden die Tests nachts und früh morgens durchgeführt und die Ergebnisse für die anschließende Auswertung in einer Datenbank gesammelt. Datentransfers mit GridFTP wurden etwas später ebenfalls regelmäßig nachts durchgeführt, da der Datentransfer Einfluss auf die Ansprechbarkeit der Frontendknoten haben kann. Die Frontenknoten werden von den Benutzern auch zum Abschicken ihrer Jobs auf dem Cluster benötigt.

Ein weiterer Aspekt dieses Arbeitspaketes ist die performante Anbindung von Benutzern, die sehr große Datenmengen für ihre Berechnungen auf den bwGRiD Ressourcen transferieren müssen, wie z.B. BioQuant[9]. In diesem Fall liegen die Daten auf lokalen Datenspeichern von BioQuant vor, die aufgrund der physikalischen Distanz zu den bwGRiD Rechenressourcen speziell angebunden werden müssen. Insgesamt beläuft sich der Datenbestand der Institution auf ein PByte, wobei ein einzelner Satz eine Größe von mehreren TByte erreichen kann. Um eine effektive Berechnung der BioQuant-Daten im bwGRiD zu gewährleisten, muss unter Berücksichtigung der zugrunde liegenden Datenmengen, eine breitbandige Verbindung mit geeigneten Protokollen realisiert werden. Hierzu wurde vom Rechenzentrum der Universität Heidelberg in Kooperation mit BioQuant ein Infrastrukturkonzept erarbeitet und mögliche Lösungsansätze diskutiert.

---

[8] Iperf wurde entwickelt von NLANR /DAST als eine moderne Alternative zur Messung der maximalen Bandbreite von TCP und UDP Verbindungen, `http://iperf.sourceforge.net` [aufgerufen: 31.04.2012]

[9] BioQuant: Center for Quantitative Analysis of Molecular and Cellular Biosystems at Heidelberg University, `http://www.bioquant.uni-heidelberg.de` [aufgerufen: 02.05.2012]

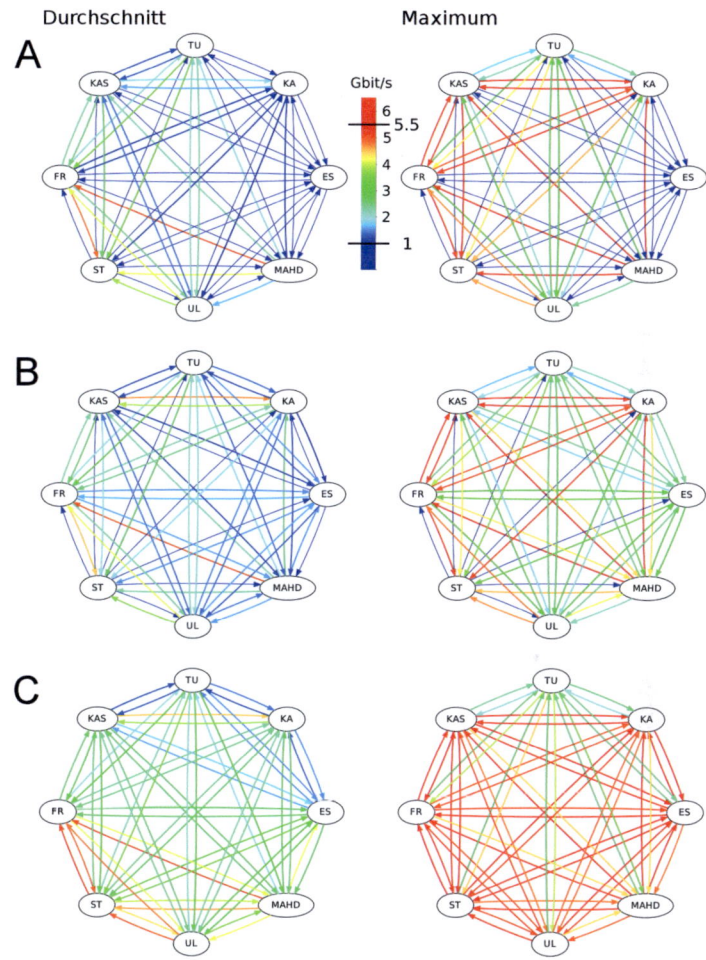

Abbildung 1: Netzwerkdurchsatz im (**A**) Februar 2012 (30.1. - 4.3.2012 / Kalenderwoche 5-9), (**B**) März 2012 (5.3. - 1.4.2012 / Kalenderwoche 10-13) und (**C**) im April 2012 (2.4. - 29.4.2012 / Kalenderwoche 14-17). Die Ergebnisse in den Reports beziehen sich zur Zeit lediglich auf die TCP Verbindungen.
Abkürzungen der Standorte:
ES = Esslingen, FR = Freiburg, KA = Karlsruhe, KAS = Karlsruhe Storage,
MAHD = Mannheim / Heidelberg, ST = Stuttgart, TU = Tübingen, UL = Ulm

Nachdem im Mai 2012 der BioQuant-Speicher (LSDF[10]) von „Scale-out File Services" (SoFS) zu IBM „Scale Out Network Attached Storage" (SO-NAS) umgestellt wurde, sind die ursprünglich für SoFS erarbeiteten Ansätze nicht mehr anwendbar. Eine immer noch verfügbare Lösung stellt dennoch der Zugriff auf das LSDF als Block Device dar. So wäre es möglich, einen freien Storage-Bereich als Block Device an den Cluster anzuschließen. Jedoch müsste dann jeder Datensatz vor dem Berechnen auf den Cluster und die Ergebnisse wieder zurück kopiert werden. Ob der resultierende Vorteil durch die Anbindung des LSDF als Block Device die Nachteile der doppelten Datenhaltung und der langen Transferzeiten durch die Kopiervorgänge überwiegt, ist fraglich.

Für eine Anbindung via NFS über eine breitbandige IP-Verbindung erwarten wir eine akzeptable Performanz. Zusätzlich wird ein Zwischenspeichern der Daten auf den bwGRiD-Clustern in Betracht gezogen. Die Visualisierung der Netzwerktests hat Transparenz geschaffen, um die Anbindung der einzelnen Standorte miteinander besser vergleichen zu können. Die aus den Messungen resultierenden Daten dienen der realistischen Einschätzung bezüglich des Datentransfers für die Umsetzung eines landesübergreifenden Schedulings, wie es im Rahmen der ergänzenden Maßnahmen angedacht ist. Zukünftig werden Lösungen evaluiert, um die großen Datenmengen, wie sie im bwGRiD-Projekt entstehen, zu verwalten.

3.5 Arbeitspaket 4.1 – Verbreitung, Förderung, Schulung und Zugang

Die zentralen Fragestellungen, die im Rahmen des Arbeitspaketes beantwortet werden sollen, lauten: Welche Informationen werden benötigt, um Zugang zu dem bwGRiD zu bekommen? Wie können diese Informationen so aufbereitet werden, dass die notwendigen Prozeduren um beispielsweise ein Grid-Nutzer-Zertifikat zu beantragen, so beschrieben werden, dass sie einfach, verständlich und nachvollziehbar sind? Der Fokus der Zielgruppe liegt auf Benutzer (-gruppen), die entweder bislang noch nicht mit

---

[10] LSDF: Large Scale Data Facility for Life Sciences, `http://www.bioquant.uni-heidelberg.de` [aufgerufen: 18.05.2012]

dem bwGRiD gearbeitet haben oder die aus wissenschaftlichen Bereichen kommen, die nicht klassischerweise mit HPC-Ressourcen operieren. Beide Benutzer (-gruppen) benötigen individuelle Konzepte und Lösungen, um mit dem bwGRiD produktiv arbeiten zu können. Diese werden im Rahmen des Arbeitspakets 4.1 erarbeitet und entwickelt.

Zugang, Förderung und Schulung Die inhaltliche und visuelle Aufbereitung der gesamten Prozedur, die notwendig ist, um ein Grid-Nutzer-Zertifikat zu beantragen, war eine der ersten Maßnahmen in dem Arbeitspaket 4.1. Dieses Grid-Nutzer-Zertifikat wird benötigt, um grundsätzlich Zugriff auf die bwGRiD-Ressourcen zu bekommen – entweder über die Konsole oder über webbasierte Zugänge wie das bwGRiD Wissenschaftsportal. Allerdings ist die Beantragung ein mehrstufiger, recht umständlicher und daher fehleranfälliger Prozess. Gerade für Benutzer, die bislang keine Erfahrungen im Umgang mit HPC-Ressourcen haben, ist dies eine Einstiegshürde, die nicht förderlich für die Akzeptanz des bwGRiDs ist. Die komplette Aufarbeitung dieser Prozedur führte zur Entwicklung einer Schritt-für-Schritt Anleitung, die sowohl als Webseiten als auch in gebunden in Form eines „Handbuchs bwGRiD" vorliegen. Sämtliche Masken sind als Screenshots abgebildet und enthalten farbige Markierungen und Erklärungen, welche Daten an welcher Stelle eingetragen werden müssen. Mit dieser Schritt-für- Schritt-Anleitung konnte speziell für Benutzer aus „nicht-klassischen" Bereichen der Zugang zu dem bwGRiD erheblich vereinfacht werden.

Für die Planung und Durchführung von wissenschaftlichen Projekten auf den bwGRiD-HPC-Ressourcen sind Informationen zur Softwareausstattung an den jeweiligen Standorten von essentieller Bedeutung. Nur so kann auch eine effiziente Nutzung der Ressourcen gewährleistet werden. Aus diesem Grund wurde ein web-basiertes System entwickelt, um eine aktuelle Übersicht über die an den Standorten verfügbare Software liefern zu können, ohne dass die Benutzer bereits ein Grid- Nutzer-Zertifikat benötigen. Der „Cluster Software Browser" (CSB)[11] arbeitet mit zwei Komponenten: ei-

---

[11] CSB: Cluster Software Browser, `http://www.bw-grid.uni-freiburg.de/software` [aufgerufen: 14.05.2012]

nem Software-Agenten, der auf allen Standorten die dort verfügbare Softwareliste zusammenstellt und sie an eine zentrale Stelle übermittelt und einer Weboberfläche, die die gesammelten Informationen grafisch aufbereitet. Der Software-Agent wird dazu manuell gestartet und meldet sich mithilfe eines Grid-Nutzer-Zertifikat der Reihe nach auf allen Standorten an. Dort wird die Ausgabe des Programmes `modules` eingelesen und in entsprechende Datenstrukturen umgewandelt, die an eine zentrale Stelle (dem Webserver, der auch die grafische Oberfläche bereitstellt) zur Speicherung übertragen werden. Die grafische Oberfläche bildet ein webbasiertes Interface, mit dessen Hilfe nach beliebigen Softwarenamen oder innerhalb bestimmter Anwendungsgebiete gesucht werden kann. Die Weboberfläche kann in die lokalen Content-Management-Systeme der bwGRiD-Standorte eingebaut und an das jeweilige Corporate Design angepasst werden. Auf diese Weise können sich interessierte Benutzer schon im Vorfeld erkundigen, ob die benötigte Software in der entsprechenden Version vorliegt - und wenn ja, an welchen Standorten.

Verbreitung Neben Aufgaben zu Zugang, Förderung und Schulung hinsichtlich des bwGRiDs, stellt die Verbreitung einen weiteren Schwerpunkt des Arbeitspaktes dar. Es werden kleine lokale Veranstaltungen mit interessierten (potenziellen) Anwendergruppen regelmäßig durchgeführt, die relativ kurzfristig organisiert werden können. In diesem Zusammenhang wird zum ersten Mal in der Geschichte des bwGRiD-Projektes vom 23. Mai bis 25. Mai 2012 am Standort Freiburg in Kooperation mit dem „Black Forest Grid" (BFG) eine Konferenz stattfinden, auf der sowohl Anwender als auch Betreiber ihre Arbeit vorstellen. Mit dieser Konferenz werden mehrere Ziele verfolgt: (1) die Sichtbarkeit des bwGRiD-Projektes wird durch entsprechende Einladungen und Werbung deutlich erhöht, (2) die Nutzer des bwGRiDs bekommen die Möglichkeit, ihre Projekte einem interessierten Fachpublikum vorzustellen und die Betreiber der Infrastruktur können interessante Entwicklungen vorstellen und (3) es soll die Vielfalt der fachlichen Schwerpunkte der Benutzer dargestellt und der persönliche Austausch zwischen Benutzern und Betreibern intensiviert werden. Die Veranstaltung ist mit einer Gesamtdauer von zweieinhalb Tagen konzipiert und wird mit einem internen Treffen der Projektmitglieder beginnen. Am Nachmittag des ersten Tages beginnt der öffentliche Teil der Konferenz mit Grußworten und Vorträgen zu generellen Fragestellungen rund um das Grid-Computing. Der zweite Tag ist den Anwendern und Administratoren gewidmet: dort werden wissenschaftliche Projekte, die aus den unterschiedlichsten Fachbereichen stammen und die auf dem bwGRiD gerechnet wurden, einem breiten Fachpublikum vorgestellt. Dabei wird es Vorträge zu linguistischen Problemstellungen genauso wie Vorträge über die neuesten Techniken zur Programmierung von spezieller Hardware wie den GPGPU-Karten geben. Der dritte Tag beendet die Konferenz mit einer praktischen „Hands-On Session", bei der interessierte Benutzer unter fachkundiger Anleitung ihre Grid-Nutzer-Zertifikate beantragen oder andere praktische Probleme gemeinsam mit den Administratoren lösen können.

Neben der Durchführung der Konferenz wurden auch von allen interessierten Anwendergruppen aus dem gesamten Bundesland Beiträge zu einem Konferenzband eingesammelt. Dieser Konferenzband soll einen Einblick in die Vielfalt der aktuellen Projekte ermöglichen und auch eine Art „Zustandsbericht" darstellen.

Alle Maßnahmen, die im Rahmen des Arbeitspaketes 4.1 entwickelt werden, dienen der Verbesserung der Integration von neuen Benutzern und der Verbesserung des Austausches von Informationen rund um das bwGRiD-Projekt. Dabei wird jedes Mal die Perspektive der Benutzer eingenommen, um die notwendigen Angebote optimal auf die Bedürfnisse der Anwender hin zu entwickeln.

3.6 Arbeitspaket 4.2 – Integration zusätzlicher wissenschaftlicher Nutzer und Fachgruppen mit speziellen Anforderungen

Eines der Ziele des bwGRiD-Projektes ist die Bereitstellung von HPC-Ressourcen für ein möglichst breites Anwenderspektrum. Dies ist durch die zu Beginn des Projektes beschaffte Basis-Hardwareausstattung zwar gewährleistet, jedoch sollen auch neue Anwender aus HPC-fernen Fachgebieten mit speziellen Anforderungen sowohl im Bereich der Hard- als auch Software an das bwGRiD herangeführt werden. Dazu wurde im Rahmen der ergänzenden Maßnahmen das Arbeitspaket 4.2 erarbeitet. Durch die Beschaffung und Eingliederung spezialisierter Hard- und Software sowie das Erarbeiten individueller Nutzungskonzepte sollen Anwender mit speziellen Anforderungen in das bwGRiD integriert werden. Die Koordination des Projektes für das bwGRiD übernimmt der Standort Tübingen.

Seit Beginn des bwGRiD-Projektes begannen einige Standorte mit der Integration eigener Hardware-Komponenten in die ursprünglich homogene Basisausstattung ihrer HPC-Cluster, wobei die Gewährleistung der Interoperabilität zwischen den einzelnen Standorten zwingend erforderlich war. Solche heterogenen Erweiterungen durch Integration von spezialisierten Hardwarearchitekturen steigern nicht nur die Attraktivität einzelner Standorte, sondern auch die des gesamten bwGRiDs. Insbesondere wenn die zusätzlichen Ressourcen dem gesamten Clusterverbund zur Verfügung gestellt werden. Diese können dadurch die optimale Hardware für die Lösung ihres Problems ermitteln und anschließend auch verwenden. Im besten Fall führt dieses nicht nur zu einer Nutzung der entsprechenden Hardware, sondern auch zu anwenderfinanzierten Neuanschaffungen, welche anschließend in die entsprechenden bwGRiD-Cluster integriert werden können.

Unabhängig davon profitieren allerdings alle Nutzer allein schon durch die Entlastung der Basis-Hardware. Ferner ermöglicht das Konzept der heterogenen Hardware-Erweiterung die Evaluation verschiedener Rechnerarchitekturen im Produktionsbetrieb und die Erstellung spezieller Nutzungskonzepte bei Neuanschaffungen. Der intensive Erfahrungsaustausch zwischen Nutzern und Betreibern fördert auch den Aufbau von Kernkompetenzen einzelner Standorte im Bereich Hard- und Software, von denen das gesamte bwGRiD-Projekt profitiert.

Die Standorte Freiburg, Esslingen, Mannheim/Heidelberg, Stuttgart und Tübingen haben im Laufe des Projektes die Grundausstattung ihrer Cluster durch Betreiber- und Anwender-finanzierte Hardware kontinuierlich erweitert (Abbildung 2). In vielen Fällen steht die neue Hardware dem gesamten bwGRiD zur Verfügung. So wurden am Standort Freiburg 18 Knoten mit größerem Hauptspeicher (16 x 24 GByte, 1 x 256 GByte, 1 x 512 GByte) von dem Lehrstuhl für Quantenoptik und Statistik angeschafft, in das bwGRiD-

Standorte	# Knoten	CPU/GPU	RAM (GByte)
Esslingen	2	PowerXCell 8i, 3.2Ghz(2x2 Kerne)/ 16 SPUs	8
	16	Intel Xeon X5550, 2.67GHz (2x4 Kerne)	
Freiburg	8	Intel Xeon X5650X5550, 2.66GHz (2X6 Kerne) / Nvidia Tesla M2090** (1x512 Kerne)	24
	4	Intel Xeon E5520, 2.27GHz (2x4 Kerne) / Nvidia Tesla C1060* (2x240 Kerne)	
	1	AMD Opteron 8360 SE, 2.44GHz (8x4 Kerne)	512
		AMD Opteron 8384, 2.64GHz (8x4 Kerne)	256
Heidelberg	28	Intel Xeon E5440, 2.83GHz (2x4 Kerne)	16
Stuttgart	8	Intel Xeon 5472, 3.00GHz (2x4 Kerne) / Nvidia Quadro FX 5800 (240 Kerne)	8
	24	Intel Xeon L5530, 2.4GHz (2x4 Kerne)	72
	18	AMD Opteron 6172, 2.1GHz (2x12 Kerne)	
Tübingen	16	Intel Xeon 5150, 2.66GHz (2x2 Kerne)	32
	8	Intel Xeon 5355, 2.66GHz (2x4 Kerne)	
		Intel Xeon 5150, 2.66GHz (2x2 Kerne)	16
	1	Intel Xeon E7-4830, 2.13GHz (4x8 Kerne) / 6,5 TByte Storage	512
	2	AMD Opteron(TM) Processor 6274, 2.2GHz (16*4 Kerne) / 2 x 2TByte Storage	256
	7	AMD Opteron(TM) Processor 6274, 2.2GHz (16*4 Kerne) / 2 x 2TByte Storage	512

* 2x Tesla S1070 mit je 4x C1060 (2x4 GByte RAM) | ** intern verbaut (6 GByte RAM)

Abbildung 2: Zusätzliche Hardware des bwGRiDs (Stand: 21.05.2012)

Cluster integriert und allen Grid-Nutzern uneingeschränkt zur Verfügung gestellt. Gleiches gilt in Esslingen für die Maschinen mit den PowerXCell-Prozessoren und in Tübingen für 24 Knoten mit bis zu 32 GByte Hauptspeicher. Der Standort Stuttgart stellt allen Nutzern acht Knoten mit GPU Beschleunigerkarten für die interaktive Nutzung und grafische Auswertung zur Verfügung, ebenso der Standort Freiburg, der 4 Knoten mit je zwei Tesla-GPU-Beschleunigerkarten in sein bwGRiD-Cluster integriert hat. Weiterhin wurden aus Mitteln des RZ-Freiburg acht Dell M610x Blades beschafft, die mit, vom Lehrstuhl für biomolekulare Dynamik finanzierten, M2090 GPU Grafikarten ausgerüstet worden sind. Zwar stehen diese Maschinen dem gesamten bwGRiD zur Verfügung, aber den Mitgliedern des Lehrstuhls wird eine erhöhte Priorität eingeräumt. Die restlichen in Abbildung 2 aufgeführten Ressourcen in Heidelberg und Tübingen stehen denjenigen Arbeitsgruppen exklusiv zur Verfügung, die sie finanziert haben.

Die Integration heterogener Hardware in die Basis-Ausstattung des bwGRiDs tangiert jedoch verschiedene Aspekte des Betriebsmodells in unterschiedlicher Weise. Die Hardware und die Nutzungs-Policies (Nutzungsbedingungen) müssen im Scheduling-System für die Nutzer transparent abgebildet werden, ohne dabei die Interoperabilität des Grids zu beeinträchtigen. Entsprechende Konzepte sollen im Rahmen des Arbeitspaket 4.2 entwickelt und umgesetzt werden. Ein weiterer Aspekt betrifft die zentrale Bereitstellung von Softwaremodulen für das bwGRiD. Insbesondere ist die Frage zu klären, ob die mit der Bereitstellung von Standard-Softwaremodulen beauftragen Personen auch für die Bereitstellung der Module für spezielle Hardwarearchitekturen wie GPUs verantwortlich sind. Ferner muss auch geprüft werden, inwieweit die Nutzung der unterschiedlichen Hardwarearchitekturen über das bwGRiD-Portal ermöglicht werden soll. Dazu ist in jedem Fall eine entsprechende Integration in das Ressourcenmanagement in das Portal erforderlich, die zum Teil schon abgeschlossen ist.

Obwohl das bwGRiD-Projekt im Dezember 2012 offiziell ausläuft, wird der Ausbau einiger Cluster geplant. An verschiedenen Standorten werden die bwGRiD-Cluster noch über das offizielle Projektende hinaus betrieben. Dennoch werden jetzt nur noch Komponenten angeschafft, die gegebenenfalls eigenständig betrieben werden können oder sich auch in die HPC-Cluster des Nachfolgeprojektes integrieren lassen.

3.7 Arbeitspaket 4.3 – Anwendersoftware-Kompetenz-Netzwerk

Das Arbeitspaket 4.3 legt den Schwerpunkt auf die im bwGRiD verfügbare Software. Software ist eine der Kernkomponenten für eine erfolgreiche Nutzung des bwGRiDs. Ohne eine ansprechende, umfangreiche und verfügbare Softwareausstattung ist es sehr schwer, neue Benutzer für das bwGRiD zu gewinnen und Bestehende im System zu halten. Die Verteilung von Standard-Software soll verbessert und vereinheitlicht werden, um an möglichst allen Standorten eine homogene Umgebung für den Benutzer bereitzustellen. Durch eine stärkere Automatisierung und Routinen zur automatischen Funktionsprüfung der Software soll sich der Wartungsaufwand für die lokalen Administratoren reduzieren. Gleichzeitig soll auch verstärkt spezielle Software für einzelne Benutzer auf das Grid gebracht werden. Der dazu zur Verfügung gestellte Installationssupport hilft dem Benutzer in allen Phasen dieses Prozesses, angefangen von der Anpassung und Kompilierung der Software bis hin zur Installation und zur Problembehebung während der Laufzeit. Neben dieser durch bwGRiD-Mitarbeiter angebotenen Unterstützung sollen die Benutzer auch untereinander in Kontakt gebracht werden, um sich gemeinsam über die in Verwendung befindliche Software auszutauschen. Hierzu werden entsprechende web-basierte Kommunikationsmöglichkeiten geschaffen. Alle genannten Punkte bedingen eine verbesserte Präsentation der bwGRiD-Software und deren Möglichkeiten nach außen. Zu diesem Zweck muss die Webseite aktualisiert, übersetzt und insbesondere das Softwareangebot übersichtlich dargestellt werden. Für die Koordinierung der Aufgaben wurde in Konstanz die Stelle eines Software-Koordinators geschaffen.

Die beschriebenen Ziele im Arbeitspaket gliedern sich in vier wesentliche Meilensteine. Der erste Meilenstein im Bereich Software-Verteilung ist die Schaffung eines entsprechenden Repositorys mit Mechanismen zur Verteilung. Für diesen Meilenstein, der bis Juli 2012 erreicht werden soll, stellte sich nach eingehender Analyse heraus, dass zuerst ein vernünftiger Überblick über den Soll- und Ist-Zustand der Software auf den einzelnen Knoten vorliegen muss. Gleichzeitig müssen diese Informationen auch über eine Schnittstelle für andere Anwendungen im bwGRiD verfügbar sein. Aus diesem Grund haben wir uns vor der Arbeit an diesem Meilenstein im Projekt entschlossen, zuerst eine Software-Datenbank zu entwickeln, die diese Information ermittelt, aufbereitet und sowohl intern als auch extern zur Verfügung stellt. Diese Datenbank wird an das Portal angedockt, das dabei als bewährtes Framework für die zu entwickelnden Softwarekomponenten dient. Die so ermittelten Daten werden dann über einen bereits in Freiburg entwickelten Software-Browser komfortabel, übersichtlich und sortierbar auf der bwGRiD-Webseite für die Benutzer dargestellt. Bei der internen Verwendung werden die Daten genutzt, um Unterschiede zwischen dem Soll- und dem Ist-Zustand darzustellen und den lokalen Administrator aufzufordern, die neue verfügbare Software zu installieren. Dieser automatisch generierte Überblick macht das manuelle Verfolgen der Softwareliste obsolet. Als zweiter Meilenstein im Bereich der verbesserten Bereitstellung von Software ist die Bereitstellung von automatischen Testroutinen für Juli 2013 vorgesehen. Für diesen Meilenstein haben bisher nur grundlegende

Überlegungen stattgefunden und in einem ersten Schritt eine Vereinheitlichung der Notation von mitgelieferten Testcases in den beschreibenden
Module-Dateien der Softwarepakete erreicht. Außerdem wurde als Vorstu-
fe für automatisierte Tests ein Mechanismus integriert, der ein gegenseiti-
ges manuelles Testen neuer Software beinhaltet. Als weitere Maßnahme im
Rahmen des Installationssupports wurde die Webseite um die Beschreibung
von Software, deren Installation und möglicher Probleme erweitert. Damit
wird eine öffentlich sichtbare Seite geschaffen, auf der sowohl Benutzer
als auch Mitarbeiter jederzeit nachlesen können, was bei der Installation
von bestimmter Software zu beachten ist. Durch das gute Google-Ranking
der universitären Seiten ergibt sich als Nebeneffekt eine gute Werbung für
das bwGRiD bei Personen, die allgemein nach der Software suchen. Auf
Nachfrage von Benutzern wurden bereits mehrere Softwarepakete individuell gebaut und im bwGRiD zum Einsatz gebracht. Der vierte Meilenstein
schließt an den Installationssupport an und soll den Benutzern die Möglichkeit geben, sich selber über Software auf einer geeigneten Plattform auszutauschen. Als Moderator fungiert dabei der Software-Koordinator, der auch
in diesem Benutzerforum aktiv Support geben soll. Da der Meilenstein erst
für Juli 2013 vorgesehen ist, wurde hier bisher nur als Vorarbeit die Über-
setzung der Webseite ins Englische durchgeführt. Die bevorzugte Sprache
der meisten Benutzer im bwGRiD ist englisch und eine gewünschte Diskussion kann nur in dieser Sprache forciert werden. Um eine homogene
Einbettung in die bestehende Webseite zu gewährleisten, muss diese logi-
scherweise dann auch in englisch zur Verfügung stehen.

4 Fazit

Durch das bwGRiD-Projekt wurde in Baden-Württemberg im Laufe der
letzten Jahre eine für Deutschland einzigartige HPC-Infrastruktur geschaffen, die HPC-Ressourcen für ein breites Anwenderspektrum aus der Wissenschaft im Land und darüber hinaus zur Verfügung stellt. Voraussetzung
dafür war das erfolgreiche Verbinden einzelner HPC-Standorte zu einem
Clusterverbund, unter Entwicklung und Einhaltung gemeinsamer Standards
bezüglich der Software, des Batchsystems und des Betriebskonzeptes. Nur
dadurch konnte die für das Projekt so wichtige Interoperabilität gewährleis-

tet werden, die Nutzern die gesamten Rechenressourcen flexibel und transparent zur Verfügung stellt. Die beträchtliche Anzahl an Veröffentlichungen (Referenz) aus verschiedensten wissenschaftlichen Fachrichtungen, für die die Ressourcen der bwGRiD-Infrastruktur in Anspruch genommen wurden, beweist, dass sich das bwGRiD im Laufe der Zeit zu einem unverzichtbaren Werkzeug für eine große Anzahl von Wissenschaftlern entwickelt hat. Mit dem „Ergänzenden-Maßnahmen-Paket" wurde darüber hinaus ein wichtiger Grundstein für die weitere erfolgreiche Entwicklung des HPC in Baden-Württemberg gelegt.

Nicht zuletzt durch das bwGRiD-Projekt hat das HPC eine herausragende Stellung im Land erlangt und stärkt durch die Bereitstellung seiner Computing-Ressourcen für die wissenschaftliche Gemeinschaft den Wissenschaftsstandort Baden-Württemberg.

Geomechanical Reservoir Modeling – a geological application of high-performance computing

Karsten Fischer,* Andreas Henk†

Albert-Ludwigs-Universität Freiburg
Technische Universität Darmstadt

Abstract: Tectonic stresses affect the optimal exploitation of hydrocarbon and geothermal reservoirs in numerous ways. Amongst others, wellbore stability and the orientation of hydraulically induced fracs depend on the recent in situ stresses. The local stress field can vary substantially in magnitude and orientation due to faults or changing rock types. In order to obtain a robust pre-drilling prediction of in situ stress fields and fracture networks, geomechanical reservoir modeling incorporates the specific reservoir geometry, the remote stress field, as well as the mechanical properties of all participating lithologies and faults. The numerical technique of the Finite Element Method (FEM) has the potential to describe the subsurface reservoir in sufficient detail. Reservoir dimensions, the required spatial resolution, and the amount of incorporated faults representing non-linear structural discontinuities increase the demand in computing power in a way that HPC solutions become obligatory. The bwGRiD cluster in Freiburg eventually allowed us to calculate a geomechanical FE-model of an entire reservoir comprising over 3.8 million elements, three lithological layers with individual rock mechanical properties, and more than 80 faults cross-cutting the reservoir. Job-specific performance statistics of differently sized models and multiple runs on various servers reveal interesting aspects regarding the impact of processor type, way of parallelization and GPU acceleration on the computing time of our models. These insights facilitate future work with the bwGRiD and other HPC clusters.

1 Introduction

Compressive stress is ubiquitous in the interior of the earth. The scientific field of Geomechanics is the geological study of the behavior of soil and

---

* karsten.fischer@geologie.uni-freiburg.de
† henk@geo.tu-darmstadt.de

rock under a given state of stress. Geomechanical aspects play an important role for the optimal exploration and production of a variety of reservoir types, for instance in conventional and unconventional hydrocarbon reservoirs, in geothermal reservoirs, but also when it comes to underground sequestration of CO2 (CCS – carbon capture and storage). Amongst others, wellbore stability, the orientation of hydraulically induced fracs and - especially in fractured reservoirs - permeability anisotropies depend on the recent in situ stresses.

While the regional tectonic stress field is mostly dictated by plate tectonics, the local state of stress in a reservoir is affected by faults, as well as vertical and lateral lithological changes, i.e. contrasts in rock mechanical properties (e.g., [Zoback2007, Fjaer2008]). Observations from surface and subsurface studies indicate that such heterogeneities can substantially modify the local magnitudes and orientations of the three principal stresses. In some fault-controlled reservoirs, for example, local stress orientations differing by up to $90°$ from the regional trend have been reported for individual fault compartments [Yale2003].

Such stress perturbations characterize not only the present-day in situ stress regime in a reservoir. Similar, but differently oriented local stress deviations must have existed during past tectonic stages, when the tectonic regime and, hence, paleo-stresses differed in magnitude and orientation from the present situation. Such paleo-stress field perturbations at times of fracture formation and reactivation were responsible for the spatial variations in fracture orientation, fracture type and fracture density observed today.

In order to minimize exploration risks and optimize drilling, a reliable, ideally "pre-drilling" prediction of tectonic stresses and fracture networks is desirable.

2 Geomechanical Modeling

A reliable prognosis requires the incorporation of the specific reservoir geometry, the recent and paleo remote stress field, as well as the mechanical properties of all participating rock types and faults as detailed as possible. The Finite Element Method (FEM) represents an appropriate numerical technique to account for complex reservoir geometries, inhomogeneous material distributions and nonlinear material behavior. Within the Research Project 721 of the German Society for Petroleum and Coal Science and Technology (DGMK), the potential of 3D geomechanical reservoir models for a robust prediction of stress fields and fracture networks is examined using a gas reservoir in the North German Basin as case study.

Figure 1 shows the general workflow for 3D geomechanical reservoir modeling. The ideal input data base is a reservoir model based on depth-converted 3D seismics and geometrically consistent with all available data, for example, a Petrel® project. Calibration data must be independent from the input data and are used to compare the modeling results of the geomechanical FE-model to field observations. The final results can be visualized anywhere in the model by contour and vector plots for all stress and strain quantities that can be derived from the respective 3D tensors. Furthermore it is possible to plot graphs showing the variation of a stress quantity along a pre-defined path through the model. This could be used to evaluate potential drilling paths, for instance.

Following preliminary parameter studies and a first basic model, the buildup of a large and detailed 3D geomechanical reservoir model is carried out. This model covers the entire reservoir area of the case study and includes not only the lithological layer of the reservoir, but also the rock layer above and beneath it, which are called over- and underburden, respectively. These two layers were incorporated to reduce the impact of boundary conditions on the central layer of the reservoir horizon. Based on reservoir-specific data, individual rock mechanical properties are derived and applied to each layer. In total, the three layers of the model cover a thickness of 1.6 km and account for a horizontal reservoir area of more than 700 km^2.

Almost all faults that were interpreted from 3D seismic data and are available in the provided datasets have been incorporated into the model. This leads to more than 80 faults and at most of them, vertical displacements lead to juxtaposition of the mechanically different layers. The faults are implemented as contacts between separately meshed fault block volumes and are modeled with two dimensional contact elements. These ele-

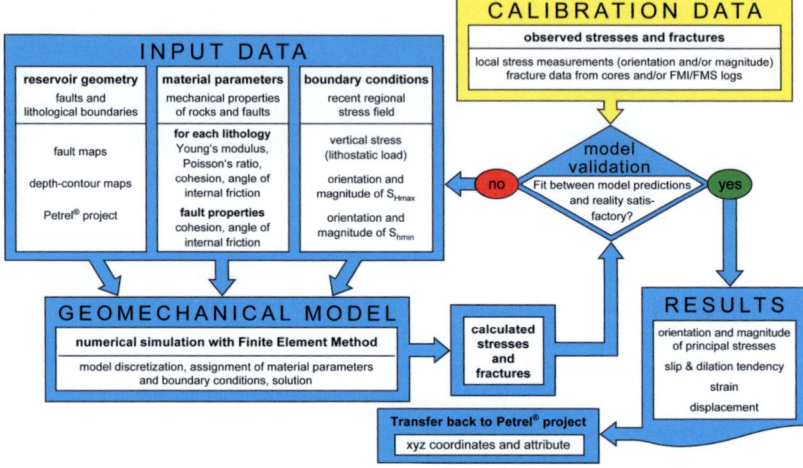

Figure 1: Workflow to set up and calibrate a geomechanical reservoir model for prediction of in situ stresses and fracture networks.

ments allow the application of Coulomb friction and thus a non-linear behavior of the faults. Moreover, they can finally provide fault-specific shear and normal stresses as results revealing their behavior in a distinct state of stress.

The boundary conditions of the model comprise the vertical stress of the overburden on top of the model, while the bottom of the model is fixed along the depth axis. Horizontal stresses are generated by displacements, whose values are calibrated to obtain the characteristic horizontal stress magnitudes published for the region of the reservoir in the North German Basin [Roeckel2003].

3 Application of the bwGRiD as HPC solution

All models within the preliminary parameter studies and the first basic model could be calculated on a local workstation. However, those models included only one set of mechanical parameters, i.e. one type of material, 4-15 faults, and no more than about 1 million elements.

The bwGRiD enabled us to build a full-scale reservoir model with an outstanding complexity, regarding for instance the number of faults and especially the spatial resolution. While the rather thin central layer of the reservoir horizon is divided vertically into 4 element layers, the much thicker over- and underburden are each divided into 6 element layers. In combination with a horizontal element size of 100 m this yields more than 3.81 million elements in total. Figure 2 shows one of more than 200 very differently sized fault blocks of the model elucidating the layering and the high spatial resolution. It has to be kept in mind that the reservoir covers an area of several hundreds of square kilometers. Together with the large amount of non-linear contacts representing faults, this large and detailed 3D geomechanical model would result in absolutely unacceptable computing times when calculated on the available local workstation (Intel Xeon Quad-Core CPU, 12 GByte RAM).

Within the DGMK Research Project 721, the commercial FE-code Ansys® (Ansys Inc., Houston, USA) is used for pre- and post processing, as well as for solving the models. This highly facilitated the usage of the bwGRiD, because Ansys® 13 SP1 had already been installed on all clusters. Inside Ansys®, modeling is done using the Mechanical APDL (Ansys Parametric Design Language), which results in script files comprising a section for pre-processing, solution specifications, and post-processing. These script files are read into Ansys® and are solved as batch jobs using the sparse matrix direct solver.

A portlet programmed for the bwGRiD Portal Project by the very obliging and helpful IT service of the University of Freiburg was used for submitting ANSYS Mechanical jobs to the grid. This portlet is accessible via web browser and allows users to upload the Mechanical APDL script files as well as to select the desired number of nodes, cores, type of parallelization and required main memory. The selectable queues depend on the applied job specifications. After submitting the job, the portlet can be used for monitoring and to download the result files after the job is done. Most calculations were done on the bwGRiD Freiburg, mainly due to the higher

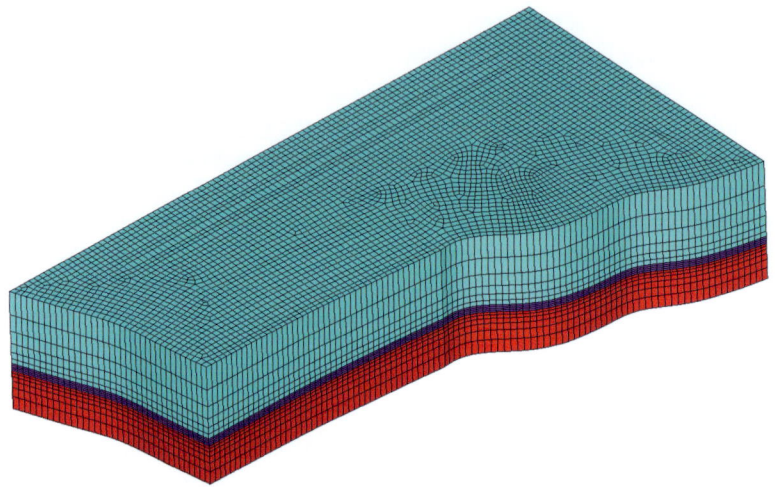

Figure 2: One fault block of the final 3D geomechanical FE-model showing the layer of the overburden (turquoise), reservoir horizon (violet), and underburden (red) divided vertically into six, four and six element layers, respectively. The horizontal element size is 100 m. Both non-planar faces to the front are vertical fault surfaces. The final large reservoir model incorporates more than 200 fault blocks and accounts for a horizontal reservoir area of more than 700 km^2.

variety of special hardware structures and the very fast troubleshooting.

During the work on the bwGRiD, many different hardware configurations were tested and used. The most frequently used servers and those yielding very interesting insights are listed in Table 1.

Before Ansys$^®$ starts with the calculation of a model, the solver checks for the number of equations that have to be solved and for the amount of main memory available. If enough physical memory is available to accommodate all solver data, the model is calculated in the in-core memory mode, which most often results in the fastest solution time. In case this is not possible, the solver runs in the optimal out-of-core memory mode, in which data is swapped from the RAM onto the hard drive to achieve a good bal-

Model	CPU	Cores	RAM	GPU
Dell PowerEdge M610x	Intel Xeon X5650 / 2.66 GHz	12 (2x6)	24 GB	-
HP ProLiant DL785 G5	AMD Opteron 8360 / 2.44 GHz	32 (8x4)	512 GB	-
HP ProLiant DL785 G5	AMD Opteron 8384 / 2.64 GHz	32 (8x4)	256 GB	-
Nvidia Tesla S1070	Intel Xeon E5520 / 2.27 GHz	8 (2x4)	24 GB	GT 200 2x240

Source: http://www.bwgrid.uni-freiburg.de/hardware

Table 1: Hardware of the bwGRiD cluster at the University of Freiburg that was most frequently used for geomechanical modeling.

ance of memory usage and hard drive usage in order to obtain an efficient solution time.

The amount of solver data and, thus, the required amount of memory for in-core calculation rises with an increasing number of elements. However, the relatively high density of non-linearly behaving contacts (i.e. faults) amplifies the amount of solver data extensively. For instance, a small model built in the same way as the large reservoir model, covering only the north-western part of the reservoir and comprising about 880,000 elements and 12 faults, already requires 92 GByte RAM for in-core calculation. Hence, the ProLiant server providing 512 GByte RAM and 32 cores was regarded as the most promising system to calculate the large reservoir model at the shortest solution times (s. Table 1).

All other systems have to calculate in the out-of-core mode due to the limited amount of memory. However, they were interesting for other reasons. While the PowerEdge server comprises the fastest CPUs on the cluster, the Tesla S1070 could provide insights into the performance boost resulting from GPGPU-based acceleration, which is supported by Ansys® since release 13.0.

4 Results

In total, three models are calculated using the bwGRiD: the large, full-scale reservoir model with 120 m and 100 m horizontal element size, as well as a small submodel with a horizontal element size of 70 m covering only the northwestern part of the reservoir.

Figure 3 shows a top view on a cross section plane through the reservoir horizon of the submodel contoured with the distribution of the maximum horizontal stress. This plot reveals characteristic stress perturbations of 2-3 MPa at intersections of faults, strong curvatures and their tips. Moreover, interacting perturbations of neighboring faults can affect the stress magnitudes in a larger surrounding area.

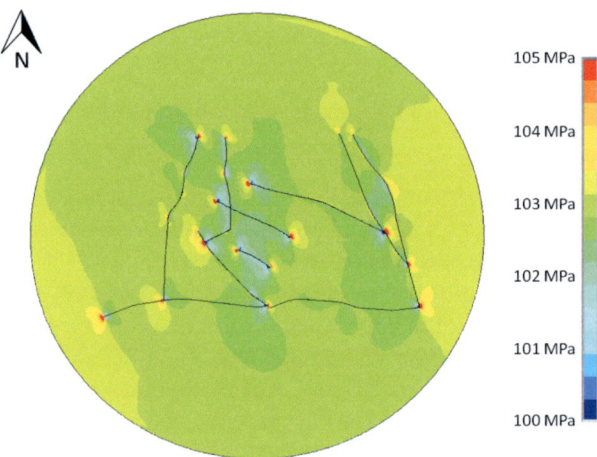

Figure 3: Top view of a cross section plane through the small submodel contoured with the distribution of the magnitudes of the maximum horizontal stress in [MPa]. The diameter of this model is 18 km.

The results of the submodel match those of the large reservoir model, due to the exact same buildup and material parameters, and are now compared to actual stress measurements in the stage of calibration.

Furthermore, the numerous calculations of the three models on various hardware configurations and settings yielded insights into solver performance and those factors influencing the solution time the most. Specific statistics are provided by Ansys® for every calculated batch job. These include, for instance, the time spent for pre-processing, solving the model and post-processing, as well as the equation solver computational rate and effective I/O rate. However, the following findings relate exclusively to our geomechanical FE-models and not to "common" FE-models in structural mechanics.

Concerning the way of parallelization, only symmetric multiprocessing (SMP) resulted in acceptable solution times for our models. This is most probably due to the relatively high amount of non-linear contacts, which increase the required communication between the individual tasks. Table 2 summarizes and compares the maximum and average equation solver effective I/O and computational rates from jobs calculated with SMP parallelization on different systems.

	HP ProLiant DL785 G5 (in-core / 32 cores)	Dell PowerEdge M610x (out-of-core / 12 cores)	Nvidia Tesla S1070 (out-of-core / 8 cores)
Maximum equation solver effective I/O rate	1873.7 MB/s	534.0 MB/s	79.7 MB/s
Average equation solver effective I/O rate	1703.7 MB/s	317.8 MB/s	57.8 MB/s
Maximum equation solver computational rate	20.858 Gflops	49.299 Gflops	33.597 Gflops
Average equation solver computational rate	19.714 Gflops	44.744 Gflops	24.074 Gflops

Table 2: Overview on the equation solver effective I/O rates and computational rates listed by Ansys®. All jobs considered in this table were calculated using SMP parallelization and always with the number of cores listed on top.

As expected, the in-core memory mode yields by far the fastest I/O rates, whereas the jobs calculated out-of-core show a strong dependence of this rate to the specific system (s. Table 2). The overview in Table 2 further demonstrates that - at least for calculating our models - Intel's Xeon CPUs yield significantly higher computational rates of the equation solver than the Opteron CPU from AMD.

The computational rate and the effective I/O rate of the equation solver do both affect the solution time of a model directly. The amount of impact can be elucidated by a direct comparison using the final reservoir model comprising "only" a horizontal element size of 120 m and about 2,650,000 elements. This direct comparison, summarized in Table 3, indicates that the computational rate of the equation solver is much more important than its effective I/O rate. However, other hardware differences of the compared system might be relevant as well.

	HP ProLiant DL785 G5	Dell PowerEdge M610x
Parallelization	SMP	SMP
Cores	32	12
CPU Type	AMD Opteron 8360 2.44 GHz	Intel Xeon X5650 2.66 GHz
Allocated Memory	353.68 GB	19.16 GB
Equation Solver Computational Rate	20.733 Gflops	49.299 Gflops
Equation Solver Effective I/O Rate	1873.7 MB/s	361.6 MB/s
Solution Time	1d 05h 42min	14h 30min

Table 3: Direct comparison between the in-core (left) and out-of-core (right) calculation of the final reservoir model. The significantly shorter solution time for the out-of-core calculation emphasizes the large impact of the equation solver computational rate.

The final reservoir model comprising the highest horizontal resolution of 100 m and about 3,810,000 elements could not be calculated in-core, because of the memory requirements of 520 GByte. Its solution on the HP

ProLiant DL785 G5 using SMP parallelization with 32 cores took 2 days, 18 hours and 5 minutes (out-of-core memory mode).

A direct comparison concerning the GPU acceleration was done using the small submodel. The exact same model was solved on the Nvidia Tesla S1070 with and without the contribution of the GPU units, which resulted in calculation times of 152 minutes and 191 minutes, respectively.

The GPU acceleration thus only saves about 20% of solution time. The reasons for this rather small acceleration, however, are manifold and require further investigations.

5 Outlook

The following stage in the DGMK Research Project 721 covers the calibration of the final geomechanical reservoir model. This will include multiple calculations, which will be done again on the bwGRiD cluster in Freiburg. In addition, future research projects addressing geomechanical modeling will benefit from the experiences gained on the bwGRiD as HPC solution.

References

[Fjaer2008] E. Fjaer, R. M. Holt, and P. Horsrud. *Petroleum Related Rock mechanics*. Elsevier Science and Technology, 2008.

[Roeckel2003] T. Röckel and C. Lempp. The state of stress in the north german basin; der spannungszustand im norddeutschen becken. *Erdöl Erdgas Kohle*, 119:73–79, 2003.

[Yale2003] D.P. Yale. Fault and stress magnitude controls on variations in the orientation of in situ stress. *Geological Society, London, Special Publications*, 209(1):55–64, January 2003.

[Zoback2007] M.D. Zoback. *Reservoir Geomechanics: Earth Stress and Rock Mechanics Applied to Exploration, Production and Wellbore Stability*. Cambridge Press, 2007.

Acknowledgements

This work is part of DGMK Project 721 "Prediction of tectonic stresses and fracture networks with geomechanical reservoir models" funded by Exxon-Mobil Production Deutschland GmbH, Gaz de France Suez E&P Deutschland GmbH and RWE Dea AG. Their support is gratefully acknowledged.

Scalability Study of HiFlow^3 based on a Fluid Flow Channel Benchmark

Vincent Heuveline,* Eva Ketelaer,† Staffan Ronnas,‡
Mareike Schmidtobreick,§ Martin Wlotzka¶

Engineering Mathematics and Computing Lab (EMCL)
Karlsruhe Institute of Technology (KIT)

Abstract: Exploiting the compute power of high performance computing clusters efficiently is a key ingredient in order to solve large, fully coupled systems modeled by partial differential equations with high accuracy. We study strong and weak scalability properties of the parallel Finite Element software package HiFlow^3 for a challenging instationary 3D fluid flow problem. For this benchmark study, we ran several simulations with up to 10 millions of unknowns using up to 512 cores on the bwGRiD cluster in Karlsruhe. For large problem sizes, the software package showed good characteristics regarding efficiency and speedup.

1 Introduction

Numerical simulations often play a key role in the analysis of complex physical and technical processes. Many real world phenomena can be modeled mathematically by partial differential equations (PDEs). Examples include the numerical simulation of tropical cyclones which influence the global weather forecast, as well as computational studies of the human respiratory system. Performing accurate simulations

* vincent.heuveline@kit.edu
† eva.ketelaer@kit.edu
‡ staffan.ronnas@kit.edu
§ mareike.schmidtobreick@kit.edu
¶ martin.wlotzka@kit.edu

often relies on computational resources only available on high performance computing (HPC) platforms. Approximate solutions of the underlying system of PDEs can be computed using appropriate numerical discretization methods. A common discretization approach is the Finite Element Method (FEM), which usually results in large, sparse, and fully coupled linear systems with up to several millions of unknowns. In order to be able to solve such large problems, it is essential to use highly scalable finite element software.

In this paper we analyze weak and strong scalability properties of the HiFlow^3 Finite Element package [Heuveline2010] developed at the Engineering Mathematics and Computing Lab (EMCL). This software platform aims at providing efficient and accurate solvers for complex models. The study is based on a 3D channel flow benchmark problem defined by the DFG [Turek1996]. It is defined as a fluid flow problem inside a rectangular channel containing a block-shaped obstacle. This benchmark has previously been performed by a large community using a variety of discretization methods and numerical solvers with a strong emphasis on the accuracy of the solution. On the one hand the benchmark is a challenging problem for numerical simulations, and on the other hand there are published results giving a point of comparison for the quality of our solutions. Our study was carried out on the bwGRiD cluster located in Karlsruhe using up to 512 cores distributed over 64 nodes.

In Section 2, the mathematical problem, the solution method and implementation are described. Additionally, in this section the setup for the scalability study is presented. Section 3 is dedicated to the presentation of the results, as well as their analysis. A conclusion and outlook are given in Section 4.

2 Benchmark Formulation

In this section, we present the mathematical setup on which our scalability study is based and depict how we validated the benchmark implementation. The second part of the section gives an overview of the test setup.

2.1 Mathematical Problem

The considered benchmark assumes a three dimensional instationary flow around a block-shaped obstacle in a channel as described in [Turek1996], see Fig. 1. We assume the liquid to be an incompressible Newtonian fluid and model the flow by the Navier-Stokes equations

$$u_t - \nu\Delta u + (u\cdot\nabla)u + \frac{1}{\rho}\nabla p = 0, \quad \text{in } \Omega\times[0,T],$$

$$\nabla\cdot u = 0, \quad \text{in } \Omega\times[0,T],$$

where u denotes the velocity field, p the pressure variable and $\Omega\subset\mathbb{R}^3$ holds. At the inflow Γ_{in} (1a) we set the boundary condition to a Poiseuille profile, at the outflow Γ_{out} (1b) we choose the natural or do-nothing boundary condition and at the solid walls of the channel $\Gamma_{wall} := \partial\Omega\backslash(\overline{\Gamma_{in}\cup\Gamma_{out}})$ (1c) we impose homogeneous Dirichlet boundary conditions (no-slip conditions). As initial condition we set the velocity to zero inside of Ω (1d).

$$u = g, \quad \text{on } \Gamma_{in}\times[0,T], \quad (1a)$$
$$(-\mathcal{I}p+\nu\nabla u)\cdot n = 0, \quad \text{on } \Gamma_{out}\times[0,T], \quad (1b)$$
$$u = 0, \quad \text{on } \Gamma_{wall}\times[0,T], \quad (1c)$$
$$u = 0, \quad \text{in } \Omega\times\{0\}, \quad (1d)$$

where

$$g(0,y,z,t) = \left(16U_m yz\frac{(H-y)(H-z)}{H^4},0,0\right)^{\top}.$$

The height and width of the channel $H = 0.41\,m$ and the maximum inflow speed $U_m = 2.25\,m/s$ are chosen as in [Turek1996], which yields the Reynolds number $Re = 100$. We discretize this equation with an FEM, see e.g. [Girault1986]. The channel is discretized by hexahedral cells, resulting in the initial mesh covering the computational domain which is shown in Fig. 1.

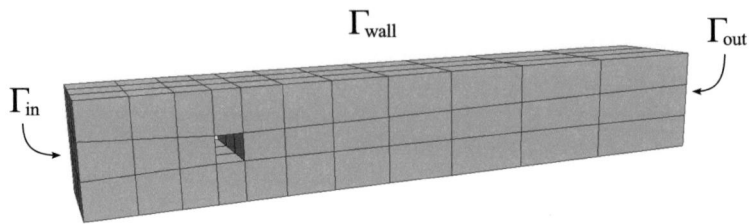

Figure 1: The initial mesh which is a coarse discretization of the computational domain with 96 cells.

The computations for the scalability study were done on meshes resulting from different levels of global refinement applied to the initial mesh. The number of mesh cells and degrees of freedom resulting from these refinements are given in Table 1.

The parallelization concept of HiFlow^3 is based on domain decomposition, as described in [Heuveline2011, Ronnas2011]. In this study, the partitioning of the mesh was computed with the METIS graph partitioner [Karypis2006]. For the spatial discretization of the model problem, we applied a continuous Galerkin FEM. We used the Taylor-Hood element pair, i.e. Q_2-elements for the velocity and Q_1-elements for the pressure. These elements satisfy the discrete inf-sup condition, and thus guarantee stability [Girault1986].

Refinement Level	# Mesh Cells	Problem size, i.e. # DoFs
2	6,144	170,688
3	49,152	1,296,256
4	393,216	10,098,432

Table 1: Information on the number of cells and the number of degrees of freedom (DoFs) that different meshes have. Hereby the mesh level describes how often the mesh has been refined globally on the basis of the initial mesh.

For the time discretization, we used the Crank-Nicolson method applied to an equidistant partitioning of the time interval. We applied Newton's method to the resulting discrete non-linear problems. In each Newton step, we used a right-preconditioned GMRES-method [Saad2003] to solve the linearized system. An incomplete LU-decomposition from the ILU++ library [Mayer2007, Mayer2008] was employed as a preconditioner. The stopping criteria for both the non-linear Newton solver and the linear GMRES solver were set to a relative tolerance of 10^{-6}. This ensures that the residual norm of both the Newton iteration as well as the GMRES iteration decreases by six orders of magnitude compared to the residual of the starting solution, respectively.

The whole solution process was implemented using HiFlow^3, besides the already mentioned mesh partitioning and the preconditioner library.

For this benchmark no analytical solution and no experimental data are available for comparison. In order to obtain a good indication for the accuracy of the benchmark implementation, we compared the drag coefficient of the obstacle to the results of simulations performed with other software by other researchers as listed in [Turek1996]. We computed the drag coefficient in each time-step by evaluating face integrals as described in [John2002]. The initial mesh, see Fig. 1, was globally refined four times. The benchmark was solved in the time interval [0s, 8s] with a time-step size of 0.025s, i.e. 320 time-steps. For the maximum drag coefficient we get 4.84 which lies in the interval of [4.31, 4.88] from [Turek1996]. The authors of that paper expected a time-periodic solution at a Reynolds number of 100. Here, we made the same observation as in [John2002], namely that the numerical solution tends to a stationary solution instead, which is another indication that our benchmark implementation works correctly.

2.2 Setup of Scalability Tests

We study strong and weak scalability for the following benchmark setup. As benchmark metric, we measure the total run-time of the first ten time-steps of the solution process. The problem size is associated to the successively globally refined meshes mentioned in Subsection 2.1. The refinement levels of the mesh and their resulting problem sizes, i.e. the number of unknowns are listed in Table 1.

This benchmark was done on the local part of the bwGRiD-cluster in Karlsruhe. This system is a x86-cluster featuring 10 Blade centers each of which contains 14 HS21 XM Blades. Each node has two quad-core Intel Xeon E5440 (Harpertown) processors with 2.83 GHz clock frequency and 16 GByte main memory. The nodes are connected via Infiniband. The operating system is Scientific Linux 5.5.

We executed the simulation with up to 512 cores; for more details see Table 2. Furthermore we took into account the following two limiting factors with respect to the dependency between the refinement levels and the number of cores. On the one hand the memory available on a computing node is important: a minimum number of nodes is needed to cover the memory required by the solver. On the other hand, problem instances with lower refinement levels require less computational effort, which makes the use of a large number of cores meaningless.

3 Results and Analysis

We consider strong and weak scaling, which are the two common concepts of scalability in HPC. In both cases, the total run-time on different numbers of processors is compared. For the strong scaling, the total problem size is fixed, while for the weak scaling the problem size per process is kept constant.

3.1 Strong Scalability

For the strong scalability, we analyzed the speedup and efficiency for each refinement level. The speedup $S(p, N)$ of a parallel execution

Nodes x Cores			Run-time [sec]			# of GMRES iter.		
			Level 2	Level 3	Level 4	Level 2	Level 3	Level 4
1	x	1	2,391	27,517		438	778	
1	x	2	1,470	14,076		1,239	2,376	
1	x	4	906	8,078		1,664	2,510	
1	x	8	605	5,887		2,155	2,819	
2	x	8	345	3,074		2,657	2,976	
4	x	8	226	1,644		3,306	3,214	
8	x	8		1,027	10,752		4,133	5,306
12	x	8			6,923			5,234
16	x	8			5,539			5,520
32	x	8			3,023			5,770
64	x	8			2,007			6,652

Table 2: The run-time in seconds and the total number of GMRES iterations needed over the whole solution process. The benchmark was run with different numbers of cores and different levels of refinement of the intial mesh.

with p processors is defined as

$$S(p,N) = \frac{T(p,N)}{T(1,N)} \, ,$$

where $T(p,N)$ is the run-time for an execution with p processors and problem size N. The efficiency is defined as

$$E(p,N) = \frac{S(p,N)}{p} \, .$$

Fig. 2 and Fig. 3 show the obtained speedup and Fig. 4 shows the efficiency of our three test series. Note that for the level 4 test series, these quantities are computed relatively to the execution with $p = 64$ processors, since it was not possible to run these tests with fewer processors due to the limited memory of the computing nodes.

There are two aspects which generally degrade the efficiency of our test runs as the number of processors is increased. First, for solving

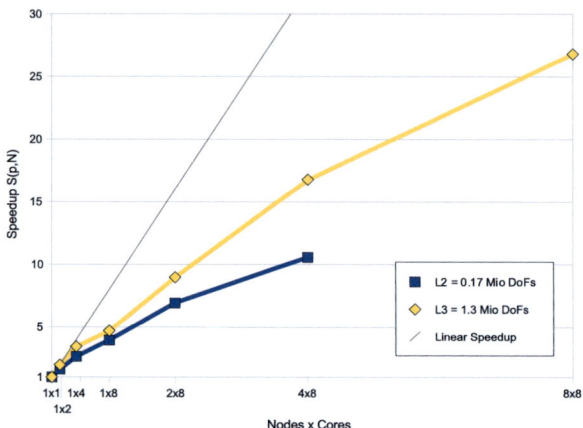

Figure 2: The speedup of the benchmark is plotted for levels of refinement 2 and 3. As reference point the sequential run is used.

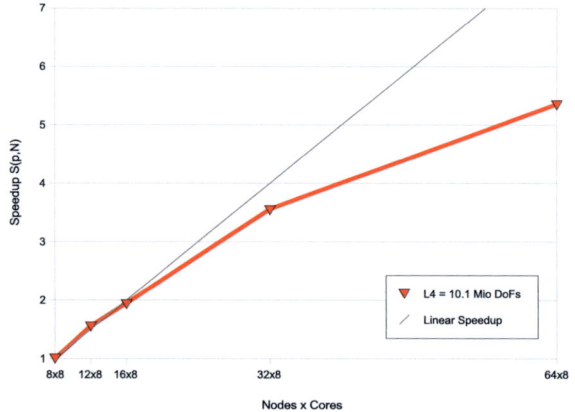

Figure 3: The speedup of the benchmark is plotted for the level 4 refinement. The test run with the lowest possible core number (64 cores) is used as reference point.

the linear systems, communication and synchronization is necessary in every iteration of the GMRES solver, since the systems are fully coupled. The computational domain is divided into the same number of subdomains as the number of processors used. Second, the incomplete LU factorization is applied as a block-Jacobi preconditioner. This means that the couplings from different subdomains are neglected in the preconditioning step. Therefore the preconditioner becomes less effective the more subdomains we have, since more information about the couplings between the unknowns is ignored. In consequence, the GMRES solver needs to perform more iterations to achieve the desired stopping tolerance, which can be seen by comparing the number of GMRES iterations in Table 2.

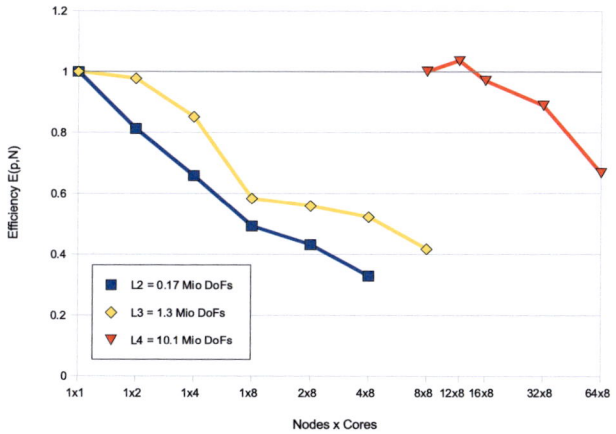

Figure 4: The efficiency of the benchmark for three levels of refinement. The efficiency of the test run with the lowest possible core number is set to 1, the other tests are based on these, respectively.

The problem sizes of the level 2 and 3 series are small enough to run the tests on one processor as a basis for the evaluation of the efficiency. The efficiency decreases to less than 50% for these two series when increasing the number of processors to 32 and 64, respectively. In addition to the effects regarding the linear solver and preconditioner mentioned above, the computation to communication ratio decreases when using more processors, and therefore the level 2 series with the smallest problem size yields the lowest efficiency. For the level 3 series we observe a better efficiency due to its larger problem size.

The level 4 series shows a better efficiency than the other two series, but it should be kept in mind that this is measured with respect to a different reference, and therefore not directly comparable. For 96 processors, we even observe a superlinear speedup, which corresponds to the fact that fewer GMRES iterations are needed on 96 cores compared to 64 cores. When increasing the number of processors to 128 and 256, the efficiency remains at high values of 97% and 89%, respectively. For a decomposition onto 512 processors, the computation to communication ratio is lowered so that the efficiency decreases to 67%.

3.2 Weak Scalability

For the weak scalability, we want to keep the problem size per core constant. Hence, we increase the problem size, namely the number of DoFs N, and the number of cores p by the same factor s and compare the run-times $T(p, N)$:

$$\mathcal{R} := \frac{T(s \cdot p, s \cdot N)}{T(p, N)}.$$

To evaluate the weak scalability, we compare the run-times from Table 2 of runs where the number of cores are increased by a factor of eight, and the number of DoFs are increased by a factor of about 7.7, which we obtain naturally by the global mesh refinement.

For example, we can compare the run-time of $T(2 \times 8, L3) = T(16, 1.3 \cdot 10^6)$ and $T(1 \times 2, L2) = T(2, 0.17 \cdot 10^6)$ which gives $\mathcal{R} = 2.09$. Assuming a perfect scaling the run-time should remain constant, so that $\mathcal{R} = 1$. Results for selected comparisons from Table 2 are shown

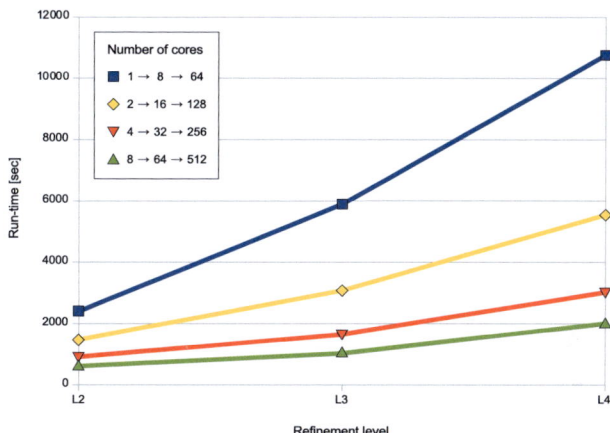

Figure 5: Comparison sequences of the run-times of jobs in order to obtain a measure for weak scalability, where the number of cores and DoFs are increased by a factor of 8 and 7.7, respectively.

in Fig. 5. Each curve stands for a sequence of run-times where the number of cores is multiplied by 8 from level to level. The number of cores for level 2 is taken from $\{1, 2, 4, 8\}$, respectively, for each line. The run-times increase by factors varying from 1.70 to 2.46 when comparing level 2 and 3 and from 1.80 to 1.95 when comparing level 3 and level 4. However, as mentioned in Subsection 3.1, the workload is not completely determined by the number of unknowns, due to the increase in the number of GMRES iterations with an increased degree of parallelization.

3.3 Scalability Results

The obtained results for the strong and weak scalability show a decrease in speedup and efficiency as well as a non-constant behaviour of the ratio $\mathcal{R}$. This can be explained by two aspects. Firstly, the main influence results from the mathematical characteristics of the block-Jacobi preconditioner as described in Subsection 3.1. Secondly, one cannot expect much better efficiency with a large number of processors for the small problem sizes of the level 2 and 3 test series. Due to memory limitations of the cluster, it was not possible to run the tests with a refinement level higher than level 4, i.e. number of DoFs $N = 10,098,432$.

4 Conclusion

In this paper we presented the mathematical setup of the scalability benchmark implemented with the HiFlow^3 Finite Element package. We executed different tests with varying numbers of cores and different problem sizes. Based on the run-times, the weak and strong scalability were analyzed. Our conclusion is that both the weak and the strong scalability are highly satisfactory and correspond to the expected behaviour of a mature parallel FEM software package. It turns out that the behaviour of the block-Jacobi preconditioner has a strong impact on the decrease of the scalability. Improvements with respect to more efficient preconditioning techniques are planned and will be included in a new release of HiFlow^3. An extension of this benchmark on larger machines considering larger problems will be the subject of further research.

References

[Girault1986] V. Girault and P.-A. Raviart. *Finite element methods for Navier-Stokes equations : theory and algorithms.* Springer series in computational mathematics. Springer, Berlin, 1986.

[Heuveline2010] H. Anzt, W. Augustin, M. Baumann, H. Bockelmann, T. Gengenbach, T. Hahn, V. Heuveline, E. Ketelaer, D. Lukarski, A. Otzen, S. Ritterbusch, B. Rocker, S. Ronnas, M. Schick, C. Subramanian, J.-P. Weiss, and F. Wilhelm. Hiflow3 – a flexible and hardware-aware parallel finite element package. EMCL Preprint Series, 2010. 06:1-36.

[Heuveline2011] H. Anzt, W. Augustin, M. Baumann, T. Gengenbach, T. Hahn, A. Helfrich-Schkarbanenko, V. Heuveline, E. Ketelaer, D. Lukarski, A. Nestler, S. Ritterbusch, S. Ronnås, M. Schick, M. Schmidtobreick, C. Subramanian, J.-P. Weiss, F. Wilhelm, and M. Wlotzka. Hiflow3 - a hardware-aware parallel finite element package. In *5th Parallel Tools Workshop*. Springer, accepted.

[John2002] V. John. Higher order finite element methods and multigrid solvers in a benchmark problem for the 3d navier-stokes equations. *International Journal for Numerical Methods in Fluids*, 40(6):775–798, 2002.

[Karypis2006] A. Abou-Rjeili and G. Karypis. Multilevel algorithms for partitioning power-law graphs. In *20th International Parallel and Distributed Processing Symposium, 2006. IPDPS 2006.*

[Mayer2007] J. Mayer. A multilevel crout ilu preconditioner with pivoting and row permutation. *Numerical Linear Algebra with Applications*, 14(10):771–789, 2007.

[Mayer2008] J. Mayer. Symmetric permutations for i-matrices to delay and avoid small pivots during factorization. *SIAM J. Sci. Comput.*, 30(2):982–996, March 2008.

[Ronnas2011] S. Ronnås, T. Gengenbach, E. Ketelaer, and V. Heuveline. Design and implementation of distributed meshes in hiflow3. In C. Bischof, H.-G. Hegering, W. E. Nagel, and G. Wittum, editors, *Competence in High Performance Computing 2010*, pages 61–71. Springer Berlin Heidelberg, 2012.

[Saad2003] Y. Saad. *Iterative methods for sparse linear systems.* SIAM, Society for Industrial and Applied Mathematics, Philadelphia, 2nd edition, 2003.

[Turek1996] S. Turek and M. Schäfer. Benchmark computations of laminar flow around cylinder. In E.H. Hirschel, editor, *Flow Simulation with High–Performance Computers II*, volume 52 of *Notes on Numerical Fluid Mechanics*, pages 547–566. Vieweg, 1996. co. F. Durst, E. Krause, R. Rannacher.

Acknowledgments

We thank Mehmet Soysal for his constant technical support as administrator of the bwGRiD cluster in Karlsruhe. Further the authors thank Prof. Dr. Rudolf Lohner and Dr. Marcel Kunze for their kind support in the preparation of this paper.

CART Trees and Random Forests in Linguistics

Ulrike Schneider*

Albert-Ludwigs-Universität Freiburg

Abstract: This paper investigates in how far usage-based factors, observable in bigram frequencies, transitional probabilities and other measures of association, influence the placement of hesitations in English. I focus on the placement of filled and unfilled pauses as well as discourse markers in the context of prepositional phrases. The approach taken here makes use of classification and regression trees (CART) and random forests implemented in R. Results indicate that there are frequency effects in the data: more coherent structures are less likely to be interrupted than infrequent sequences with low internal attractions.

This paper is a loose summary of the more detailed argument presented in [SchneiderInPreparation].

1 Introduction

A central question in cognitive linguistics is how utterances are planned. Do we go ahead word by word filling a grammatical frame? In the case of a phrase like *in the blue box*, it is well imaginable that a speaker retrieves all words separately from the mental lexicon and puts them in sequence as he plans the phrase. If the speaker were, however, planning a phrase like *in the United States*, which is structurally very similar to the first, he could still be expected to go about differently. While he has separate entries in the lexicon for *united* and *states*, there are reasons to expect that he additionally has a combined entry for *United States*, which he can insert into his phrase as a block or 'chunk'. While *United States* is a comparatively frequent expression, sequences may not even need to be frequent to be 'chunked'.

* ulrike.schneider@frequenz.uni-freiburg.de

The speaker may rarely talk about something which happened *in the olden days*, yet *olden days* is likely to be chunked, because, nowadays, the archaic word *olden* can only be combined with *days*. Finally, some expressions are expected to be chunked, because their semantics are non-compositional, which means that, as in the case of *on the other hand*, the meaning of the whole expression cannot be deduced from the meaning of the individual words in it. So, while linguists working in a usage-based framework generally agree that "a large amount of language is not constructed from 'basic' structures and a lexicon, but occurs in sequences [...] that are more or less fixed in form" ([Hunston2000, p. 7]), there is yet no consensus about the conditions necessary for a sequence to get chunked. Neither is there agreement on the common size or nature of chunks (cf. for example [Biber2004], [Bybee2007], [Ellis2003], [Wray2002]).

One way to determine the conditions which facilitate chunking is to look at hesitations in spoken language (cf. [Biber2004], [Erman2007], [Kapatsinski2005], [Fox2010], [Shriberg1996]). It is highly unlikely for a speaker to interrupt longer words to hesitate. Utterances such as **door uh knob* or **neighbour uh hood* are highly unlikely, because the speaker retrieves the entire word as one unit from the mental lexicon. Consequently, if chunks are also retrieved 'pre-assembled' from the lexicon, neither should they be interrupted by hesitations.

However, the model, as described up to this point, is somewhat oversimplistic, as it is unlikely that there is a strict division between words and chunks. Rather, we are dealing with a cline: activating one word in the lexicon always leads to the activation of others which hold some relation to the initially activated one. The stronger the mutual activation between a pair or sequence of words, the easier for a speaker to retrieve it in combination and the less likely the sequence is to be interrupted by hesitations.

The present paper analyses phrases in spoken language where the speaker needs to hesitate. The analysis is based on the assumption that language planning is always slightly ahead of actually uttering the planned words, so that speakers are subconsciously aware of upcoming planning trouble before they have reached the 'trouble spot' in their utterance. Consequently, within a limited range of words, the speaker has a choice of where to halt for a moment to plan the next part of the utterance. I hypothesise that frequency-based factors determine where the speaker pauses. Hence I investigate the role co-occurrence frequencies and other probabilistic factors play in chunking. The present publication focusses on the computational aspects of the study (for a more in-depth analysis see [SchneiderInPreparation]).

2 Design

In the present study, chunking strength is measured at the bigram level; bigram being defined as two consecutive words which do not cross sentence boundaries. A word, in turn, is defined as any word-form with an attached part-of-speech tag, separated by spaces from other word-forms. Hence, in a structure like the following

it_PRP 's_BES crazy_JJ. i_PRP do_VBP n't_RB believe_ VB it_PRP.

it 's, do n't and *believe it* would be considered bigrams while *crazy i* would not. All bigrams are drawn from the *Switchboard NXT* corpus ([NXTSwitchboardCorpus2008]), a collection of American telephone conversations between strangers, collected by Texas Instruments in 1990/91. I am not working with the actual recordings, but with an annotated transcription of the corpus, which contains a total of 830,000 words. It is furthermore time-aligned, making it possible extract unfilled pauses.

The following frequency-based and probabilistic measures of association serve as predictors of hesitation placement:

w.freq - Word frequency: How often the word occurs in the corpus.

bi.freq - Bigram frequency: How often the bigram occurs in the corpus.

TPD - Direct transitional probability: The probability of the second word given the first; unidirectional (cf. [Kapatsinski2005, p. 6/7]).

TPB - Backwards transitional probability: The probability of the first word given the second, unidirectional (cf. [Kapatsinski2005, p. 6/7]).

MI - Mutual Information score: Assesses how much more often the two words in the bigram occur together than would be expected by chance; bidirectional ([Wiechmann2008, p. 264/5]).

G - Lexical gravity G: Bidirectional measure similar to MI, though additionally taking into account the restrictions grammar imposes on the distributions of words in language ([Daudaravicius2004]; [Gries2010]).

In summary, hesitation placement will be predicted by comparing frequencies and probabilistic properties of the bigrams in close proximity of the hesitation. This is, however, only possible if hesitations in comparable contexts are selected. For the present study, contexts were therefore limited to prepositional phrases with the structure 'Preposition Determiner Noun'. This includes phrases such as *during the dinner* or *in that regard*. All 1,440 hesitations occurring within or immediately preceding these prepositional phrases were extracted from the corpus. The context considered for analysis consists of the three words in the phrase (w1 to w3), the two bigrams in the phrase (bi1 and bi2; e.g. *during the* and *the dinner*) as well as the word preceding the phrase (w0) and the bigram containing w0 and w1 (bi0). This leaves three 'slots' for the speaker to place a hesitation: before the first word in the phrase (position1), before the second word (position2) and before the third (position3). As this represents a non-binary research question, binomial regression was not an option. Hence CART trees and random forests were chosen as methods of regression. The following sections will discuss their computation as well as their advantages and disadvantages when applied in linguistics.

3 Study I: CART Trees

Classification and regression trees (CART), which are also known as "conditional inference trees" (cf. [Hothorn2006]), are a non-parametric approach to regression ([Strobl2009, p. 5/6]). This data-driven method has a number of advantages: It can handle multinomial outcomes, complex interactions, unbalanced designs as well as collinear predictors and large numbers of predictors ([TagliamonteToAppear, p. 22,30]).

The algorithm 'grows' trees through recursive binary partitioning of the data, with the aim to create ever purer 'branches', i.e. subgroups of the data. At every splitting point, the algorithm selects the predictor best suited to reduce impurity and the optimal splitting point for this predictor ([Baayen2008, p. 149]; [Strobl2009, p. 8]). All branches end in terminal 'leaf' nodes which jointly make up the entire data-set ([Baayen2008, p. 149]). The more complex the model, the more splits and consequently terminal leaves are in the tree ([Hothorn2006, p. 13]). The final sequence of splits reflects non-linear and non-monotone associations ([Strobl2009, p. 6]) as well as interactions ([Baayen2008, p. 154]; [Strobl2009, p. 11]).

In this paper, the CART mechanism applied is the `ctree` package for R ([Hothorn2006]). Unlike previous algorithms, `ctree` is claimed neither to overfit ([Strobl2009, p. 10]) nor to favour predictors with many possible splits ([TagliamonteToAppear, p. 21]; [Strobl2009, p. 30]).

Figure 1 shows the resulting tree. Nodes are numbered from one through 17. At each split, the selected predictor is given and branches are labelled for whether they contain predictor values above or below the splitting point. The diagrams at the bottom represent terminal leaves. In each leaf, the most frequent outcome (hesitation in position1, 2 or 3) shows the model's prediction for the entire leaf. Out of a total of n=1,440 data points, this tree predicts 924 correctly, which corresponds to a misclassification rate of 35.83 per cent.

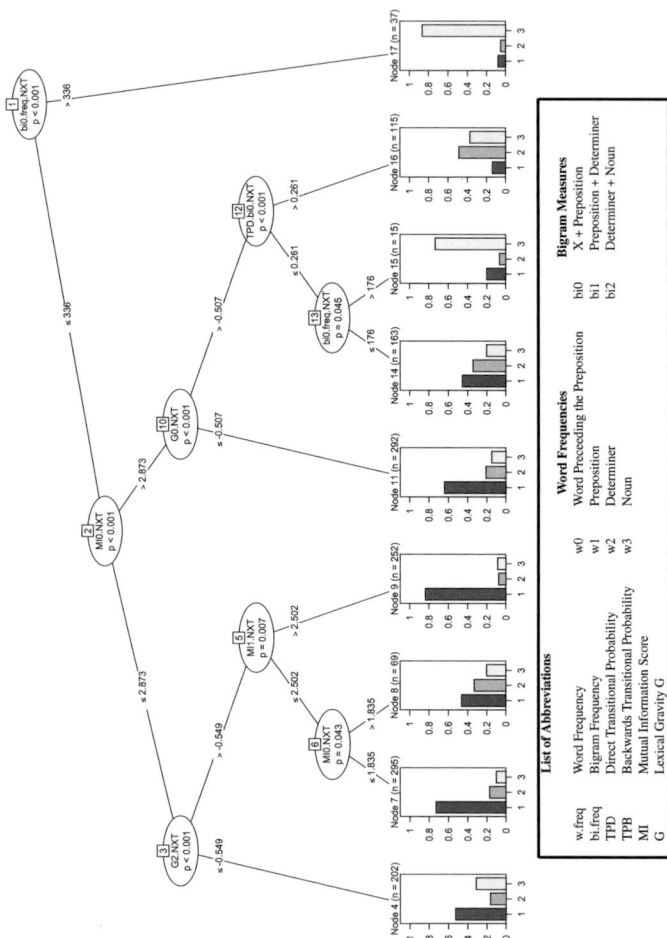

Figure 1: Ctree for Hesitation Placement in the Structure 'Preposition Determiner Noun'

`Ctree` does not provide a correlation coefficient or the variance resolution. Consequently, the performance of the model needs to be assessed in comparison to a 'baseline model', which predicts all data points to have the same realisation as the most frequent outcome ([Baayen2008, p. 153]). Here, hesitations are preferentially placed before the preposition, which corresponds to position1. The baseline model would therefore predict position1 throughout, thus classifying 847 outcomes correctly (misclassification rate: 41.18 per cent). The tree's performance is evaluated by comparing the number of correct and wrong classifications of the tree (847 vs. 516; observed) to those of the baseline model (924 vs. 516; expected) in a chi^2 test of significance. The p-value of $p < .0001$ shows that the `ctree` model preforms highly significantly above baseline. In addition, the residuals of the chisquared test provide a more cautious assessment of the `ctree`'s performance. Residuals with a value exceeding two indicate a significant difference. In the present case, residuals are 2.65 and -3.16, indicating a significantly improved number of correct predictions (positive value) and a significantly lower number of misclassifications (negative value)[1].

As noted before, speakers tend to place hesitations before the preposition, i.e. before the phrase, indicating an influence of structural factors. The tree, however, reveals that the tendency to place hesitations at the phrase boundary increases the lower the attraction within bigram0, that is between the preposition and the word preceding it. Apart from this, strong attraction between the words in bigram0 means that the preposition is easily predictable given the word preceding it. This is particularly the case in node 17. Finally, the tree shows that hesitation placement before the preposition can also be caused by strong cohesion within the phrase (for a complete analysis, see [SchneiderInPreparation]).

The choice of predictors in the tree furthermore indicates that more complex measures of association do not generally outperform simpler ones. While the Mutual Information score and lexical gravity G feature the most in the tree, bigram frequency and direct transitional probability were also selected.

---

[1] I acknowledge the help of Sascha Wolfer who suggested this way to compare model performances.

A great advantage of CART trees is the resulting clustering of the data, which allows for further analyses of the linguistic properties of the structures in such homogenous groups as, for example, nodes nine and 17. On the downside, `ctree` does not plan ahead; all splits are only locally optimal ([Strobl2009, p. 17]). Furthermore, reliance on a single tree with only locally optimal splits means that minor changes in the dataset can lead to different splits in the tree, thus leading to variation in the predictions ([Strobl2009, p. 13]).

4 Study II: Random Forests

The aforementioned issues resulting from the use of a single tree can be avoided by generating a range of trees, each based on a subsample of the data points and predictors ([TagliamonteToAppear, p. 21]; [Strobl2009, p. 15/6]). This option is offered by random forests. In the present study, the forest generating mechanism applied is the `cforest` command in the party package for R ([Hothorn2006]; [Strobl2007]; [Strobl2008]). For each data point, prediction weights across all trees are averaged (R Documentation [help function] for cforest {party}, [TagliamonteToAppear, p. 22]).

While `ctree` analyses can be computed on home office computers, `cforest` is computationally intensive. Depending on the number of trees in the forest, the number of predictors and the complexity of the model, running `cforest` on a home computer can be rather time-consuming, if not computationally infeasible. The present model with 1,440 data-points and 20 predictors (all numeric, except *hesitation type*) tends to crash in R version 1.42 for Mac (release 2.13.1) on a MacBookPro (2.26 GHz Intel processor; 4 GByte RAM) if more than 1,000 trees are grown. Due to the resources and technical support of the bwGrid, these problems could be resolved. If run on one node in the grid (nodes=1:ppn=8), scripts were stable and ran in up to 48 hours (for 1,000 forests of different sizes, see below).

The following is a overview of the fitting and results of a `cforest` analysis of the influence of frequency-based predictors on hesitation placement in the context of the structure 'Preposition Determiner Noun'. Procedure, scripts and interpretation are based on [Strobl2009], [Shih2011] and [TagliamonteToAppear]. For more details see [SchneiderInPreparation].

For a forest, which ideally fits the data, the "number of randomly pre-selected variables" ('mtry'; R Documentation [help function] for cforest {party}) and the number of trees ('ntree') need to be adjusted. There is no standard procedure for either adjustment. For mtry, "[t]he square root of the number of variables" ([Strobl2009, Supplement:3]) has been suggested as a default. Consequently, in the present study, which considers 20 predictors, mtry was fixed at 5. Concerning ntree, it is commonly suggested to use as many trees as computationally feasible ([Goldstein2011, p. 20]; [Genuer2008, p. 16/7]; [Shih2011, p. 3]). The ctree model above, however, suggests that trees resulting from the present analysis may not be too complex. So, forests with several thousands of trees may not be required. To see whether ever larger forests lead to improved results, 100 forests of 100, 500, 1,000, 2,000, 3,000, 4,000, 5,000, 6,000, 7,000, 8,000 trees each (all with mtry= 5) were grown. Results can be seen in Figure 2. At first, variation decreases with increasing forest size. Though from about 2,000 trees on, variation does not significantly decrease further and the mean is near stable. To be cautious, ntree was fixed at 3,000.

The average forest with mtry= 5 and ntree= $3,000$ predicts 1035 of the 1440 outcomes correctly, corresponding to a misclassification rate of 28.13 per cent. The chi-squared test shows that the cforest performs significantly better than the baseline model ($p < .0001$). Also, the residuals of 6.46 and -7.72 show that the number of correct predictions has significantly increased.

Results from cforest can be somewhat "over-optimistic" ([Strobl2009, p. 19]). Therefore, it is more realistic to rely on more conservative results offered by the 'out-of-bag' (OOB) observations ([Strobl2009, p. 19,29]). Each tree in a forest is fitted to a random subsample of the data points; all remaining observations form the OOB set ([Strobl2009, p. 19]). In the present study of hesitation placement in prepositional phrases (mtry= 5, ntree= $3,000$), OOB predictions average 928 correct classifications (misclassification rate of 35.56 per cent). Despite being more conservative than the original cforest result, this still highly significantly exceeds the performance of the baseline model ($p < .0001$, residuals: 2.78 and -3.33).

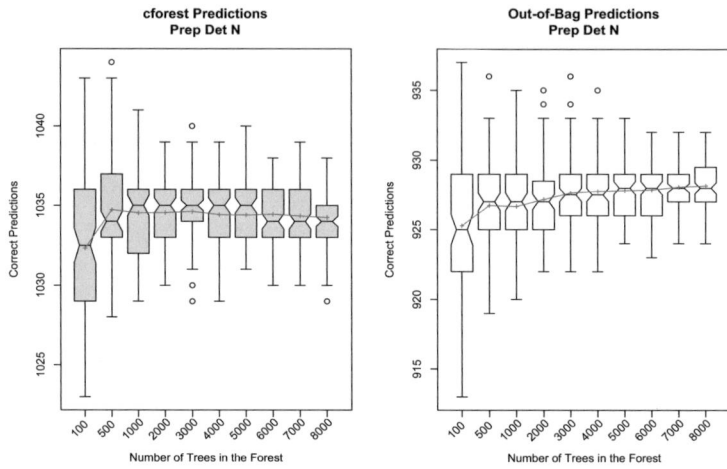

Figure 2: Correct Predictions for 'Preposition Determiner Noun' at Different Forest Sizes

Like `ctree, cforest` can be used to evaluate the influence of individual predictors. Though, unlike the individual trees, forests cannot be visualised, so predictors need to be ranked with the additional function `varimp` (permutation variable importance measure, part of the `party` package). `Varimp` scores provide a "relative ranking" of predictors ([Shih2011, p. 2]), which is not comparable across studies ([Strobl2009] as published in *Psychological Methods*:336). It works by converting individual predictors to non-significant predictors and comparing the resulting change in predictive accuracy ([TagliamonteToAppear, p. 21/2]).

The score of non-significant predictors is close to or even below zero ([TagliamonteToAppear, p. 23]). Therefore, "[a]ll variables whose importance is negative, zero or has a small positive value that lies in the same range as the negative values, can be excluded from further exploration" ([Strobl2009, p. 31]). The directionality of the effect cannot be deduced from `varimp` results.

`Varimp` has the additional option to adjust "for correlations between predictor variables", so that "[t]he resulting variable importance score is conditional in the sense of beta coefficients in regression models" (R Documentation [help function] for cforest party). This option could not be chosen here, mainly because the script crashed even at 16 GByte RAM.

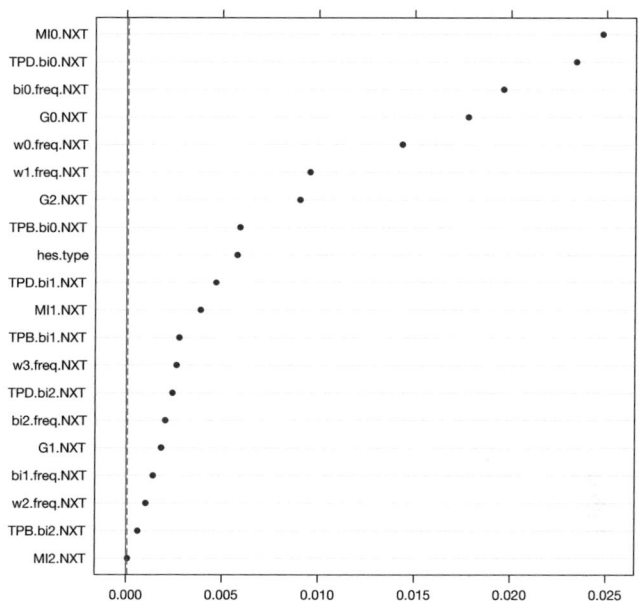

Figure 3: Variable Importance of Predictors for Hesitation Placement in 'Preposition Determiner Noun'

Figure 3 shows the results of `varimp` for the previously described forest. In line with the single tree analysed above, the variable importance ranking shows that measures relating to the 'X + Preposition' bigram have the strongest effect on hesitation placement. Contrary to what the `ctree` model suggested, MI0 actually outperforms the frequency of bigram0. Furthermore, the role of some word frequencies is far more significant than suggested by the `ctree` model. So, the general hypothesis that more complex measures of association perform better at predicting hesitation placement is not confirmed.

5 Summary and Conclusion

This paper focussed on a statistical methodology. It points out that recursive partitioning, particularly when applied in ensemble methods, offers a solution for multinomial problems in linguistics. Results show that word and bigram frequencies as well as transitional probabilities, the Mutual Information score and lexical gravity G are predictive of hesitation placement in prepositional phrases. Consequently, hesitation placement is not only governed by grammatical, but also by frequency-based factors. For a theory of chunking, this implies that hesitations can serve as indicators of chunk boundaries. Results furthermore allow conclusions about the importance of individual predictors. While simple co-occurrence frequency was not the best predictor, no one predictor clearly outperformed the others. As a conclusion, it can be assumed that high bigram frequency alone is not a sufficient condition for chunking.

This paper showed that combining single trees with random forests can be a useful procedure in linguistic analyses, as it combines the clustering offered by trees with the more stable analysis of random forests. It also showed how linguists can profit from the computational possibilities offered by cluster computing.

References

[Baayen2008] R. H. Baayen. *Analyzing Linguistic Data. A Practical Introduction to Statistics using R.* CUP, Cambridge, 2008.

[Biber2004] D. Biber, S. Conrad, and V. Cortes. If you look at... : Lexical bundles in university teaching and textbooks. *Applied Linguistics*, 25(3):371–405, 2004.

[Bybee2007] J. Bybee. *Frequency of Use and the Organization of Language.* OUP, Oxford, 2007.

[Daudaravicius2004] V. Daudaravičius and R. Marcinkevičienė. Gravity counts for the boundaries of collocations. *International Journal of Corpus Linguistics*, 9(2):321–348, 2004.

[Ellis2003] N. C. Ellis. *Handbook of Second Language Acquisition*, chapter Constructions, chunking, and connectionism: The emergence of second language structure. Blackwell, Oxford, 2003.

[Erman2007] B. Erman. Cognitive processes as evidence of the idiom principle. *International Journal of Corpus Linguistics*, 12(1):25–53, 2007.

[Fox2010] B. A. Fox, Y. Maschler, and S. Uhmann. A cross-linguistic study of self-repair: Evidence from English, German and Hebrew. *Journal of Pragmatics*, 42:2487–2505, 2010.

[Genuer2008] R. Genuer, J.-M. Poggi, and C. Tuleau. Random forests: some methodological insights. *Rapport de Recherche*, 6729:1–32, 2008.

[Goldstein2011] B. A. Goldstein, E. C. Polley, and F. B. S. Briggs. Random forests for genetic association studies. *Statistical Applications in Genetics and Molecular Biology*, 10(1):1–34, 2011.

[Gries2010] S. Th. Gries and J. Mukherjee. Lexical gravity across varieties of English: An ICE-based study of n-grams in Asian Englishes. *International Journal of Corpus Linguistics*, 15(4):520–548, 2010.

[Hothorn2006] T. Hothorn, K. Hornik, and A. Zeileis. Unbiased recursive partitioning: A conditional inference framework. *Journal of Computational and Graphical Statistics*, 15(3):651–674, 2006.

[Hothorn2006a] T. Hothorn, P. Buehlmann, S. Dudoit, A. Molinaro, and M. van Der Laan. Survival ensembles. *Biostatistics*, 7(3):355–373, 2006.

[Hunston2000] S. Hunston and G. Francis. *Pattern Grammar: A Corpus-Driven Approach to the Lexical Grammar of English*. Benjamins, J., Amsterdam/Philadelphia, 2000.

[Kapatsinski2005] V. M. Kapatsinski. Measuring the relationship of structure to use: Determinants of the extent of recycle in repetition repair. *Berkeley Linguistics Society*, 30:481–92, 2005.

[NXTSwitchboardCorpus2008] *NXT Switchboard Corpus Public Release 2008*. Linguistic Data Consortium. Catalog #LDC2009T26, Philadelphia, 2008.

[SchneiderInPreparation] U. Schneider. *Frequency, Hesitations and Chunks. What Does the Placement of Hesitations Tell us About the Nature of Chunks?* PhD Thesis, in preparation.

[Shih2011] S. S.-y. Shih. Random forests for classification trees and categorical dependent variables: An informal quick start R guide, 2011.

[Shriberg1996] E. Shriberg and A. Stolke. Word predictability after hesitations: A corpus-based study. *Proceedings of the International Conference on Spoken Language Processing (Vol.3)*, pages 1868–1871, 1996.

[Strobl2007] C. Strobl, A.-L. Boulestreix, A. Zeileis, and T. Hothorn. Bias in random forest variable importance measures: Illustrations, sources and a solution. *BMC Bioinformatics*, 8(25), 2007.

[Strobl2008] C. Strobl, A.-L. Boulestreix, T. Kneib, T. Augustin, and A. Zeileis. Conditional variable importance for random forests. *BMC Bioinformatics*, 9(307), 2008.

[Strobl2009] C. Strobl, J. Malley, and G. Tutz. An introduction to recursive partitioning: Rationale, application and characteristics of classification and regression trees, bagging and random forests. *University of Munich, Department of Statistics, Technical Report Number 55. (Including Supplement)*, pages 1–42, 2009.

[TagliamonteToAppear] S. A. Tagliamonte and R. H. Baayen. Models, forests and trees of York English: *Was/were* variation as a case study for statistical practice. to appear.

[Wiechmann2008] D. Wiechmann. On the computation of collostruction strength: Testing measures of association as expressions of lexical bias. *Corpus Linguistics and Linguistic Theory*, 4(2):253–290, 2008.

[Wray2002] A. Wray. *Formulaic Language and the Lexicon*. CUP, Cambridge, 2002.

GBDP on the grid: a genome-based approach for species delimitation adjusted for an automated and highly parallel processing of large data sets

Jan P. Meier-Kolthoff^{1} *†, Alexander F. Auch^{2}†,
Hans-Peter Klenk^{1}, Markus Göker^{1}

^{1}Leibniz Institute DSMZ - German Collection of Microorganisms and
Cell Cultures, Braunschweig
^{2}Eberhard-Karls-Universität, Tübingen, Germany

Abstract: The GBDP approach (Genome Blast Distance Phylogeny) is a digital, genome-based method for the calculation of distances between organisms that can be further utilized for the inference of phylogenetic trees. Moreover, it is a technological advancement over the tedious and error-prone wet-lab technology DNA-DNA hybridization (DDH), on which the prokaryotic species concept is ultimately based. GBDP provides for an exact calculation of distances between pairs of entirely or partially sequenced genomes. These are compared using local-alignment tools such as BLAST and the resulting intergenomic matches subsequently transformed into a genome-to-genome distance (GGD). The Genome-to-Genome Distance Calculator (GGDC) web service is implementing the GBDP approach and is publicly available under http://ggdc.gbdp.org/. We advanced the GBDP approach by developing a high-performance cluster (HPC) version that is capable of executing large amounts of genome comparisons by using the parallel nature of compute grids, such as the bwGRiD. Pairwise distances for a novel exemplary data set of 15 eukaryotic Basidiomycota genomes – about order of magnitude larger than common prokaryotic genomes – were calculated, a phylogenetic tree reconstructed and subsequently analysed. The new implementation is boosting the conduction of large genome-based experiments and can thus provide new and even more detailed phylogenetic insights into groups of organisms for which genomic data are available. Benchmarks revealed that the total computation time of the Ba-

---

* E-mail of corresponding author: jan.meier-kolthoff@dsmz.de
† These authors contributed equally to this work

sidiomycota data set is almost negligible (within 1h) due to the linear speed-up
provided by the cluster.

1 Introduction

This article describes an HPC (high-performance cluster) implementation
of Genome-Blast Distance Phylogeny [Henz2005, Auch2006, Auch2009,
Auch2010, Auch2010a], a bioinformatics approach for the calculation of
distances between completely or partially sequenced genomes. GBDP is a
basis for the inference of phylogenetic trees or networks and can also be
used as a technically improved genome-sequence-based alternative for tedious and error-prone wet-lab techniques such as DNA-DNA hybridization
(DDH).

The 2011 EHEC outbreak in Germany and other European countries
called to mind that a quick identification and classification of pathogenic
microorganisms is of utmost importance for proper reactions to such crises
[Beutin2012]. Knowledge about key properties such as infectious spread-
ing, antibiotic resistances, optimal growth conditions and morphology help
to develop a proper cure and to eliminate or at least to reduce the risk of
new infections. For this and other reasons, one important sub-discipline in
biology is taxonomy; the identification and classification of species according to a given scheme. In recent decades, microbial taxonomy was richly
informed by phylogenetics, the study of evolutionary relatedness among
groups of organisms on the basis of molecular sequencing data. It reached
a preliminary climax in 1977 when Carl Woese used the DNA sequence of
the 16S ribosomal subunits of bacterial strains to introduce a revolutionary
classification scheme that contained the *Archaea* as a third domain along
with *Bacteria* and *Eucaryota* [Woese1977]. These ribosomal sequences are
ancient and distributed over all lineages of life with little or no horizontal
gene transfer. However, the more 16S sequences were obtained from both
Bacteria and *Archaea* the more they turned out not to be suitable as sole
universal phylogenetic marker [Klenk2010], i.e., sequences among some
microbial groups are almost identical (high conservation), although the underlying organisms are only distantly related. Hence, new approaches were
required and finally became apparent with the advent and rapid advances in

whole-genome sequencing [Mardis2011]. These offered new perspectives for genome-based identification and classification of microorganisms: by using whole genomes – or at least a large number of gene-families – the phylogenetic resolution can be substantially increased [Henz2005].

This principle led to the aforementioned development of the Genome-Blast Distance Phylogeny approach (GBDP) that was originally devised in 2005 [Henz2005] and subsequently improved. The latest installation of the software is especially designed for the use on high-performance clusters – such as those provided by bwGRiD [bwgrid2012] – and thus capable of handling large data sets. The underlying principle of the GBDP software itself is as follows: in the first step two genomes A and B are locally aligned using tools such as BLAST [Altschul1990], which search for local similarities and thus produce a set of high-scoring segment pairs (HSPs; these are intergenomic stretches matching up to a certain extent). In the second step, information contained in these HSPs (e.g., the total number of identical base pairs) is transformed into a single genome-to-genome distance value (GGD) by the use of a specific distance formula. In principle, GBDP could as well process proteomic data instead of genomic ones.

We describe the basic principle of the GBDP approach and the extensions necessary for running it on compute clusters. Finally, we demonstrate the implementation on the basis of an exemplary data set of fungal genomes. These eukaryotic genomes are by an order of magnitude larger than those of *Bacteria* and *Archaea* thus making the computation of intergenomic distances a more challenging task. We observed that the GBDP implementation is able to handle input of this size without requiring any extra adjustments to the algorithms. We further assessed the general suitability of our grid-based implementation for this kind of analyses and could confirm that the highly parallel nature of the bwGRiD is boosting studies of the aforementioned kind: overall computation times are significantly reduced, allowing our experiment to be completed within a single hour; computations that would have taken days – if not weeks – on a standard desktop PC.

2 Materials and Methods

2.1 The GBDP principle

The GBDP approach has been discussed in several publications [Henz2005, Auch2006, Auch2009, Auch2010, Auch2010a], thus, we will only describe the basic mechanisms and principles of the algorithm. The pipeline is primarily subdivided into two phases: in the first phase, a genome X is BLASTed against a genome Y and vice versa. Here, the term "BLASTed" denotes the application of one out of six supported local-alignment programs: BLAST+ [Camacho2009], NCBI-BLAST [Altschul1990], MUMmer [Kurtz2004], BLAT [Kent2002], WU-BLAST [Altschul1990] and BLASTZ [Schwartz2003]. The resulting matches between both genomes are called high-scoring segment pairs (HSPs). In a second phase, GBDP is filtering these HSPs according to one out of three available algorithms: "greedy", "greedy-with-trimming" or "coverage". Each one of these is accounting differently for special cases such as overlapping HSPs (i.e., two HSPs that share a specific part within the query or subject genome). Briefly, the algorithms define (i) whether the smaller overlapping HSP is removed (called "greedy"; can lead to information loss but computationally fast), (ii) the overlapping parts are merged ("greedy-with-trimming"; also prevents overlapping genome parts to be considered twice but is more compute-intense) or (iii) only the amount of the genome is accounted that is actually covered by HSPs. At the end of the second phase, these matches are transformed to a single distance value $d(X,Y)$ by applying one out of ten available distance formulas (d_0 to d_9). These formulas are basically different flavours of how distances between genomes can be computed on the basis of their respective HSP sets. For example d_4 and d_5 are preferable when dealing with partially incomplete genomes, whereas d_1 and d_7 (and their logarithmized variants d_3 and d_9) are especially suitable if two complete genomes are significantly differing in size (see [Auch2010] for detailed descriptions). Optional is the generation of bootstrap or jackknife replicate distances, which is based on a random sampling of the above mentioned HSPs (prior to the distance calculation). The GGDC can be requested to compute these replicates by adding either a bootstrap or jackknife generator object to the YAML request (see

Fig. 3). These sampling implementations should not be confused with the type of bootstrapping/jackknifing that is usually applied to multiple sequence alignments.

Regarding the implementation, the first phase is encapsulated in a so-called "match request" which triggers the aforementioned comparison of two genomes and finally provides the results in a standardized output format (see below for details). In turn, the latter output is read during the second phase and used by a separate "distance request" to finally compare distance values that are also stored in a proper output format. The division into these two types of requests is due to the fact that distance requests can be conducted under different settings without requiring the matches requests to be repeated. This procedure is saving both computation and storage resources.

2.2 Adjusting GBDP for the bwGRiD

The GBDP software was originally devised to be run on local machines, thus requiring a couple of extensions to the initial concept [Auch2010a]. The final workflow of the new pipeline is shown in Fig. 1. The following list summarizes the requirements of the implementation and how they were finally embedded into the bwGRiD environment.

Languages The GBDP software is written in Java (1.5+) whereas the grid-related part (e.g., for the scheduling) is implemented in the Ruby language (1.8.7+).

Interfaces All request and output files are uniformly provided in the YAML cross-language format – a human-readable data serialization format (http://www.yaml.org/). This allowed us to upload and/or download data to and from the bwGRiD. Fig. 2 and 3 show sample requests and output files for both match and distance calculations.

Bulk generation of the request Most of the phylogenomic analyses conducted on the bwGRiD are based on comparably large sets of genomes thus requiring an automated generation of match and distance requests as well as a simultaneous validation of the genome files' for-

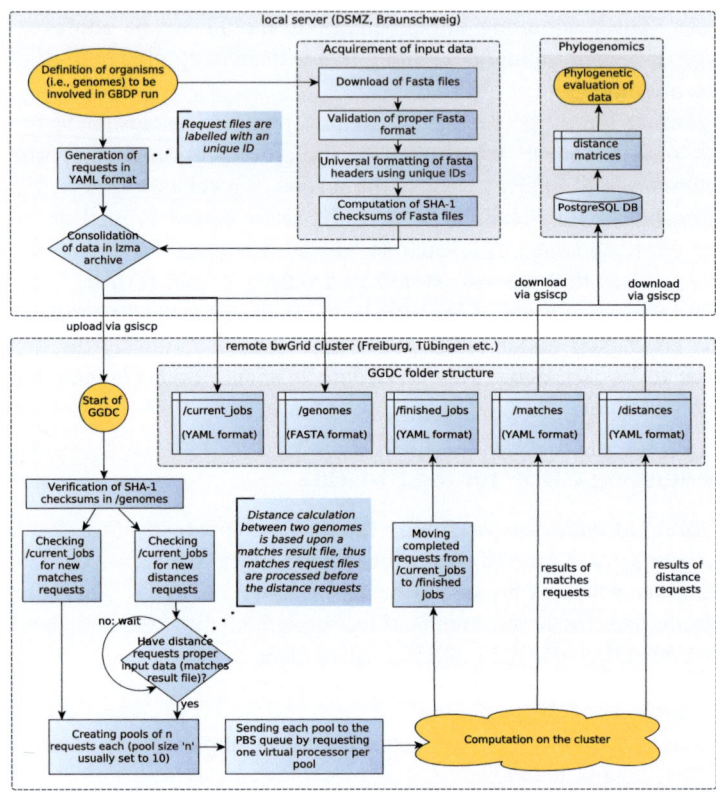

Figure 1: The GBDP pipeline as embedded on the grid. The pipeline is subdivided into three fully automated steps: (i) preparation of input data (both request and FASTA files) and upload to the grid, (ii) start of the GGDC software and submission of jobs to the PBS queue and, (iii) download of the results to the local server and final phylogenetic analysis. Even though the use of the grid infrastructure is preferable, the GBDP software can be run on any type of server or local PC. In that case, the requests are processed consecutively.

mat before the data is transferred to the grid. For each FASTA file an SHA-1 checksum is computed that can be verified once the file has been transmitted to the remote site (i.e., bwGRiD). Moreover, genome files and genome parts are internally represented by unique IDs to avoid the problem of mislabelled or duplicate genome parts.

Job dispatcher Match and distance requests as well as FASTA files are the initial input for the Genome-to-Genome Distance Calculator software (GGDC) – the software which is implementing the aforementioned GBDP approach. The Job dispatcher facility checks the available requests and validates the SHA-1 checksums of the uploaded FASTA files. Afterwards the requests are pooled (default pool size is 10), i.e. they are assigned to one virtual processor on the grid and consecutively executed. On the background of large sets of requests, this strategy substantially reduces the number of virtual processors that have to be requested. The dispatcher task can be either triggered on the grid by a cron job or from an arbitrary external logic.

2.3 GBDP-based phylogenetic analysis of 15 species from the Basidiomycota phylum

Together with the Ascomycota, Basidiomycota is one of two large phyla that comprise the subkingdom Dikarya within the kingdom Fungi [Hibbett2007]. We queried the Genomes Online Database [Pagani2012] for all species from the Basidiomycota phylum and restricted the outcome to those for which genomic data was available. Seven strains were marked as "complete and published" whereas eight strains were in state "incomplete". Genomic data was downloaded from NCBI for 15 strains including incomplete ones (see Tab. 1); GBDP is capable of calculating distances even between these types of data [Auch2010].

As next step, all 105 distinct pairwise distances between these genomes had to be calculated. This means that 105 match requests had to be completed, followed by the same number of distance requests. By default, the GBDP software calculates intergenomic distances under all distance formulas d_0 to d_9, thus resulting in a separate distance matrix for each of them.

```
 1  ——— ! BlastJob
    jobId: 1
 3  outputDirectory: matches
    EValueThreshold: 10.0
 5  localAlignmentTool: !! BlastPlusWrapper
      lowComplexityFilter: 1
 7    softMasking: 1
      wordLength: 11
 9    maskedBlastDbAlgorithm: dustmasker
      dbSoftMaskingAlgorithmId: 11
11
    genomes:
13  — ! Genome
      name: Coprinopsis_cinerea_okayama7_130
15    genomeId: 7
    — ! Genome
17    name: Cryptococcus_neoformans_B_3501A
      genomeId: 6
```

```
    ———
 2  jobId: 1
    genomeId1: 6
 4  genomeId2: 7
    matchCollections:
 6  — ! MatchCollection
      querySequenceId: 6::20546
 8    hitSequenceId: 7::20614
      matches:
10    — ! Match
        alignmentLength: 1874
12      bitScore: 2480.9185
        eValue: 0.0
14      hitEnd: 2038
        hitStart: 3902
16      identity: 1688
        queryEnd: 2005279
18      queryStart: 2003429
```

Figure 2: A sample match request (**left**) with the resulting output (**right**) in YAML format. Line 12 in the match request denotes an array of the two genomes to be compared, whereas line 5 defines a hash table containing settings under those the genomes are locally aligned. Line 9 in the output file defines an array of BLAST hits. For convenience the BLAST statistics are also contained in the matches output file (not shown). The files can be found at `http://www.bw-grid.de/projekte/`.

These matrices were used for the phylogenetic reconstruction, using an improved minimum-evolution approach (FastME [Desper2002]). The resulting trees were compared with the NCBI classification of the included organisms to assess their accuracy in representing evolutionary relationships. NCBI is not an authoritative source for taxonomy but already includes recent improvements of the higher-order classification of fungi [Hibbett2007]. Comparison was done using the c-score [Henz2005, Auch2006] which corrects for the insufficient resolution of the classification-based reference tree.

2.4 Benchmark setup

On the one hand we measured (i) the total execution time (walltime) for each of the aforementioned 105 matches and 105 distances requests, and (ii)

```
     ── !DistanceJob
 2   jobId: 106
     matchesJobId: 1
 4   distanceAlgorithms:
     − Trimming
 6   eValueFilterThreshold: 0.01
     outputFile: 106_distances.yaml
 8   genomes:
     − !Genome
10     name: Coprinopsis_cinerea.fna
       genomeId: 7
12   − !Genome
       name: Cryptococcus_neoformans.fna
14     genomeId: 6

16   replicateGenerator: !BootstrapGenerator
       numberOfReplicates: 100
18     randomSeed: 10027302
```

```
     ── !DistanceData
 2   distanceAlgorithm: Trimming
     jobId: 106
 4   matchesJobId: 1
     replicateId: 0
 6   taxonId1: 6
     taxonId2: 7
 8
     distanceEntries:
10   − distance: 0.99
       distanceType: D0
12     status: OK
       variance: 3.784E−12
14     ...
     − distance: 8.23
16     distanceType: D9
       status: OK
18     variance: 1.914E−4
```

Figure 3: A sample distance request (**left**) with the resulting output (**right**) in YAML format. Line 8 of the distance request denotes an array of two genomes. Line 4 defines a list of algorithms that should be applied during the distance calculation. The additional computation of bootstrap or jackknife replicates can be activated by adding either a "!BootstrapGenerator" or "!JackknifeGenerator" object (here: bootstrap replicates are requested). In the distance output file, the distance values for all ten distance formulas (d_0 - d_9) are listed (in this example only d_0 and d_9). Bootstrap or jackknife replicate distances are numbered according to a replicate ID (line 5). The files can be found at `http://www.bw-grid.de/projekte/`.

the file sizes of the YAML files containing the match results. On the other hand, we approximated the intergenomic search space of each genome pair by calculating the product of both genomes' lengths. We investigated if and how the execution time was affected in dependence of search space size and, secondly, assessed whether the latter also affected the size of the match results. For means of a better interpretation of the results we added information on the relatedness of the denoted genome pairs by calculating patristic distances from the NCBI taxonomy tree of the 15 Basidiomycota genomes.

Strain	Size (Mb)	GOLD ID	NCBI accession
Phanerochaete chrysosporium RP-78	29	Gc00187	AADS00000000
Cryptococcus neoformans JEC 21	19	Gc00247	AE017341
Ustilago maydis 521	20	Gc00507	AACP00000000
Malassezia globosa CBS 7966	8.7	Gc00704	NZ_AAYY00000000
Laccaria bicolor S238N-H82	74	Gc00714	NZ_ABFE00000000
Postia placenta MAD 698-R	59	Gc00946	NZ_ABWF00000000
Schizophyllum commune H4-8	52	Gc01524	NZ_ADMJ00000000
Cryptococcus neoformans gattii R265	17	Gi00179	AAFP00000000
Malassezia restricta CBS 7877	4.7	Gi01942	AAXK01000000
Moniliophthora perniciosa FA553	12	Gi00175	ABRE00000000
Coprinopsis cinerea okayama 7#130	36	Gi01113	AACS00000000
Mixia osmundae IAM 14324	13	Gi07938	BABT00000000
Cryptococcus neoformans var. *grubii* serotypeA H99	19	Gi00180	AACO02000000
Cryptococcus neoformans B-3501A	20	Gi00177	NZ_AAEY00000000
Puccinia graminis tritici CRL 75-36-700-3	87	Gi01690	AAWC01000000

Table 1: Strains from the Basidiomycota phylum used in the GBDP analysis. Information as retrieved from the GOLD database [Pagani2012]. The genome status is either "complete and published" (if the GOLD ID starts with "Gc") or "incomplete" (if the ID starts with "Gi"). The genome sizes are provided in mega base pairs (Mb). The genomic data can be downloaded from http://www.ncbi.nlm.nih.gov/sites/genome/.

All calculations were made on the bwGRiD cluster in Freiburg which is made up of 140 nodes, each one equipped with an IBM-Bladeserver HS21XM containing two Intel Xeon E5440 CPUs (Harpertown) with a clock frequency of 2.83 GHz. Moreover, each node comes with 16 GByte of main memory.

3 Results

3.1 Phylogenetic analysis of the Basidiomycota data set

The resulting branch support was uniformly high (see Fig. 4 for an example), but the c-scores varied, depending on the distance formula used and to a much lesser degree on whether "greedy", "greedy-with-trimming" or "coverage" was used. The lowest c-scores of 0.333 (i.e., the least correspondence with the reference classification) were obtained with formulas d_4 and d_5, the highest c-scores of 0.917 with formulas d_3 and d_9. Whether "greedy", "greedy-with-trimming" or "coverage" was used did not affect the c-scores of formulas d_3 and d_9.

One of the best trees is shown in Fig. 4. The subphyla (Pucciniamycotina: *Mixia* and *Puccinia*; Ustilaginomycotina: *Malassezia* and *Ustilago*; Agaricomycotina: all other included organisms) are all well recovered. The sole discrepancy with the NCBI classification is that *Phanerochaeta* and *Postia* ("Agaricomycetes incertae sedis") are placed within Agaricales, closer to the other Agaricales than *Schizophyllum*. Their names are boxed in Fig. 4. Because this discrepancy is caused by organisms of uncertain taxonomic placement ("incertae sedis"), the GBDP phylogeny might well be regarded as in full agreement with the classification.

3.2 Benchmark results

The total execution time of all match requests added up to 19.75 hours and that of the distance requests was 59.9 hours. The average execution time of all match requests was about 11 minutes and that of the distance requests about 34 minutes. The average size of all match results was about 40 MByte (total size: 4 GByte). Fig. 5 shows the benchmark results.

4 Discussion

4.1 Phylogenetic analysis

Distance formulas d_4 and d_5 (which is the logarithmized version of d_4) ignore the genome lengths and only relate the total HSP length and the total number of identical base pairs within HSPs to each other; in contrast, d_3 and

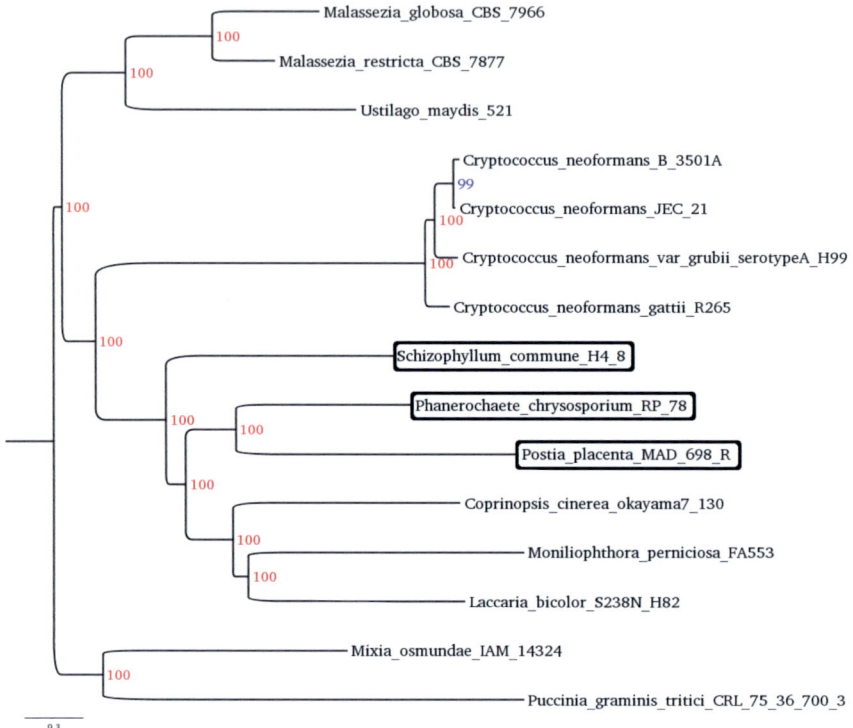

Figure 4: GBDP-based phylogeny of 15 Basidiomycota genomes reconstructed with FastME. The following GBDP settings were used: BLAST+ with default settings, trimming algorithm and distance formula d_9. The root was set via mid-point rooting [Farris1972]. The boxed species names are conflicting with the NCBI classification, but only with respect to taxa of uncertain position.

d_9 are both logarithmized distances and either relate the total HSP length or the total number of identical base pairs within HSPs to the smaller of the two respective genome lengths. When comparing distantly related organ-

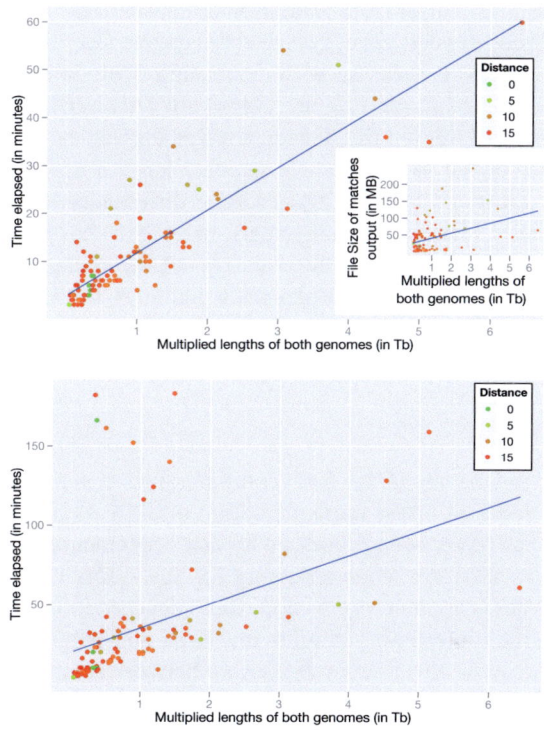

Figure 5: Benchmarks regarding the performance of both matches (top) and distance requests (bottom). In both cases, the size of the intergenomic search space affects the execution time as well as the size of the matches output files (fan-like shape). The right plot contains eight striking outliers with respective total times above 100 minutes opposed to a comparably small search space (< 2Tb). In order not to base the interpretation of the data solely on a search space criteria, we also determined the taxonomic distance (as provided by the NCBI taxonomy) as an additional one (green=low, red=high). Both figures were created using the R package ggplot [Wickham2009].

isms, d_4 and d_5 may suffer from saturation effects because the HSPs are reduced to matches between strongly conserved genes. For this reason, d_4 and d_5 distances may even decrease with decreasing evolutionary relatedness. The main benefits of d_4 and d_5 are elsewhere [Auch2010, Auch2010a]. Conversely, logarithmizing the distances helps against saturation, and using the smaller of the two respective genome lengths as the denominator in the distance formula corrects against huge differences between genome sizes [Henz2005]. Hence, the relative performance of the distance formulas in the phylogenomic problem studied here is not surprising, given previous results [Henz2005, Auch2006]. Eukaryotic genomes, however, were tested here for the first time, whereas earlier work with GBDP was restricted to prokaryotes or organelles of eukaryotes.

4.2 Benchmarks

The use of 15 eukaryotic (Basidiomycota) genomes was a special test case for the presented grid-based implementation of GBDP as these comparably big genomes had never been processed by that implementation before, thus we entered new territory when assessing the scalability of the algorithms and the hardware (e.g., memory usage). GBDP succeeded in processing this data and provided interesting insights into time and space complexity: in general, we can assume a linear relationship between search space size and the elapsed time for both types of requests. If the work load of a cluster is low, the cluster can process all requests in less than an hour, virtually providing for a linear speed-up.

However, some outliers were detected among the computed distance requests which cannot be explained by the mere size of the respective input data they used (matches). Here, other effects must have occurred that might be due to the partial incompleteness of some genomes. A closer look at the internal structure of these files revealed a high number of sequences (i.e., headers) – ranging from hundreds to thousands of sequences – and thus might have influenced the way GBDP is internally processing hits and transforming them to distance values. Moreover, the time measurement for each request ranges from the process' starting time till the time when the result file was completely written to the file system; measurement errors at any of these stages might also be the case. Thus, a detailed benchmarking of all the steps performed in a single request could presumably provide more explanations to the aforementioned outliers. On the background of this data set, the taxonomic relatedness only had a minor effect on the computation time.

The benchmark results provide for an estimated a priori calculation of both the expected computation time as well as the order of magnitude of the resulting matches files' sizes. Hence, this information can be used to plan the requirements of future GBDP-based experiments.

4.3 Outlook

GBDP is using local-alignment tools such as BLAST+ for processing match requests. As the latter is providing multi-core support these could also be utilized for speeding-up the overall execution time. Even more speed-up would be achieved with highly-optimized GPU-BLAST software suites [Vouzis2011]. Even though the local alignment phase isn't a computational bottle-neck right now, optimized BLAST could be beneficial in the near future if more complete genomes are sequenced, especially from eukaryotes. In cooperation with Marek Dynowski (Rechenzentrum, University of Freiburg) and Kevin Körner (Zentrum für Datenverarbeitung, University of Tübingen) we are currently working on a GGDC portlet for the bwGRiD. The portlet is targeting the following aspects and features:

- The aforementioned grid-based GGDC variant should be provided to the scientific community as a high-throughput tool. By means of a web-based graphical user interface (similar to the web service already available on http://ggdc.gbdp.org/), users should be able to set-up and launch their HPC-based experiments.

- The conduction of large GBDP-based data sets/experiments in a relatively small amount of time should be possible, thus accessing new types of scientific questions that had previously only been possible in theory.

- Providing large amount of disk space even beyond common user quotas. Data management will be totally left to the portal, thus relieving the user from this tedious task. Data will be always available via a job monitoring and download portlet.

- Generation of match and distance requests: the portlet should translate the user-defined genome comparisons to the YAML request format as required by the GGDC.

- Recycling of results: in order to avoid the repetition of popular genome comparisons which have already been triggered by other users before, the results of match and distance requests could be stored in a central repository such as the bwGRiD storage located at the Karlsruher Institut für Technologie (KIT). However, a concept for this kind of central data management has to be developed beforehand and should preferably consider a broader spectrum of features. The latter would positively affect the development of new applications as these could recourse to existing infrastructure via an universal application programming interface (API).

- GGDC's job submission system will be adopted for grid computing using the GATLET library (http://gatlet.scc.kit.edu/). The presented implementation is currently devised for sending requests to a single cluster and is thus only using a specific part of the grid instead of dynamically sending jobs to those cluster(s) having the smallest work load at a particular time. This would provide for an additional speed-up and, in principle, even allow for the processing of even larger data sets. Notifications would be brought to the user in a similar manner as already implemented on http://ggdc.gbdp.org/.

- A permanent software infrastructure should be established that would directly benefit from future hardware extensions such as those provided by follow-up projects of the successful bwGRiD service.

The work presented here allows for a clearly optimistic view regarding GBDP's suitability for the processing of large (eukaryotic) genomes. Since each genome comparison is independent of the others, these calculations perfectly fit to the distributed, node-based architecture of compute clusters. The highly parallel processing of genomic data sets thus leads to a dramatically reduced overall computation time, paving the way for experiments that have practically been impossible before.

Bibliography

[Altschul1990] S Altschul, W Gish, W Miller, E Myers, and D Lipman. Basic local alignment search tool. *J Mol Biol*, 215(3):403–410, 1990.

[Auch2006] A. F. Auch, S. Henz, B. Holland, and M. Göker. Genome BLAST distance phylogenies inferred from whole plastid and whole mitochondrion genome sequences. *BMC bioinformatics*, 7(1):350, 2006.

[Auch2009] A. F. Auch. *A phylogenetic potpourri – Computational methods for analysing genome-scale data*. PhD thesis, Universität Tübingen, Wilhelmstr. 32, 72074 Tübingen, 2009.

[Auch2010] A. F. Auch, M. von Jan, H.-P. Klenk, and M. Göker. Digital DNA-DNA hybridization for microbial species delineation by means of genome-to-genome sequence comparison. *Standards in Genomic Sciences*, 2(1):117–134, 2010.

[Auch2010a] A. F. Auch, H.-P. Klenk, and M. Göker. Standard operating procedure for calculating genome-to-genome distances based on high-scoring segment pairs. *Standards in Genomic Sciences*, 2(1):142–148, 2010.

[Beutin2012] L. Beutin and A. Martin. Outbreak of Shiga Toxin-Producing Escherichia coli (STEC) o104:h4 Infection in Germany Causes a Paradigm Shift with Regard to Human Pathogenicity of STEC Strains. *Journal of Food Protection*, 75(2):408–418, 2012.

[Camacho2009] C. Camacho, G. Coulouris, V. Avagyan, N. Ma, J. Papadopoulos, K. Bealer, and T. Madden. BLAST+: architecture and applications. *BMC Bioinformatics*, 10(1):421, 2009.

[Desper2002] R. Desper and O. Gascuel. Fast and Accurate Phylogeny Minimum-Evolution Principle. *Journal of Computational Biology*, 9(5):687–705, 2002.

[Farris1972] J. S. Farris. Estimating phylogenetic trees from distance matrices. *American Naturalist*, 106(951):645–667, 1972.

[Henz2005] S. R. Henz, D. H. Huson, A. F. Auch, K. Nieselt-Struwe, and S. C. Schuster. Whole-genome prokaryotic phylogeny. *Bioinformatics*, 21(10):2329–2335, 2005.

[Hibbett2007] D. S. Hibbett, M. Binder, J. F. Bischoff, M. Blackwell, P. F. Cannon, O. E. Eriksson, S. Huhndorf, T. James, P. M. Kirk, R. Lücking, H. T. Lumbsch, F. Lutzoni, P. B. Matheny, D. J. McLaughlin, M. J. Powell, S. Redhead, C. L. Schoch, J. W. Spatafora, J. A. Stalpers, R. Vilgalys, M. C. Aime, A. Aptroot, R. Bauer, D. Begerow, G. L. Benny, L. A. Castlebury, P. W. Crous, Y.-C. Dai, W. Gams, D. M. Geiser, G. W. Griffith, C. Gueidan, D. L. Hawksworth, G. Hestmark, K. Hosaka, R. A. Humber, K. D. Hyde, J. E. Ironside, U. Kõljalg, C. P. Kurtzman, K.-H. Larsson, R. Lichtwardt, J. Longcore, J. Miadlikowska, A. Miller, J.-M. Moncalvo, S. Mozley-Standridge, F. Oberwinkler, E. Parmasto, V. Reeb, J. D. Rogers, C. Roux, L. Ryvarden, J. Paulo Sampaio, A. Schüßler, J. Sugiyama, R. G. Thorn, L. Tibell, W. A. Untereiner, C. Walker, Z. Wang, A. Weir, M. Weiss, M. M. White, K. Winka, Y.-J. Yao, and N. Zhang. A higher-level phylogenetic classification of the Fungi. *Mycological Research*, 111(5):509–547, 2007.

[Kent2002] W. Kent. BLAT – the BLAST-like alignment tool. *Genome Res*, 12(4):656–664, 2002.

[Klenk2010] H.-P. Klenk and M. Göker. En route to a genome-based classification of Archaea and Bacteria? *Systematic and Applied Microbiology*, 33(4):175–182, 2010.

[Kurtz2004] S. Kurtz, A. Phillippy, A. L. Delcher, M. Smoot, M. Shumway, C. Antonescu, and S. L. Salzberg. Versatile and open software for comparing large genomes. *Genome biology*, 5(2):R12, January 2004.

[Mardis2011] E. R. Mardis. A decade's perspective on DNA sequencing technology. *Nature*, 470(7333):198–203, 2011.

[Pagani2012] I. Pagani, K. Liolios, J. Jansson, I-M. Chen, T. Smirnova, B. Nosrat, V. M. Markowitz, and N. C. Kyrpides. The Genomes OnLine Database (GOLD) v.4: status of genomic and metagenomic projects and their associated metadata. *Nucleic acids research*, 40(Database issue):D571–D579, January 2012.

[Schwartz2003] S. Schwartz, W. J. Kent, A. Smit, Z. Zhang, R. Baertsch, R. C. Hardison, D. Haussler, and W. Miller. Human - Mouse Alignments with BLASTZ. *Genome Research*, 13(1):103–107, 2003.

[Vouzis2011] P. D. Vouzis and N. V. Sahinidis. GPU-BLAST: using graphics processors to accelerate protein sequence alignment. *Bioinformatics*, 27(2):182–188, 2011.

[Wickham2009] H. Wickham. *ggplot2: elegant graphics for data analysis*. Springer New York, 2009.

[Woese1977] C. R. Woese and G. E. Fox. Phylogenetic structure of the prokaryotic domain: The primary kingdoms. *Proceedings of the National Academy of Sciences*, 74(11):5088–5090, 1977.

[bwgrid2012] BwGRiD. Member of the German D-Grid initiative, funded by the Ministry of Education and Research and the Ministry for Science, Research and Arts Baden-Wuerttemberg (2007-2012). Technical report, Universities of Baden-Württemberg, 2012.

Acknowledgment

Many thanks are addressed to Marek Dynowski, Rechenzentrum, University of Freiburg, and Werner Dilling, Zentrum für Datenverarbeitung, University of Tübingen, for granting access and for their technical support related to the compute clusters of the bwGRiD [bwgrid2012].

Funding

This work was supported by the German Research Foundation (DFG) SFB/TRR 51, which is gratefully acknowledged. The funders had no role in study design, data collection and analysis, decision to publish, or preparation of the manuscript.

Emulation-as-a-Service – Requirements and Design of Scalable Emulation Services for Digital Preservation

Isgandar Valizada,* Klaus Rechert,† Dirk von Suchodoletz‡

University of Freiburg

Abstract: The goal of digital preservation activities is to research sustainable access strategies to digital objects over a long time period. The *bwFLA – Functional Long-Term Access* project develops automated workflows for object ingest and access using emulation of original software environments. However, emulation of obsolete software environments is usually a non trivial task, because it requires good knowledge on setup and preparation of the aforementioned environments, e.g. operating systems/old software as well as detailed knowledge on emulators. Since emulation in digital preservation is becoming a mainstream activity in archives and libraries, the demand for ready-made and easy-to-use emulation services is growing. In order to provide a large variety of user-friendly emulation services, especially in combination with authentic performance and user-experience, a distributed system model and architecture is required, suitable to run on a heterogeneous Grid or Cluster infrastructure. In this article we develop requirements and a system model for emulation-as-a-service, suitable for a distributed environment thus encouraging the division of labor. The design and architecture are discussed based on a real-life use-case example.

1 Introduction

Digital preservation (DP) is a rather new field of research in computer, archival and library sciences, addressing the problem of how to maintain access to data over long periods of time. Migration and emulation are

---

* isgandar.valizada@rz.uni-freiburg.de
† klaus.rechert@rz.uni-freiburg.de
‡ dirk.von.suchodoletz@rz.uni-freiburg.de

possible solution strategies to that problem [Thibodeau2002]. While migration adapts digital artifacts to the actual digital working environments, emulation does not alter the object but re-enacts its original software and hardware environment. Emulation is a key strategy in DP for ensuring that digital objects can be rendered in their native environments and thus maintain their original "look" and "feel" [Verdegem2006], [vSuchodoletz2010], [Guttenbrunner2010] as in most cases the applications or operating systems developed by the format vendors or software producers are the best candidates for handling a specific object of a certain type [Rothenberg1995].

Besides rendering of digital content, emulation can also be used to perform format migration using the content's original creation environment. Previous work demonstrated the feasibility of migration services using the approach of interacting automatically with the original interactive based software environments [Rechert2009].

However, some important requirements should be taken into account when dealing with emulation. The additional emulation layer requires significant CPU time and main memory. Furthermore, specialized knowledge on the preparation of digital content and its environment is also important. The same applies for the preparation and maintenance of the emulators used. Thus, to lower the barriers in using emulation services and help in the solution of a number of technical, legal and privacy issues of the artifacts and the original environments, a separation of the actual service and the user interface is desirable.

Hence, in order to provide a cost-efficient and scalable emulation service model, a large scale computing backend (e.g. Grid or Cluster) paired with a service model recently developed as so-called Cloud Software-as-a-Service (SaaS) model [Vaquero2009] could be used. The paper further focuses on the above points in more detail and is structured as follows. After briefly discussing the concept of emulation in digital preservation we introduce a novel service-model for emulation. Further, we discuss the general structure and functional requirements for central technical components like an abstract emulation module. The general design focuses creating independent modules, which can be deployed and run as atomic units within a network cluster. Based on the proposed design we present a real world use-case leveraging emulation as a format migration tool. Finally, open questions concerning preservation planning, policies and administration are addressed.

2 Emulation SaaS

As emulation services compiled from a wide variety of software components and workflows are often too complex to be handled by an average user who simply wants to render a certain artifact, remote access to a cluster or cloud SaaS could provide a solution. Ideally, instead of installing a huge number of software packages which are difficult to maintain even for a small number of platforms, the user should simply be able to install a single or mobile application to access today's and future services abstracting from and translating the actual capabilities of the chosen remote platform. This could therefore lead to a solution which allows access to a 1985 home computer, a game running on an Atari ST emulator, access to mid-2000 Linux, Windows or Solaris desktops, access to Nintendo Wii and some modern 3D games just through the same application representing a front-end interface to the emulation services. Specifically, this application has also to adapt to different input/output methods.

Remote access to emulation (services) has been discussed and researched for a while [Rechert2009]. Although more and more devices became mobile, they are still not powerful enough when compared to the advances in the area of desktop computers over the last 25 years for example. They are usually limited by battery technology and requirements concerning dimensions. Tablet devices and smart phones thus do not fancy the desktop CPU, RAM and hard disk capacity and typically run different operating systems than their big counterparts. Nevertheless, more and more people like to access today's and past systems via their mobile devices.

Remote access to virtual machines and emulation can significantly help to separate content from the user accessing it. This concept is not new but often deployed in business environments using restricted terminal services. The corresponding architecture simply hides the complexity of the original environments and their components using the controlled environment of the service provider. Thus, no intellectual properties, bound software components and artifacts should be required to be transferred to the user side. The artifacts bitstream, including network traffic of distributed applications, never leave the cluster or cloud environment and only the renderings are transfered. The components required in order to reproduce an original or some compatible environment for the artifact do not need to be shipped and installed on the users' systems thus avoiding the related challenges. For instance, the KEEP emulation framework [Lohman2011] demonstrates the legal and technical challenges faced, when the original environment needs to get deployed on the user's machine.

3 Scalable and Distributed Services for DP

Distributed services for digital preservation were at the core of the PLAN-ETS project [Farquhar2007] which introduced the "Interoperability Framework" [King2009] as a Web service based architecture for the creation and execution of complex distributed DP workflows. Thanks to this, complex preservation scenarios and specialization of cooperating institutions became possible. *bwFLA*, a joint project of universities, state-libraries and state-archives, adopts these ideas and defines processes and workflows for ingestion of and access to complex digital objects.

Using scalable architectures is a rather new phenomenon within the DP research community [Strodl2011], [King2011]. However, motivated by the rising number and complexity of digital objects, the development of scalable DP services received additional attention. This set of problem is tackled, for instance, by the SCAPE project[1] which develops scalable services for the planning and execution of preservation actions. The goal is the development of an open source framework capable of orchestrating semi-automated workflows for large-scale, heterogeneous collections of different types of digital artifacts, e.g. for non-uniform media objects [Schmidt2011].

In order to provide scalable emulation services, deployable in a Grid or Cluster environments, specific DP requirements and use-cases need to be adopted for a distributed environment. Furthermore, a service-model is

---

[1] Scalable Preservation Environments, `http://www.scape-project.eu/`.

required to integrate these services into exiting frameworks and make them accessible to a large audience.

3.1 Emulation: A Functional Approach to Digital Preservation

The concept of emulation is not new to computer science. Emulators have existed for quite some time. Therefore, the list the available emulators is long and covers a fairly wide range of areas. Prominent examples for hardware emulation provided by the open source community are projects like QEMU [2], Dioscuri [3], MESS [4] or MAME [5] [vdHoeven2008].

Generally, hardware emulation represents a software implementation of CPU functionality combined with a complete system architecture. E.g. it can include a reimplementation of common hardware components of a given obsolete computer system thus providing the broadest approach to emulation. Consequently, neither applications nor operating systems need to be rewritten in order to remain accessible in the future. By concentrating on the emulation of ancient computer architectures and the configuration of obsolete operating systems running on them, emulation could significantly reduce the future preservation action tasks, because the number of the architectures and systems altogether is quite small compared to the number of applications and digital object types/formats currently in use (cf. Fig. 1).

These special properties of an emulation approach could therefore serve as a motivation for having a distributed service model for DP. However, in order to run emulation in a distributed environment and to provide ready-made, easy-to-use emulation services, two additional design aspects need to be addressed:

- Independent atomic modules need to be developed, which are responsible for running emulation sessions. When running the modules in parallel, shared resources are to be managed and coordinated (if there are any). These might include, for example, the allocated

---

[2] QEMU Open Source Processor Emulator, http://qemu.org/.
[3] Dioscuri – The Modular Emulator, http://dioscuri.sourceforge.net/.
[4] Multi Emulator Super System, http://mess.org/.
[5] Multiple Arcade Machine Emulator, http://mamedev.org/.

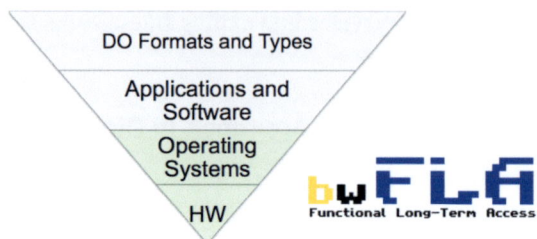

Figure 1: bwFLA project focus: Reducing the effort of preservation planning by concentrating on a small set of digital objects to be preserved.

network ports for external connection to the underlying emulated environments in cases of the parallel sessions running on the same machine.

- In order to develop a distributed service model, mechanisms for remote user interaction (e.g. mouse clicks, keyboard input) and streaming of the rendered result (e.g. video and audio-output) need to be present.

4 Use-Case Example: Migration-through-Emulation

Performing format migrations as part of preservation action manually for every digital object is not a feasible strategy when large quantities of objects need to be processed, as it would become a time-consuming and costly task. Migration-through-Emulation describes the concept of using the original software environments of designated digital objects for their migration to newer formats, whereas recreation of such environments is done by using hardware emulation. This approach avoids the often impossible alteration and adaptation of outdated migration tools to present-day environments, allowing the tools to be run in their original environments. An abstract and generalized migration-through-emulation workflow is depicted in Figure 2. The numbers represent atomic steps applied to the object passing through the workflow. To make the recreation of original digital environ-

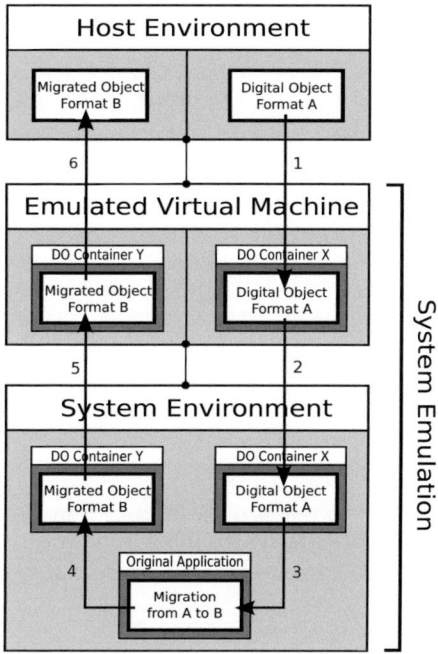

Figure 2: bwFLA Migration-through-Emulation workflow.

ments usable in standard mass migration workflows, a separation of related complex pre-configurations and convenient user access was implemented [vSuchodoletz2011], making mass migrations available via network.

A considerable amount of migration tools represent GUI-based applications possessing the capability of exporting/saving the loaded digital objects in a format other than their initial one. Such tools are therefore geared solely to human interaction (mouse clicks/movements, key strokes) when performing object migrations. Hence, in such cases the duration of migrations is additionally extended by the need of such interactions even if they are performed automatically using interactive session replaying.

Therefore, scaling up to thousands or even millions of objects of the same type, the total runtime of a linear single migration session handling all these objects might last a considerable amount of time. For such cases it would make sense to massively parallelize the involved workflows and use Cluster or Grid infrastructures. In order to run migration-through-emulation workflows the required software and hardware dependencies have to be resolved for the designated object. This can be formalized by using the concept of viewpaths (VP) [vdHoeven2009]. A viewpath describes the complete software and hardware stack required for the object (e.g. applications, drivers, operating systems, hardware devices). In a second step a VP needs to be instantiated, i.e. a running instance of the corresponding environment needs to be created using a suitable hardware emulator and the installable/runnable software dependencies of the object.

5 Software Design

The architecture of an emulation module providing the above-mentioned remote emulation services should be directed towards easy extendibility allowing the wrapping of a given emulator functionality with minimal programming efforts.

Since most of the emulators are command line based applications, their invocation differs mostly in the formation of respective command line parameters. This implies that the major functionality of a specific emulation module stays the same regardless of the emulator used. However, the cases in which a given emulator application also supports a run-time communication with a calling side in order to, for example, change a removable device should be considered separately.

Generally, an emulation module should support the capabilities that allow the user to initiate/terminate the emulation session, attach/detach a given container and obtain connection information allowing the interactive control of the emulated environment. Any other capabilities are not to be excluded during the design phase but should not be considered as substantial when considering the task of object rendering or migration.

Another important consideration is that the emulation module should avoid possessing the knowledge of any kind of viewpath schemes. The motivation behind such a design is that a slight change in the representation/understanding of what a viewpath is would result in the re-implementation of emulation module functionality. The design of the emulation module isolated from such knowledge on the other hand would increase the modularity of a preservation system allowing the calling side to perform only atomic, emulation related operations.

Object Transport Containers   The transportation of data to/from the emulated environment is a crucial capability that the emulation module must possess in order to support object rendering and/or migration [vSuchodoletz2010]. This is due to a fact that the installable dependency objects contained in the VP of a given object must be first injected into the operating system from the host system of the emulation module in order to allow for the formation of the object's native environment. Additionally, in case of migration, the resulting migrated object must be extracted from the emulated environment.

There are two main possibilities for such data exchange: via storage media devices and transportation via network interfaces. The first case represents an interesting possibility but is limited in its practical application since it requires rather complex network related configurations both inside and outside of the emulated environment, which are hard to be automated in a feasible way.

The second case is handled by the usage of so-called "containers". Containers are data files internally structured according to a given storage medium they represent. An example could be a 1.44 MByte sized binary file formatted according to FAT16 file system, in which case such a file would represent a virtual floppy disk. Usually, emulators provide a convenient way for attaching such virtual device files simply using a pair of command line parameters.

Containers can be of different media type, file system format and capacity. Generally, three main operations should be supported for any container, namely: container creation, data injection and data extraction. In practice, however data extraction features can not always be provided in a feasible way. E.g. extraction from optical devices like ISO CD-ROM disks would require an extra software layer in the guest system in order to allow data writing.

Remote Access to Emulation The possibility of direct user control of the emulated environment is another important requirement for the emulation module as certain manual interactions might be necessary for object rendering/migration in each specific case. Some existing emulators like QEMU already have this requirement fulfilled, enabling run-time access to the virtual screen and input devices.

6 Conclusion and Outlook

Usage of emulation in DP is unavoidable when it comes to ensuring the original "look & feel" of a digital object in its native environment. A cluster or cloud operation model allows to separate the artifact and its environment from the actual rendering the user will experience. This requires a convenient interface to the various emulators and virtual machines, which should optimally conform to a common standard. Providing emulation as a public service with a convenient user interface would allow even unexperienced users to get hands-on practice on emulation techniques in DP, bringing more attention and further contributions to it.

Complex setups might be required, for example, in cases of networked computer games or linked business processes. The network applications, like online games or content management systems consisting of a single or multiple servers and (many) clients connecting to these servers can run in a controlled manner and be shielded from the outside world environment. This would even allow to create and maintain certain states of a given business process, database or game, e.g. before or after some "major event".

With the ever-changing technology in IT the adaptation of emulators to every new platform and device hitting the market can be avoided. The user would just need a generic remote access client made available for a wide range of different architectures. This would allow memory and other content holding institutions to offer remote access to their artifacts more easily, independently of them being early years computer games, a wide range of outdated operating systems or other platforms like game consoles.

Furthermore, other hand a cloud SaaS could also help to solve the challenge of providing access to copyrighted material without releasing it to the user, making the implementation of privacy policies much easier.

Additionally, a service based model through a predefined API would allow programmatic incorporation of emulation within more sophisticated custom preservation workflows thus making it possible to integrate these services in other digital preservation related projects.

However, more practical experiments are required in order to identify main challenges in deploying emulation in a distributed environment like Grid or Cluster. The presented ideas are work in progress and will be tested and refined throughout the bwFLA project.

Bibliography

[Farquhar2007] Adam Farquhar and Helen Hockx-Yu. Planets: Integrated services for digital preservation. *International Journal of Digital Curation*, 2(2), 2007.

[Guttenbrunner2010] Mark Guttenbrunner, Christoph Becker, and Andreas Rauber. Keeping the game alive: Evaluating strategies for the preservation of console video games. *International Journal of Digital Curation*, 5(1), 2010.

[King2009] Ross King, Rainer Schmidt, Andrew N. Jackson, Carl Wilson, and Fabian Steeg. The planets interoperability framework. In *Proceedings of the 13th European Conference on Digital Libraries (ECDL09)*, pages 425–428, 2009.

[King2011] Ross King, Orit Edelstein, Michael Factor, Thomas Risse, Eliot Salant, and Philip Taylor. Evolving domains, problems and solutions for long term digital preservation. In *Proceedings of the 8th International Conference on Preservation of Digital Objects (iPRES2011)*, pages 194–204, 2011.

[Lohman2011] Bram Lohman, Bart Kiers, David Michel, and Jeffrey van der Hoeven. Emulation as a business solution: The emulation framework. In *8th International Conference on Preservation of Digital Objects (iPRES2011)*, pages 425–428. National Library Board Singapore and Nanyang Technology University, 2011.

[Rechert2009] Klaus Rechert, Dirk von Suchodoletz, Randolph Welte, Maurice van den Dobbelsteen, Bill Roberts, Jeffrey van der Hoeven, and Jasper Schroder. Novel workflows for abstract handling of complex interaction processes in digital preservation. In *Proceedings of the 6th International Conference on Preservation of Digital Objects (iPRES2009)*, pages 155–161, 2009.

[Rothenberg1995] Jeff Rothenberg. Ensuring the longevity of digital information. *Scientific American*, 272(1):42–47, 1995.

[Schmidt2011] Rainer Schmidt and Matthias Rella. An approach for processing large and non-uniform media objects on mapreduce-based clusters. In *Lecture Notes in Computer Science*, volume 7008/2011, pages 172–181, 2011.

[Strodl2011] Stephan Strodl, Petar Petrov, and Andreas Rauber. Research on digital preservation within projects co-funded by the european union in the ict programme, 2011.

[Thibodeau2002] Kenneth Thibodeau. Overview of technological approaches to digital preservation and challenges in coming years. In *The State of Digital Preservation: An International Perspective, Conference Proceedings*, pages 4–31, 1755 Massachusetts Avenue, NW, Suite 500, 2002. Council on Library and Information Resources.

[Vaquero2009] Luis M. Vaquero, Luis Rodero-Merino, Juan Caceres, and Maik Lindner. A break in the clouds: towards a cloud definition. *ACM SIGCOMM Computer Communication Review*, 39, January 2009.

[Verdegem2006] Remco Verdegem and Jeffrey van der Hoeven. Emulation: To be or not to be. In *IS&T Conference on Archiving 2006, Ottawa, Canada, May 23-26*, pages 55–60, 2006.

[vSuchodoletz2010] Dirk von Suchodoletz, Klaus Rechert, Jeffrey van der Hoeven, and Jasper Schroder. Seven Steps for Reliable Emulation Strategies – Solved Problems and Open Issues. In *7th International Conference on Preservation of Digital Objects (iPRES2010)*, volume 262, pages 373–381. Austrian Computer Society, 2010.

[vSuchodoletz2011] Dirk von Suchodoletz, Klaus Rechert, and Isgandar Valizada. Remote emulation for migration services in a distributed preservation framework. In *Proceedings of the 8th International Conference on Preservation of Digital Objects (iPRES2011)*, pages 158–166, 2011.

[vdHoeven2008] Jeffrey van der Hoeven and Dirk von Suchodoletz. Emulation: From digital artefact to remotely rendered environments. In *Proceedings of the Fifth International Conference on Preservation of Digital Objects (iPRES2008)*, pages 93–98, The British Library, St. Pancras, London, 2008. The British Library.

[vdHoeven2009] Jeffrey van der Hoeven and Dirk von Suchodoletz. Emulation: From digital artefact to remotely rendered environments. *International Journal of Digital Curation*, 4(3), 2009.

Acknowledgments

The work presented in this publication is a part of the bwFLA project[6] sponsored by the federal state of Baden-Württemberg, Germany.

---

[6] bwFLA – Functional Long-Term Access, *http://bw-fla.uni-freiburg.de/*.

Infiniband for Highspeed IP Networking

Dirk von Suchodoletz[*]

University of Freiburg

Abstract: Infiniband got originally introduced to provide high speed interconnects for compute nodes in HPC setups. It allows data exchange with very low latency using specialized hardware and protocols in multi-machine cluster configurations to close the gap to single hardware supercomputers. Infiniband can link many machines and span local networks and thus became attractive for standard IP based network applications, too. As Infiniband uses different physical and data link layer implementations it behaves differently with IP traffic and does not necessarily scale linearly for TCP connections. This paper extends the review on measurements and tweaks for 10 GbE and faster Ethernet configurations. It focuses on the Linux implementation of the OFED and mainly considers the IP over Infiniband software layer. It compares the capabilities of different Infiniband adaptors in various configurations.

1 Introduction

Scaling up a single supercomputer is often much more expensive than clustering hundreds to thousands of nodes using commodity hardware. Plus, it reaches certain physical limitations regarding the amount of multi processors or memory banks available. Unfortunately, fast machine interconnects are required for certain jobs to parallelize them onto distributed cluster nodes. The bandwidth of the ubiquitous Gigabit Ethernet (GbE) does often not fulfill a couple of requirements of High Throughput Computing (HTC) or High Performance Computing (HPC)[1] and thus needs to be complemented with special purpose components.

To fill the gap between supercomputers and compute clusters InfiniBand (IB) a switched fabric communications link was introduced [Liu2003]. IB

---

[*] dirk.von.suchodoletz@rz.uni-freiburg.de

[1] For Grid, HPC and HTC terminology and characteristics see e.g. [Montero2006].

features serial, bi-directional point-to-point connections between CPUs and for enterprise storage applications to highspeed peripherals like disks. IB is a scalable architecture and its design focuses on characteristics like low latency, throughput, quality of service and failover. The primary installations of the bwGRiD feature local DDR IB interconnects [Dynowski2012] and can be used to run specifically configured compute jobs. Nevertheless, it could be attractive to re-use this high performance infrastructure to provide traditional IP services like network filesystems over it.

This paper extends upon the *Benefits and Limitations of Highspeed Machine Interconnects* and concentrates mainly on the IP over InfiniBand (IPoIB) implementation [RFC4391, RFC4392]. Thus, it builds upon and mainly uses the same experiment setups as described there. The figures produced from the various experiments should not be interpreted in absolute terms but are to be read to compare a number of setups side-by-side. They can help to get an idea which measures need to be taken to optimize the throughput for a given scenario.

The remainder of this paper is structured as follows: The next section presents an overview on the IB standard and the hardware deployed in the different setups of IP over InfiniBand. After having established the foundation, the different experiments and optimizations are discussed in more depth, comparing the InfiniBand setups with each other. Finally, a conclusion on IB deployment scenarios is given and it will be stated which challenges will have to be faced.

2 InfiniBand Interconnects

InfiniBand was originally developed to link highspeed compute node interconnects in High Throughput Compute (HTC) clusters. To avoid overhead and reduce latency special protocols were introduced to copy data from the memory of connected nodes. As IB forms a low range network it was seen as an attractive addition to have IP traffic available on top of it. This opens up the opportunity to run a plethora of well established protocols for different network applications. As IB is still more expensive than most 10 Gbit/s components it is not expected to replace mainline HTC IP interconnects though.

2.1 Software Stack

The InfiniBand specification does not define a standard programming API. This task is left to vendors, who agreed upon a de-facto standard which is maintained by the OpenFabrics Alliance. The stack developed for FreeBSD, GNU/Linux, and MS Windows is released as "OpenFabrics Enterprise Distribution (OFED)" [OFED2012]. The OFED^2 provides tools and software for several layers, starting e.g. with the `mstflint` utility for updating the firmware of Mellanox adaptors, the kernel modules for the different adaptors and the software IPoIB layer, up to programs like `ibstatus` to check the link status of the installed IB cards up to the Open Subnet Manager `opensm`. The Intel MPI Benchmark (IMB) suite is contained as well.

Distributions like RHEL 5.5 or 6.2 already contain the relevant InfiniBand adaptor kernel drivers. They are typically of older versions than the drivers shipped with the latest OFED.

3 Experimental Setup

For the InfiniBand experiments two different sets of cluster equipment were deployed: Dual-CPU configurations of DELL PowerEdge M610 and 710. While the M610 is a blade unit in a M1000e enclosure hosting up to 16 computers, the 710 is a two height unit server machine. Both machine types can host up to two Intel XEON CPUs. The machines were configured with 24 GByte of RAM. The measurements were taken on idle machines and at least repeated ten times. The IB network was separated or simply a one-to-one connection between two host adaptors. To check that there were no specific influences during measurements each experiment was repeated at least two times on another day to see if the results were in line with the figures from the first run.

The IB network bandwidth and the capacity of the IO subsystem needs to be balanced, as IB connections are specified for data rates up to 25.8 Gbit/s per lane. The setup of the blade units was fixed with Mellanox Technologies MT26428 QDR dual-port cards. The first port of each adaptor was

---

^{2} See the OpenFabrics Alliance homepage `https://www.openfabrics.org` and the comments in [Carter2007, Auernhammer2007].

connected to a built-in Mellanox switch, the second port was unused. On all M610 blades a RedHat Enterprise Linux 5.5 was installed. This distribution is the base of Scientific Linux 5.X which is still common in many cluster setups.[3] As the newer of the HTC installations use Scientifc Linux or the RedHat Linux Enterprise 6.2 distribution by now, the 710 based experiments focus on this code base with the 2.6.32 kernel.[4]

Tests with different IB adaptors and thus the requirement of rewiring the IB network configuration were all run in the dual 710 setup with both machines configured exactly the same. To simplify the tests a number of relevant adaptors were installed at the same time:[5]

```
[root@dual-710-2 ~]# lspci
...
04:00.0 InfiniBand: Mellanox Technologies MT26428 [ConnectX VPI PCIe \
   2.0 5GT/s - IB QDR / 10GigE] (rev b0)
05:00.0 InfiniBand: Mellanox Technologies MT25204 [InfiniHost III Lx \
   HCA] (rev 20)
07:00.0 InfiniBand: Mellanox Technologies MT26418 [ConnectX VPI PCIe \
   2.0 5GT/s - IB DDR / 10GigE] (rev a0)
...
04:00.0 Network controller: Mellanox Technologies MT27500 Family \
   [ConnectX-3]
07:00.0 InfiniBand: QLogic Corp. IBA7322 QDR InfiniBand HCA (rev 01)
...
```

The first two devices in this listing are a single port QDR Mellanox and a dual port DDR card capable to be reconfigured to Ethernet mode with the `connectx_port_config` utility provided with OFED.

The PCIe slot configuration should be optimized in a way that the peripheral cards get the required number of PCI lanes.[6] Some PCIe slots are physically wired with fewer channels than the dimensions of the slot would indicate. Some of the hardware drivers such as the QLogic InfiniBand in-

---

[3] Most of the bwGRiD nodes run Scientific Linux 5.5 using a patched 2.6.18 kernel.

[4] The specific kernel version installed on both 710 servers was 2.6.32-220.el6.x86_64.

[5] This would normally would not be the case in real live setups. Plus, the optimal OFED for a given adaptor would be installed.

[6] PCIe provides typically 250 Gbit/s gross per lane.

dicate this during module loading: *ib_qib 0000:05:00.0: infinipath0: PCIe width 4 (x8 HCA), performance reduced.*

3.1 InfiniBand Hardware

The data rates specified for today's InfiniBand networks range from *double data rate* (DDR) running up to 20 Gbit/s, to *quad* (QDR) featuring 40 Gbit/s up to the recently specified *fourteen* (FDR) and *enhanced* EDR connects featuring up to 56 Gbit/s and lower latency. Some of the newer Mellanox and compatible adaptors could be reconfigured to 10 Gbit/s Ethernet mode for DDR and QDR and 10 to 40 Gbit/s Ethernet for FDR adaptors. As the physical layer implementation of IB and Ethernet differs, there are two different kernel drivers responsible to handle each low layer protocol, e.g. *mlx4_ib.ko* and *mlx4_en.ko* for the newer Mellanox DDR and QDR interfaces. Version information on the drivers can be gathered through the dmesg tool from the kernel output. The interrupt distribution is different for the IB and Ethernet modes of the cards.

```
[root@dual-710-1 ~]# cat /proc/interrupts
          CPU0      CPU1   CPU2   CPU3
   0: 5743453         0      0      0  IR-IO-APIC-edge timer
  ...
  63:        32 5014355      0      0  PCI-MSI-edge     ib_mthca (comp)
  64:         8       0      0      0  PCI-MSI-edge     ib_mthca (async)
  65:      1811     731      0      0  PCI-MSI-edge     ib_mthca (cmd)
  ...
 122:        54 9425275    397    168  PCI-MSI-edge     eth-mlx4-0
 123:         0       0      0      0  PCI-MSI-edge     eth-mlx4-1
 124:         0       0      0      0  PCI-MSI-edge     eth-mlx4-2
 125:     62502   16037      0      0  PCI-MSI-edge     mlx4_core(async)
  ...
```

Some of the IB adaptors can be configured to both network technologies. If possible the InfiniBand cards were run in Ethernet mode, too; 10 GbE for the DDR and QDR and 40 GbE for the FDR ConnectX.[7] There were no Ethernet experiments possible with the M610 enclosure setup because of

---

[7] To use the adaptors in Ethernet mode appropriate SPFs were required.

the embedded configuration of the whole system. The older DDR Mellanox DDR InfiniHost III Lx and the QLogic cards did not offer an Ethernet mode.

If a capable card is configured into Ethernet mode and the interface is brought up, then a couple of new interrupts will be listed that are labeled with the name of the network interface and a number for each interrupt line, like e.g. `eth2-0..15`. Ethernet configured adaptors behave completely like 10 or 40 GbE only adaptors with insignificant differences in performance. The bandwidth decreases to 10 Gbit/s in Ethernet mode compared to the theoretical capacity of DDR or QDR IPoIB connections and to 40 Gbit/s for FDR.

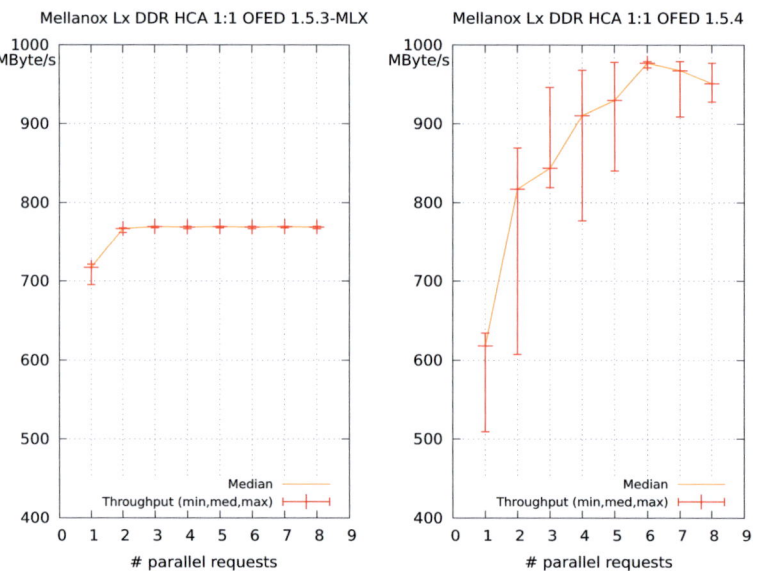

Figure 1: Different OFED versions (1.5.3 and 1.5.4) for Mellanox Lx DDR cards

```
   ...
  88:       253   461150 3481837        5  PCI-MSI-edge    eth2-0
  89:    154133 9340512 2506165   194252  PCI-MSI-edge    eth2-1
  90:    430936       0       0  7502423  PCI-MSI-edge    eth2-2
  91:       183   86702       0  8521615  PCI-MSI-edge    eth2-3
  92:     78931  114590       0   114996  PCI-MSI-edge    eth2-4
  93:    152542 8171543       0        0  PCI-MSI-edge    eth2-5
  94:    299902   14409       0   382957  PCI-MSI-edge    eth2-6
  95:    106604   92093       0        0  PCI-MSI-edge    eth2-7
  96:    376227  287081       0        0  PCI-MSI-edge    eth2-8
  97:     28983  212068       0        0  PCI-MSI-edge    eth2-9
  98:       188     433       0  3288275  PCI-MSI-edge    eth2-10
  99:    162587   31671       0        0  PCI-MSI-edge    eth2-11
 100:   2159803 1355365 1161306        0  PCI-MSI-edge    eth2-12
 101:    118366       0       0  6177263  PCI-MSI-edge    eth2-13
 102:     83014 2956963       0        0  PCI-MSI-edge    eth2-14
 103:     93259   79037       0        0  PCI-MSI-edge    eth2-15
   ...
```

To gather driver, hardware and version information it helps to filter for the relevant output of the kernel log:

```
[root@dual-710-1 ~]# dmesg | grep mthca
ib_mthca: Mellanox InfiniBand HCA driver v1.0-ofed1.5.3 (January 19, \
  2011)
ib_mthca: Initializing 0000:05:00.0
ib_mthca 0000:05:00.0: PCI INT A -> GSI 35 (level, low) -> IRQ 35
ib_mthca 0000:05:00.0: setting latency timer to 64
ib_mthca 0000:05:00.0: HCA FW version 1.1.000 is old (1.2.000 is \
  current).
ib_mthca 0000:05:00.0: If you have problems, try updating your HCA FW.
ib_mthca 0000:05:00.0: irq 65 for MSI/MSI-X
ib_mthca 0000:05:00.0: irq 66 for MSI/MSI-X
ib_mthca 0000:05:00.0: irq 67 for MSI/MSI-X
```

The ibstatus tool additionally tells of the underlying link rate of each connection, like *56 Gbit/s (4X FDR)* for full rate FDR. If the reported rate is lower than expected from the type of card, the components might either be not of the same standard, there might be cabling problems or the components do not agree properly on the highest possible connection.

With many IB adaptors installed in one machine the identification of the interfaces would be difficult, especially for the numbering of the IP interfaces. The OFED provided utility `ibdev2netdev` provides the required information.

```
[root@dual-710-1 bin]# ibdev2netdev
mlx4_0 port 1 ==> eth2 (Down)
mlx4_0 port 2 ==> eth3 (Down)
qib0 port 1 ==> ib1 (Down)
mthca0 port 1 ==> ib0 (Up)
```

"Up" is shown corresponding to the IP interface status. The kernel log is to be checked for hints if a specific interface does not come up properly. If the card is running in Ethernet mode than the port points to an Ethernet interface.

3.2 InfiniBand IP Networking

The InfiniBand fabric has its own underlying network protocol which is serviced by the Open Subnet Manager opensm. This tool is usually started as a daemon via the runlevel scripts. It can handle just one channel per thread, if more are to be serviced, it needs to be started manually to select the connection it is to handle. Without opensm running the link(s) stay(s) in the "INIT" state instead of becoming "ACTIVE", visible from the output of the `ibstatus` tool. The necessary daemons and quite a number of helper utilities are part of the OFED.

```
[root@dual-710-1 bin]# opensm
-------------------------------------------------
OpenSM 3.3.9.MLNX_20111006_e52d5fc
Command Line Arguments:
 Log File: /var/log/opensm.log
-------------------------------------------------
OpenSM 3.3.9.MLNX_20111006_e52d5fc

Entering DISCOVERING state

Using default GUID 0x5ad00000bc649
Entering MASTER state

SUBNET UP
```

The characteristics of both network types, Ethernet and InfiniBand, differ. While the Ethernet mode provides a functionality directly comparable to Ethernet adaptors, there is an added software network layer implementing IP over IB [RFC4391, RFC4392]. The IB protocol stack provides a complementary protocol to ARP which maps to the IB low level addresses. Therefore, the low-level IB network configuration has to be run before any IP connection can be configured.

With *iperf* run in single, double and quadruple streams, the resulting data transfer rates on OFED 1.5.3 were 6.32 Gbit/s each time. The data transfer rates achieved by the IMB and the tests run on IPoIB differ as expected because of the different protocols.[8] There were a couple of observations for IB networking:

- The kernel drivers and OFED version matter: Connectivity and transfer rates varied with different variants (Fig. 1, Fig. 3).[9]

- Especially interesting was the IPoIB behaviour of single thread transfers in some experiments ranging way below the expected figures, but scaling very well with parallel data streams up to nearly the results measured with the IMB on the same link. This seems to be related to the several parallel physical links which seem not to get (very well) balanced with IPoIB.

- Ethernet, if available, and IB throughput differed for the same interface card as could be expected from the different data rate specifications.

- The MTU setting plays a significant role: The usually cited MTU 2044 [RFC4391, Bortolotti2011] significantly worsens the results compared to the device's default setting of MTU 65520 (Fig. 5).

[8] See e.g. [Hoefler2007] for additional experiments and figures. A study on QDR performance can be found in [Koop2008].

[9] In the experiments the Mellanox ConnectX DDR cards did not work with the OFED 1.5.4 versions and the older Lx cards gained up to 20% more throughput with the 1.5.4 OFED compared to the version 1.5.3 shipped by Mellanox. The figures for the QDR and FDR cards, both using the same kernel driver, remained the same and fell slightly for the QLogic QDR cards. For further information check e.g. [Carter2007].

- Application layer tests for the different IB cards showed different aggregated throughput figures depending on the number of streams (Fig. 2).

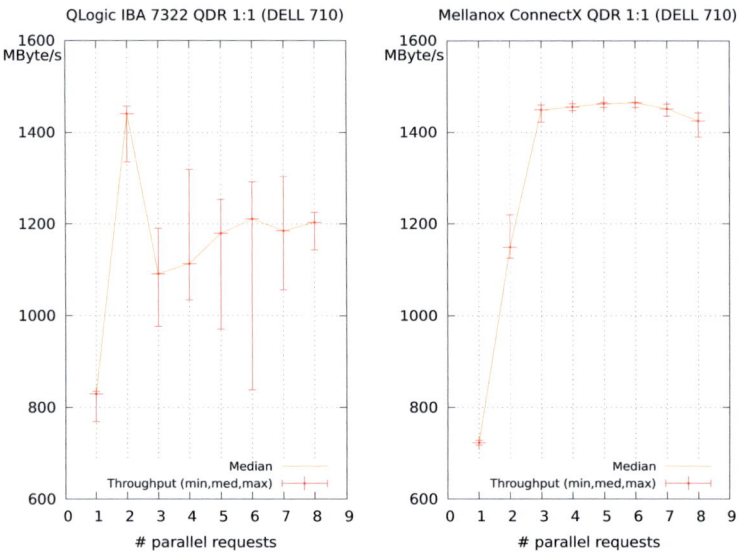

Figure 2: Mellanox ConnectX and QLogic QDR cards with OFED 1.5.3 on RHEL 6.2

Iperf test run between two identical DELL M610 blade machines with QDR IB connected over an IB switch:

```
[root@compute-24 ~]# netperf -f G -c -C -L 10.2.100.85 -H 10.2.100.84
MIGRATED TCP STREAM TEST from 10.2.100.85 (10.2.100.85) port 0 \
  AF_INET to 10.2.100.84 (10.2.100.84) port 0 AF_INET
Recv    Send    Send                       Utilization      Service Demand
Socket  Socket  Message Elapsed            Send     Recv    Send    Recv
Size    Size    Size    Time    Throughput local    remote  local   remote
bytes   bytes   bytes   secs.   GBytes  /s % S      % S     us/KB   us/KB

87380   65536   65536   10.00         1.94 6.45     8.34    0.381   0.493
```

To achieve parallel TCP connections in a very simple fashion, a bash script (`parallel-io`) was created to run `netcat` streams in parallel which are fed by `dd`. The script takes the source and destination IPs as arguments. Additionally, the number of streams and amount of data transferred in each stream can be passed onto the script.[10]

```
./parallel-io  10.2.100.82 10.2.100.83 1 2000
102400+0 records in
102400+0 records out
1048576000 bytes (1.0 GB) copied, 3.89399 seconds, 269 MB/s
Calculated total data rate 268865 KB/s, 262.220 MB/s
```

The revision and source[11] of the OFED influence the performance patterns. The QLogic card performed a bit below the Mellanox counterpart showing a divergent profile, both run on OFED 1.5.3 (Fig. 2). The results of performance were slightly lower for QLogic operated on OFED 1.5.4.1 with higher fluctuations, but there were better results for the Mellanox QDR running on RHEL 5.5 with OFED 1.5.1 (Fig. 3).

In the setup with DELL M610 blades in an DELL PowerEdge enclosure M1000e the same model of the Mellanox QDR infiniband adaptor was tested on an older RHEL 5.5 Linux with the older OFED 1.5.1 to compare the influence of different software versions (Fig. 3 left, Fig. 2 right, Fig. 4 right).

4 Ethernet vs. InfiniBand Observations

Both IB and 10 GbE provide highspeed interconnects between network nodes but use quite different physical layer implementations. IPoIB adds a layer of software to the networking stack. Generally, comparable results were expected for the higher layer logical machine-to-machine channels for both technologies. While in GbE the existing channel bandwidth was utilized independently of the parallel TCP streams, the case was different for IB (Fig. 3, 1).

---

[10] As the script calculates the absolute runtime after the last stream exited, it might under evaluate the top throughput significantly if the streams are very unbalanced.

[11] The package can either be obtained from the OFA [OFED2012] or the hardware producers like Mellanox.

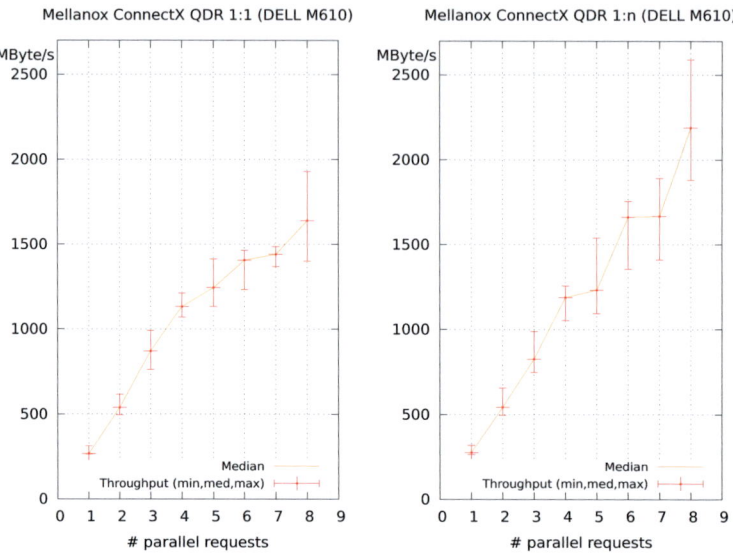

Figure 3: Mellanox QDR cards in 1:1 and 1:n setups on OFED 1.5.1 in RHEL 5.5

The characteristics were very well visible with the different Mellanox ConnectX cards, less for the InfiniHost III Lx and the QLogic (Fig. 1, 4) but not if using the *perf tools: constant 12.0 Gbit/s for 1, 2, 4 and 8 parallel streams for the Mellanox ConnectX FDR, 12.0 Gbit/s for the ConnectX QDR, 15.7 Gbit/s for the ConnectX DDR, 6.3 Gbit/s for the older Lx DDR all experiments run on OFED 1.5.3 with MTU 65520. Interestingly the results changed when using the much smaller MTU size of 2044 (figures given for the Lx DDR with the same OFED, number of parallel streams and measured transfer rates): 1 – 386 Mbits/s, 2 – 771 Mbits/s, 4 – 1.55 Gbits/s, 8 – 3.66 Gbits/s, 16 – 4.40 Gbits/s, but not reaching the throughput for the large MTU. Netperf reported 0.3 Gbit/s in the same experiment. The figures for the higher throughput standards were a bit disappointing, but matched e.g. with an average measured bandwidth value of 2324 MByte/s

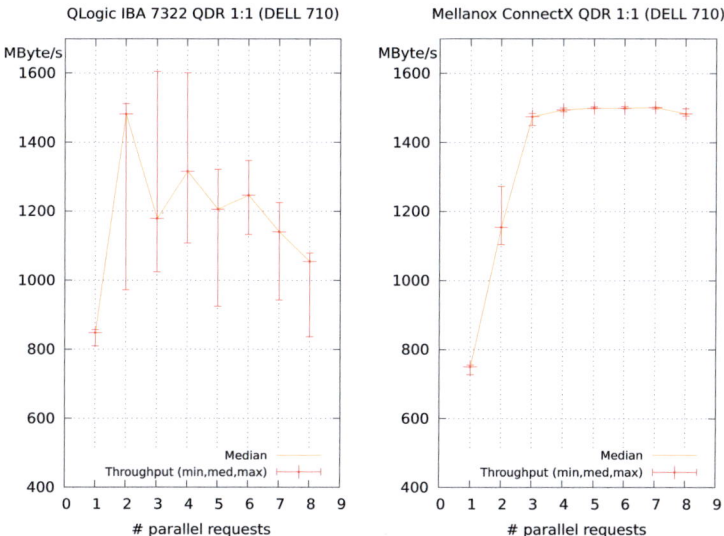

Figure 4: QLogic QDR and Mellanox ConnectX FDR cards in 1:1 on OFED 1.5.4.1 on RHEL 6.2

for a problem size of 4194304 using the QLogic QDR cards in the Intel MPI Benchmark.

Single streams at least for the Mellanox IB connection were well balanced, e.g. for six parallel streams of the FDR cards these were partially perfectly balanced reading results between 251 and 258 MByte/s.[12] The higher the fluctuation in the readings (see left of Fig. 2, 4) the more unbalanced were the parallel streams. Nevertheless, the results were not as fluctuating as with 10 Gbit/s 1:1 connections.[13]

The Mellanox QDR in 10 GbE mode achieved

8.97 Gbits/s in `iperf` in a single stream and pretty much the same with

---

[12] These figures are very different from the 10 GbE experiments executed in *Benefits and Limitations of Highspeed Machine Interconnects*.

[13] Compare this to the results of the aforementioned paper.

`netperf`. The figures for 2 and 4 parallel streams reached a median of 9.30 Gbits/s with a minimum of 8.81 Gbit/s and a maximum of 9.36 Gbit/s for six runs each.[14] There exist more performance studies for UDP over IB and Gigabit-Ethernet by [Bortolotti2009] or for Java communication stacks by [Zhang2009].

5 Conclusion

InfiniBand configurations in compute clusters become more and more commonplace. It makes sense to "re-use" them for IP based services like network filesystems as well and thus make the cluster nodes available for a wider spectrum of different compute jobs. As they require an additional infrastructure and are still comparably expensive they will not necessarily make the commonplace Ethernet obsolete if they are just considered for high performance IP interconnects.

Compared to the Ethernet world, the driver situation for IPoIB is more volatile. Different OFEDs and hardware drivers produced varying results in the throughput experiments.[15]

The Mellanox Connect-X adaptors have an interesting feature for a few scenarios as they allow to be configured to either IB or 10 GbE operation mode. The newer dual-port cards even allow to mix Ethernet and IB modes. This could be either helpful for space constrained machines offering not enough PCIe slots or to re-use outdated DDR adaptors after upgrades. The latter one requires rewiring of the setup as both technologies use a completely different physical layer. Nevertheless, there is not much advantage if those adaptors are deployed in blade enclosures. Plus, compared to their 10 Gbit/s Ethernet-only counterparts, there was no performance gain using IB cards configured to the Ethernet physical layer.

Many of the experiments and tests were run in direct machine to machine connections which are not likely to occur in real-life scenarios. They def-

---

[14] Using a 10 GbE optical switch in between slightly reduced the numbers, but this could be explained with a certain load from other traffic streams on the device.

[15] Including a non-functional IP link despite properly running IB connect. As the drivers seem less mature then in the Ethernet domain, it is worth to check out different versions for the actual hardware deployed as the performance gain could be significant.

initely lack certain aspects and thus not necessarily show the full picture. But they were meant to be set up fast and simple without requiring a full network infrastructure. The experiments showed a quite different behavior of IPoIB and Ethernet based IP connections. The IPoIB unleashes its full potential in parallel connections while there was no difference at all when many connections ran over a Gigabit Ethernet line.[16]

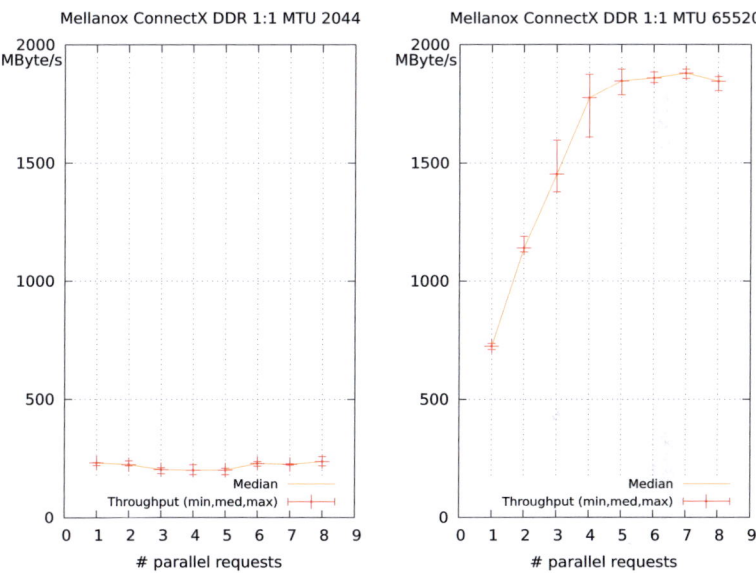

Figure 5: Mellanox ConnectX DDR cards running in 1:1 with different MTUs

As it can be expected for the highspeed connections above GbE the MTU is still a relevant factor. It has a significant influence on InfiniBand connections where the often suggested setting of 2044 is 30 times less than the device MTU being nearly the maximum of the IP packet size of today's

---

[16] The results are more volatile for the 10 GbE links as shown in the *Benefits and Limitations of Highspeed Machine Interconnects*.

drivers (Fig. 5). The optimal MTU of 65520 can be generally considered as IB networks usually span geographically limited networks with a well defined number of machines connected to them and no intermediate IP routers which might need to fragment. The TCP configuration should be optimized for low latency and jitter networks as no WAN connections need to be considered.

Bibliography

[Auernhammer2007] F. Auernhammer, A. Doering, M. Gabrani, and P. Sagmeister. Extension of an infiniband host channel adapter model and performance analysis. In *Baltic Conference on Advanced Topics in Telecommunication, Riga*, pages 55–70, 2007.

[Bortolotti2009] D. Bortolotti, A. Carbone, D. Galli, I. Lax, U. Marconi, G. Peco, S. Perazzini, V.M. Vagnoni, and M. Zangoli. Comparison of udp transmission performance between ip-over-infiniband and 10-gigabit ethernet. *IEEE Transactions on Nuclear Science*, 58:1606–1612, 2011.

[Bortolotti2011] D. Bortolotti, A. Carbone, D. Galli, I. Lax, U. Marconi, G. Peco, S. Perazzini, V.M. Vagnoni, and M. Zangoli. *IEEE Transactions on Nuclear Science*, 58:1606–1612, 2011.

[Carter2007] Steven Carter, Makia Minich, and Nageswara S. V. Rao. Experimental evaluation of infiniband transport over local- and wide-area networks. In *Proceedings of the 2007 spring simulation multiconference - Volume 2*, SpringSim '07, pages 419–426, San Diego, CA, USA, 2007. Society for Computer Simulation International.

[Dynowski2012] Marek Dynowski, Michael Janczyk, Janne Schulz, Dirk von Suchodoletz, and Sven Hermann. Das bwGRiD – High Performance Compute Cluster als flexible, verteilte Wissenschaftsinfrastruktur. In Paul Müller, Bernhard Neumair,

Helmut Reiser, and Gabi Dreo Rodosek, editors, *5. DFN-Forum Kommunikationstechnologien – Verteilte Systeme im Wissenschaftsbereich*, pages 95–105. Gesellschaft für Informatik e.V. (GI), 2012.

[Hoefler2007] Torsten Hoefler, Torsten Mehlan, Andrew Lumsdaine, and Wolfgang Rehm. Netgauge: A network performance measurement framework. In Ronald Perrott, Barbara Chapman, Jaspal Subhlok, Rodrigo de Mello, and Laurence Yang, editors, *High Performance Computing and Communications*, volume 4782 of *Lecture Notes in Computer Science*, pages 659–671. Springer Berlin / Heidelberg, 2007.

[Koop2008] M.J. Koop, Wei Huang, K. Gopalakrishnan, and D.K. Panda. Performance analysis and evaluation of pcie 2.0 and quaddata rate infiniband. In *16th IEEE Symposium on High Performance Interconnects, 2008. HOTI '08.*, pages 85–92, 2008.

[Liu2003] Jiuxing Liu, Jiesheng Wu, Sushmitha P. Kini, Darius Buntinas, Weikuan Yu, Balasubraman Chandrasekaran, Ranjit M. Noronha, Pete Wyckoff, and Dhabaleswar K. Panda. Mpi over infiniband: Early experiences. Technical Report OSU-CISRC-10/02-TR25, Computer and Information Science, Ohio State University, January 2003.

[Montero2006] R.S. Montero, E. Huedo, and I.M. Llorente. Benchmarking of high throughput computing applications on grids. *Parallel Computing*, 32(4):267–279, 2006.

[OFED2012] OpenFabrics Alliance (OFA). OpenFabrics Enterprise Distribution (OFED) – Overview, 2012.

[RFC4391] J. Chu and V. Kashyap. Transmission of IP over InfiniBand (IPoIB). RFC 4391 (Proposed Standard), April 2006.

[RFC4392] V. Kashyap. IP over InfiniBand (IPoIB) Architecture. RFC 4392 (Proposed Standard), April 2006.

[Zhang2009] Hongwei Zhang, Wan Huang, Jizhong Han, Jin He, and Lisheng Zhang. A performance study of java communication stacks over infiniband and gigabit ethernet. *IAENG International Journal of Computer Science*, 36(4), 2009.

Acknowledgements

The author would like to thank the people of the High Performance Computing group at DELL Research Labs Parmer South in Austin, Texas to provide me with all the different hardware and valuable hints and tips how to configure and run it.

Benefits and Limitations of Highspeed Machine Interconnects

Dirk von Suchodoletz,* Onur Celebioglu,† Garima Kochhar‡

University of Freiburg
DELL Computer Research Labs

Abstract: The ubiquitous Gigabit Ethernet interfaces in todays HTC clusters are getting stretched to their limits for high speed IP machine interconnects. 10 Gigabit and the forthcoming 40 or even 100 Gigabit Ethernet offer paths for upgrades but does not necessarily scale linearly for TCP connections. This paper reviews the literature on performance tweaks and measurements from a Linux administrators point of view. It discusses the relevant metrics and introduces external Ethernet loopbacks for testing and compares different setups of High Speed Ethernet connections in typical HTC setups and Internet server operation.

1 Introduction

With the rising amount of data both in filesystems and exchanged between applications, especially for High Throughput Computing (HTC) the requirements for higher bandwidth increase, too.[1] Thus, the predominant type of network interconnect, Gigabit Ethernet (GbE) can become a limitation. This paper gives an overview on and discusses the relevant parameters on network performance optimization according to the literature and the actual state on today's deployed Linux systems. As most of the upcoming HTC installations use Scientifc Linux or the RedHat Linux Enterprise 6.2

---

* dirk.von.suchodoletz@rz.uni-freiburg.de
† onur_celebioglu@dell.com
‡ garima_kochhar@dell.com
1 For the Grid, High Throughput Computing and High Performance Computing terminology and different characteristics refer to e.g. [Montero2006].

distribution the first on is based on, this paper focuses on this code base with the 2.6.32 kernel.[2]

While GbE connections are the standard for all modern server and desktop machines many mobile devices like laptops or netbooks feature such an interface too. Nevertheless, the machines have to have a fast enough IO system to actually saturate the link. The challenge is not new and can be tracked back to the first 10 and 100 Mbit/s Ethernet standards, when the machines of the respective era were not able to fully use the bandwidth available at the beginning. The network bandwidth and the capacity of the IO subsystem needs to be balanced, as e.g. the traditional PCI bus handled 133 MByte/s gross data rates at maximum, which could get easily consumed with a single unidirectional GbE connection. The problem translates to the actual set of servers run in HPC setups and cluster computing, too. Adding a 10 Gbit/s interface card does not necessarily increase the throughput by a magnitude of ten. Depending on the interface MTU configuration and the number of data streams transfered, the CPU has to generate and handle between less then 200,000 in best and over 2 Million packets in worst case.[3]

Taking the generally accepted rule of thumb for non-optimized Ethernet hardware and drivers into consideration, that one Hertz of CPU processing power is consumed to receive or send 1 bit/s of TCP data over IP links [Foong2003, Olsson2005, Leitao2009] it needs a capable processor to actually exhaust a 10 Gbit/s or even more an 40 Gbit/s Ethernet link. Generally, the actual usage scenarios of network servers could be quite different. They might exchange data between geographically distributed sites like in the bwGRiD [Dynowski2012] or run as a large volume FTP or streaming server with clients distributed all over the world. Or, they are deployed as a local file server or serve as a compute node with the need of high volume of data exchange with neighboring machines.

---

[2] The actual kernel version in use was 2.6.32-220.el6.x86_64.

[3] In the best case only full size packets of 9012 Bytes are sent, in the absolute worst case scenario having packets sent being equal or smaller than the minimum frame length of typically 520 Byte the number increases significantly. Taking the next generation 40 GbE into consideration which becomes more widely available and would be of interest to equip some special servers with the numbers simply quadruple.

There is no definite solution to optimize for all use cases at the same time. In this paper, we discuss a couple of issues to seek improved performance following a layered approach looking from the hardware layer up to the various network layers. The tests were conducted on different server hardware at the DELL Research Labs in Parmer South in Austin. The figures produced in the different tests should not be interpreted in absolute terms but are to be read to compare a number of setups side-by-side. They give an indication on what kind of tweaks actually in- or decreased the achievable bandwidth in the tests run.

The remainder of this paper is organized as follows: The section on test setup delivers an overview on the hardware used in the different setups and how the tests were run. It introduces the concept of Ethernet loopback to execute a couple of tests without the need of a second machine and additional network equipment. In the next section we go into more detail on a couple of tools useful for network performance testing. After having established the foundation, we discuss the several optimizations on the several layers in more depth, comparing different Ethernet scenarios and setups to each other. Finally, we give a conclusion which performance tweaks are overcome by actual hardware improvements and where still challenges to be faced.

2 Test Metrics and Setups

For most applications in HTC and HPC, storage and file services *throughput* is the most relevant metric, which is evident throughout the literature [Narayan2009, Leitao2009]. It is defined as the rate at which bulk data transfers can be transmitted from one host to another over a sufficiently long time period. The term has mostly the same meaning as *data transfer rate* or *digital bandwidth consumption* and is thus used synonymously. It describes the achieved average useful bit rate in a data network over a physical communication link. It is usually measured above the physical and below the network layer and therefore includes some protocol overhead and transmissions if occured. As with harddisks, the metric measurements will be used, 1 Mbit/s translating to 1,000 Kbit/s and not 1,024 Kbit/s.[4] Another metric is CPU utilization but it only relevant in some scenarios. Thus, the experiments reported in this paper mainly focus on the first one and mention the latter one for the relevant experiments if there seems to be an influence on the general networking performance. Other metrics relevant e.g. in multimedia live streaming protocols use the *round trip time* (RTT) or take the *packet jitter* into account. For webservers the time to create and tear-down a socket is a relevant measure too. These metrics are not considered further on for this paper.

For the several experiments run, a staged approach was used, starting from "external loopback", having a server-to-server direct connection then, till finally getting to full networking with network components like switches involved. This approach was designed to firstly baseline a number of machine performance parameters and secondly to rule-out the influence of active network components as certain configurations might reduce the throughput. Additionally, the external loopback helps to save on precious hardware as capable servers with 10 Gbit/s Ethernet (10 GbE) and especially 40 GbE components tend to be more pricey then wide spread industry standard equipment. The test makes machines and network cards directly comparable to each other as external influence is ruled-out. The loopback test should reveal some ground truth what a single machine is able to handle. As the same packets are sent and received on the same node, it kind of doubles the number of packets actually handled compared to an unidirectional IP packet stream between two distinguished machines.

For the tests different server equipment was deployed: Single and Dual-CPU configurations of DELL PowerEdge 610, 710 and 810. While the 610 is a one height unit server compared to the otherwise similar 710 machine which can host up to two Intel XEON CPUs, the architecture of the 810 is different. Some of the tests were re-run later on with DELL M610 blades. All machines were configured with at least 24 GByte of RAM in single CPU setup. The detailed configuration changes are described in a later

---

[4] A couple of measurements in the experiments were taken on the application layer using tools like `dd`. They will report little less data transfer rates then e.g. `*perf` utilities. `dd` gives it's transfer rates in metric values which matches the network measurement methodology.

section when optimizing the hardware layer.

To establish some baseline IO figures the dd command was executed to create a test file of 10 GByte size in machine RAM,[5] using the e.g. */dev/shm* directory.[6] dd runs in direct IO mode, different to cp. Upon successfull completion the command usually gives an estimate on transfer speed, e.g. 10240000000 bytes (10 GB) copied, 11.8114 s, 867 MB/s.

The results differ depending on the systems memory and IO performance and vary with the blocksize given. In the setup used the best results were achieved with blocksizes between 1 and 2 MByte, nearly tripling the values of smaller and still outnumbering the values of larger blocksizes above 2 MByte. Other machines behave slightly different. The idea here is just to get an estimate that the machine is fast enough to generate data or copy which is used later on in similar experiments for network transfer tests.

2.1 External Loopbacks

For the operating system kernel it usually does not make sense and thus is not possible in standard configuration to send out packets physically on one interface and receive them on another. In the standard configuration the packets are routed internally and never reach the hardware layer. The throughput and delay results could be directly compared to the loopback interface. Nevertheless, as the idea itself stirred some interest in the comunity[7], several methods are suggested to achieve such a setup:

- Trick the kernel routing table by changing the source and destination addresses "on the fly" by using Linux IPtables.[8]

- Use routing rule sets and move the local routing rule up in the stack otherwise it would be hit first every time. In older kernels of pre

---

[5] This strategy rules out the influence of harddisk performance and block caching. To obtain information on harddisk related performance parameters nmon (systems administrator, tuner and benchmarking tool) can be useful.

[6] This is TEMPFS filesystem which usually can take 50 percent of the total memory installed in standard configuration, but could be re-configured to allow more or less with mount -o remount,size=90% /dev/shm.

[7] E.g. used for IB performance measurements in [Auernhammer2007].

[8] See different blog posts on the net or see [Olsson2005].

2.6.35 this was impossible as this entry was fixed and unchangeable. This was supposed to be possible with newer kernels, but we were not able to verify the expected outcome[9] on newer Ubuntus and an OpenSuSE 12.1 featuring a recent 3.1.0 kernel.

- Apply a special loopback patch.[10]

The first method involves packet filtering and rewriting which adds to the packet handling efforts the CPU has to master. The first two methods are susceptible to general ARP problems, like that the kernel is not responding to ARP requests of locally attached interfaces. This is taken care of with the third, intrusive method. Here, a kernel patch is to be applied and the original kernel to be replaced. After rebooting into the patched kernel two new kernel interface structures appear which allow switching on the loopback:
`echo 1 > /proc/sys/net/ipv4/conf/<ifN,M>/loop`
where `if` is the actual name of the Ethernet interface and the N and M the numbers, like e.g. p4p1 and p4p2. In a next step IP addresses should be set on both interfaces which could be just point-to-point without any subnets and finally the kernel routing table is to be modified:

```
ip a a 10.0.1.1 dev p2p1
ip a a 10.0.2.2 dev p2p2
ip route replace local 10.0.1.1 dev p2p1 scope host \
  src 10.0.2.2 proto kernel
ip route replace local 10.0.2.2 dev p2p2 scope host \
  src 10.0.1.1 proto kernel
ip route show table local
```

3 Tools for Testing

The authors of [Narayan2009] give an overview on network performance measurement, discuss experiments executed by other research groups and present a couple of open source and commercially available network performance measuring tools like `iperf` and `netperf`.[11] The typical problem

---

[9] See http://lwn.net/Articles/364318.

[10] Refer to http://www.ssi.bg/~ja/\#loop for kernel patches for the different kernel versions.

[11] If referenced together we abbreviate them as `*perf`.

faced by network and server administrators is to come up with test scenarios which model at least to a certain degree the actual usage pattern a server and network is expected to experience. As this is often impossible at least a number of different experiments could be run to establish a picture on different aspects. Which tools to use depends on the actual requirements as the tools presented measure different aspects. Thus, many results produced should be not mistaken for achievable data rates in certain setups but, nevertheless, the figures will reveal some hints if a certain tweak influenced a certain test pattern.

The tools to measure data transfer rates and system performance are as varied as the metrics which might be applied. Simple benchmarks can be established using the standard commands provided with the operating system, like dd, cp or netcat (nc) if just some measures are taken on how long a file transfer takes to run and how much processor time is consumed.[12] Statistical information can be gathered with the netstat utility. For the several experiments classical network bandwidth testing and monitoring tools as well as simple network file copy experiments primarily with netcat, and file copies on mounted NFS shares were run.

The Linux kernel provides with the *packet generator* a lowlevel method already built-in [Olsson2005]. It is activated by loading the *pktgen.ko* kernel module which will spawn a kernel thread for every CPU core present in the machine. The operation of the packet generator via the */proc* interface is not very convenient, though. As most applications in HPC use TCP as the transport protocol we are concentrating on it for the remainder of this paper.

3.1 Network TCP and Application Performance

The packet generators and TCP bandwith checkers iperf and netperf are more easy to use.[13] Both tools operate in client-server mode and can

---

[12] Further tools are fio which allows as well as iometer and vdbench multithreaded operation – different to dd. They were not considered further in these experiments as not being part of the standard Linux distributions.

[13] Most distributions provide precompiled installation packets for both tools. See either http://iperf.sourceforge.net or http://www.netperf.org/netperf for further

receive multiple connections at the same time. Netperf uses two different binaries `netserver` and `netperf`. The listening server side gets activated on a specified network interface by `netserver -L 10.0.1.1`, without parameters listening on all interfaces on its standard port 12865. The client side specifies the local interface and the server side:

```
[root@localhost ~]# netperf -L 10.0.2.2 -H 10.0.1.1
MIGRATED TCP STREAM TEST from 10.0.2.2 (10.0.2.2) port 0 \
   AF_INET  to 10.0.1.1 (10.0.1.1) port 0 AF_INET
Recv    Send    Send
Socket  Socket  Message  Elapsed
Size    Size    Size     Time      Throughput
bytes   bytes   bytes    secs.     10^6bits/sec

87380   87380   87380    10.02     8613.77
```

The actual output could be configured to give either giga (G,g), mega (M,m) or kilo (K,k) byte/s or bit/s via the `-f <format>` parameter. Netperf can deliver additional information like CPU utilization on both sides with adding the options `-C -c` to the command line.

Iperf is a somewhat similar tool which uses just one binary for sending and receiving, but differently to the netserver/netperf pair the server process, activated with `iperf -s` stays in foreground and reports data rates as well. The server side reporting separates different parallel connections and does not summarize total bandwidth for all of them but just for each connection. The client side is run with `iperf -c <ip-server> [-d] [-P N]`. The option `-d` activates bidirectional transfers and `-P <number>` the number of parallel TCP streams to run.

Both tools just generate TCP packets and discard them on the receiving end, eliminating any higher layer protocols used. Thus, they can give a good estimate on the channel bandwidth between the two endpoints. This has a downside, too, as it does not really measure the network IO performance of cluster nodes or network fileservers. The application performance measured e.g. with `nc` was much lower on some of the machines tested than compared to the *perf figures. The `netcat` figures were much more inline

---

information.

with the general system performance baseline gathered with the local dd file creation and the STREAM utility [14] tests. The benchmark measures sustainable memory bandwidth in high performance computers. The memory bandwidth is heavily influenced by the architecture and the actual CPU and memory speeds. These values could be established with the dmidecode utility producing long output which could be filtered down to the significant values. In the following example, the figures for a DELL 710 system containing a single 2.9 GHz XEON CPU and six 4 GByte, 1333 MHz DIMMs are given:

```
[root@10gbe-single-133 ~]# dmidecode | grep MHz
        External Clock: 6400 MHz
        Max Speed: 3600 MHz
        Current Speed: 2933 MHz
        Max Speed: 3600 MHz
        Speed: 1333 MHz
        Speed: 1333 MHz
        Speed: 1333 MHz
        ...
```

Most of the tests involving file copies stressed single thread performance to establish what a single communicating process can expect from the given channel. Additionally, a simple shell script to initiate parallel dd-based file copies was created and used to establish parallel stream figures. There exist utilities written in C programming language like mcp[15] to achieve parallelized copy streams [Kolano2010]. As they are no part of most of the standard distributions, the package has to be compiled before it can be used.

There are system statistics tools which could be deployed to sample data over the runtime of the experiments. The mpstat utility reveals per cpu statistics and the usage of hardware and software interrupts by the system. It writes to standard output activities for each processor present in the machine, plus global average activity among all present processors. If

---

[14] STREAM source code and binaries can be downloaded here: http://www.cs.virginia.edu/stream.

[15] Multicopy, code available from http://mutil.sourceforge.net.

no specific activity has been selected, then the default report is the CPU utilization report. The usual invocation is to give the number of repetitions and the sampling interval: `mpstat 5 10` to have five seconds interval between the ten samples taken.

`vmstat` on the other hand reports the vm page information, context switch, total number of interrupts per seconds and gives information about processes, memory, paging, block IO, traps, and general cpu activity. The first report produced gives averages since the last reboot. Additional reports provide data on running sampling with similar parameters: `vmstat <interval> <samples>`. The process and memory reports are instantaneous in either case.

Another tool in this domain is `perf`, a profiler tool for Linux based systems that abstracts away CPU hardware differences. It offers a simple commandline interface which implements a set of commands like stat, record, report.[16]

4 Layers to Optimize

When trying to optimize a machine to a specific purpose there exist a number of layers which could be tweaked: *1* The machine hardware has a significant influence on the network performance as the CPU needs to be fast enough to handle the required amount of packets. The IO subsystem should be able to cope with the data streams getting in and out of the machine. Fast enough paths between storage, memory and network peripherals are required as well. *2* The network hardware is initialized and driven by kernel modules. The performance is directly influenced by how they are programmed and by how efficient they can make use of features like protocol offload provided by modern network adaptors. Plus, in multi-core systems, interrupt routing has an impact on the system load and throughput [Leitao2009]. *3* On the layers above the hardware a number of parameters like the *queue length* or the *maximum transfer unit* (MTU) can be adapted in the Ethernet interface settings. *4* The core network settings influence e.g. the size of several read and write memory buffers [Cerf2011, Gettys2011].

---

[16] Project homepage `https://code.google.com/p/kernel/wiki/PerfUserGuide`.

5 As TCP is complex, implementing a sophisticated flow control, which directly influences the network throughput, a couple of parameters might be tweaked here, too [Aggarwal2000].

While looking into 10 Gbit/s WAN networks, the authors of [Wu2010] discuss a number of measurement and performance tweaks to determine the suitability of TCP parameters such as for Jumbo Frame size and the buffer sizes of a TCP sender and receiver. The paper evaluates TCP performance measurement and network emulation tools for 10 Gbit/s highspeed optical networks. Finally, it compares the performance of TCP variants with different metrics, such as throughput and fairness. Older papers like [Schneider2007, Feng2003a] could be considered, too, but as much of them are a couple of years old, the hardware performs much better today and the operating systems got a couple of improvements on handling highthroughput packet streams. Nevertheless, changing the parameters and configuration options might optimize a given setup for a certain usage scenario.

4.1 Machine Hardware

The configuration of the machine hardware directly influences the network performance of different job patterns. Especially single threaded tasks profit from a fast CPU linked to fast memory. Comparing the, admittedly rather artificial, dd-test on different machines in different settings, the results for the 10 GByte file using the blocksize of 1 KByte file were giving at least some parameter to compare the machines to each other. The STREAM utility is another indicator to use to evaluate machines single thread performance. In the various experiments with the different machines we proved, that:

- The memory configuration is significant. The optimal number of memory channels for the architecture should be used, e.g. three for the most recent Intel XEON CPU's and chipsets. Otherwise the maximum performance will not be reached. Nevertheless, populating all memory banks often reduces the performance again as the memory will not be run at its maximum frequency for timing reasons. Thus, better use modules of larger size instead many of smaller capacity.

- A single CPU (somewhat similar to the observations in [Feng2003a]) was a little bit faster than two physical CPU's, but might be easily overcompensated with a multi-CPU configuration under higher loads. In dual-CPU configuration the BIOS setting of memory interleave mode to ON or OFF was expected to influence the results, but did not produce any statistically significant differences.

The PCIe slot configuration should be optimized in a way, that the peripheral cards get the required number of PCI lanes.[17] Some PCIe slots are physically wired with fewer channels than the dimensions of the slot would indicate. Some of the hardware drivers indicate this during module loading. A 10 GbE card would require more than four lanes in PCIe version 2 servers. 40 GbE cards often require PCIe version 3 systems to deliver full performance.

4.2 Ethernet Hardware

Every type of hardware is evolving over the time, so the same could be observed for 10 Gbit/s Ethernet. As the implementations between vendors and revisions differ, the results of the various experiments are expected to differ too. The Intel Ethernet controller Intel 82599EB e.g. performed roughly 10 to 15 % better in the experiments run than its predecessor 82598EB. A setup with two machines configured exactly the same featuring each one of the controllers resulted in better performance for one direction which reversed when the controllers were exchanged to cross-check the results. The higher and lower data transfer rate figures resulted when using the same card (82598EB or 82599EB) on each side. An equally good performance was achieved using Broadcom NetXtreme II BCM57711 adaptor together with the newer Intel card.

The peripheral hardware tells the CPU by issuing an interrupt that it needs attention, e.g. for arrived data. As the numbers of packets sent or

---

[17] PCIe provides 0.25, 0.5, 1 GByte/s in version 1, 2, 3 gross per lane in each direction. Optimally the machine supports MSI-X interrupts.

received by 10 Gbit/s adapters can trigger high IRQ activity.[18] On a multi-core system it is recommended in the literature [Leitao2009], that all interrupts generated by a device queue are handled by the same CPU core to achieve code handling locality. Nevertheless, the totally different distribution patterns of the MSI-edge interrupts of the Broadcom dual port adaptor (all routed to the same CPU) and the Intel cards (equally distributed) did not show any difference in our experiments. To avoid equal distribution over all cores, IRQ balancing needs to be disabled, or configured for the non-network peripheral serving CPUs [Leitao2009]. A userspace daemon regulates the balancing and either could be switched off completely by e.g. `service irqbalance stop` or better be configurated accordingly via */etc/sysconfig/irqbalance* file.[19] While it would be easy to blacklist the CPU core handling the network card in the Broadcom case it would be more difficult to change it for the Intel card. In the loopback experiment it achieved an insignificantly faster filetransfer in some setups but no statistically significant improvement in others.

4.3 Kernel Modules

The relevant hardware (network and Infiniband interfaces) and the network software layers are represented by kernel modules. The Ethernet adaptor modules for the Intel and the Broadcom cards delivered with the operating system (RHEL 6.2) were pretty recent. Newer versions were tried for the Intel card, but no significant improvements could be measured. The Intel module got recompiled for another reason, to test the New API (NAPI), which was to be activated by a compile time option.

Kernel modules honour a couple of module specific parameters, which could be discovered with the `modinfo` tool. One of those is the IRQ affinity shown in [Olsson2005], but no effects were measurable in the tests run on the recent machines.

---

[18] A single CPU in traditional hardware would be unable to handle the packet stream of 10 Gbit/s interfaces following [Foong2003, Olsson2005, Leitao2009]. This has changed, though, through a number of measures like protocol offload discussed later on.

[19] Different file location in different Linux distributions, for more information see `http://irqbalance.org/documentation.html`.

To significantly reduce the CPU load when receiving Ethernet frames several mechanisms were introduced like interrupt moderation or coalescing. When a new frame arrives, it gets saved in memory by the NIC, which will wait a receive delay to check if further frames get received. Then an interrupt gets generated to signal that one or more frames have been received. This strategy reduces the number of context switches the kernel has to make to service the interrupts on the penalty of added latency on frame reception. Additionally, interrupt coalescence avoids performance degregation through IRQ storms during high traffic load and thus improves the CPU efficiency if properly tuned for specific network traffic. The actual configuration is shown with `ethtool -c <if>` and set parateters with `ethtool -C <if> [adaptive-rx on|off] [rx-usecs N] [...]`.

NAPI is a feature available e.g. for the Intel 10 Gbit/s adaptors which tackles the same issue that interrupts coalescence solved with lesser impact on latency. It was introduced in the Linux kernel to improve the performance of high-speed network connections without generating interrupt storms. NAPI basically deploys a combination of interrupts and polling, which means that in phases of high traffic the device interrupts get disabled and packets are received by polling. Compliant drivers could even drop packets in the adaptor already if necessary, before reaching the kernel. In phases of relatively low traffic the kernel switches back to interrupt handling, to avoid high latencies because of device polling [Leitao2009]. Nevertheless, no significant effects could be measured in the type of experiments run.

A measure to help the kernel during high traffic phases is by increasing the receive and transmit descriptors buffer size. The default size is set to 256 the maximum possible value is 2048.[20]

5 Network Layer Optimizations

Beside the evaluation of hardware layer configuration and tweaks, there are still a couple of software layers left which are to be considered next. A couple of configuration options are made to the network interface on different

---

[20] See http://www.intel.com/support/network/sb/CS-025829.htm.

ways, others are on a more general kernel level. The latter configuration works via the */proc* interface, either via direct writing into the appropriate files or via using the `sysctl` command.

A couple of parameters could be set for the network interface directly using the `ip` command like for the MTU. Larger MTUs reduce the absolute number of packets and result in better TCP responsiveness. Jumbo frames accelerate the congestion window increase by a factor of six compared to the standard MTU [Leitao2009]. The visibility of this effect depends on the CPU and IO speed of the machine and the application used. Transmission queue size defines the buffer that holds packets which are scheduled to be sent to the card. Tuning this buffer size helps to avoid that packet descriptors are lost due to a lack of available space in memory. Depending on the type of the network characteristics, the default queue length of 1000 packets could be to small and should be raised then. A typical number given is around 3000.[21]

Another issue is the flow control on Ethernet which could be observed with the aforementioned `ethtool -a <if>` and set, e.g. `ethtool -A p4p1 autoneg off rx on tx on`. The flow control set to off on the M6220 switch resulted in 40 MByte/s throughput compared to 115 MByte/s with flowcontrol on in Gigabit Ethernet.[22]

5.1 General Network Layer

IPv6 is the next generation of the Internet Protocol which will take over from IPv4 in the next couple of years definitely reaching the HPC domain sooner or later, depending on the requirements for wider cooperation and cluster interaction. Especially because of a number of new features, new ways to (auto)configure and setup networks, the code base is much larger than IPv4. Thus, it was expected that losses in throughput will occur and the CPU will be higher utilized. In early implementations, there was a performance drop in different metrics like latency, throughput, CPU utilization and connection count measurable when using IPv6

---

[21] See the recommendations given in the literature or online.
[22] Some sources suggest to set the flowcontrol off for 10 GbE on the DELL 8024F switch.

instead of IPv4 [Ahuja2006]. Other values like socket setup time halved from IPv4 to IPv6 in Linux regarding to these measurements. A couple of experiments reported a poorer performance of Windows OS compared to Linux or FreeBSD in a number of aspects stated like in [Mohamed2006, Ahuja2006]. When network hardware gets involved in IPv6 packet routing and not just the loopback interface is used the kernel architecture plays a role too [Mohamed2006].

With the new internet protocol maturing and no significant network configuration and setup components involved in the experiments executed there was no influence of IPv6 measurable. Even the slight decrease in playload size because of the 40 Byte IPv6 header compared to standard 20 Byte IPv4 without options was not to be read from the figures produced. With rising MTUs the percentage becomes even more marginal.

5.2 Transport Layer

TCP originally developed for slow, unreliable connections is more and more used for high data rate, low delay networks [Feng2003b]. This changes some of the original assumptions like how to operate the TCP flow and congestion controls and influences the fair allocation between concurrent data flows. TCP features like Nagles Algorithm try to fill packets in order to avoid overhead of sending small packets but might hurt latency. Thus, a number of suggestions to improve TCP performance or re-implement parts of it were made. As TCP is the major transport layer protocol on the Internet changes to its algorithm might significantly change the performance and throughput within the network as well as the choice of the default TCP implementation of the major operating systems [Munir2007]. The relevance of TCP spurred quite some research in academia and industry to adapt the protocol to the changing landscape and special problem sets like high delay networks [Caini2009, Baiocchi2007]. The availability of high speed connects on the network edges produces new TCP challenges [Cohen1998]. Another kind of issues got introduced via the cell discarding algorithm in ATM networks in the beginning of the last decade [Cohen2001, Aggarwal2000]. There exist quite a number of different TCP implementations: (cu)bic, fast, reno, hstcp, vegas, westwood or compound

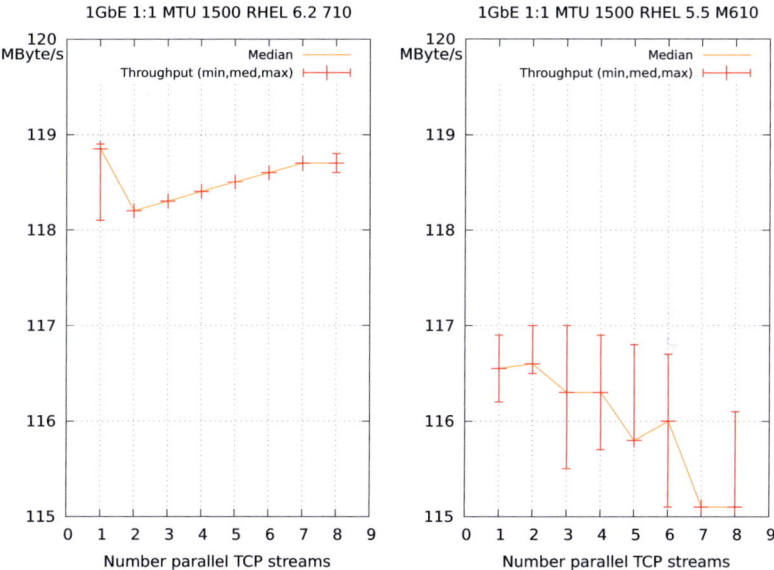

Figure 1: Well balanced TCP streams in 1:1 in 1 GbE connections in RHEL 6.2 on DELL 710 and 5.5 on DELL M610 with comparable CPU and RAM configuration

[Mo1999, Gerla2001, Baiocchi2007]. A comparison of different implementations was e.g. done by [Abdeljaouad2010]. In Linux, the kernel *proc* interface can be used to determine and change the algorithm through */proc/sys/net/ipv4/tcp_congestion_control*. Linux currently supports quite a few implementations, like (new)reno, vegas, westwood or cubic.

The default TCP algorithm in Linux is Cubic [Ha2008] which is a modified congestion control protocol with faster recovery through changing the originally linear window growth to be a cubic function in order to improve the scalability of TCP over fast and long distance networks. Another variable to set in the same location is the *tcp_window_scaling* which should be set to *0*, the default value in LAN settings and *1* in high latency WANs

[Feng2003a]. The actual picture for the high-speed LAN interconnets was mixed (Fig. 2). Single streams in the GbE connection were well balanced,

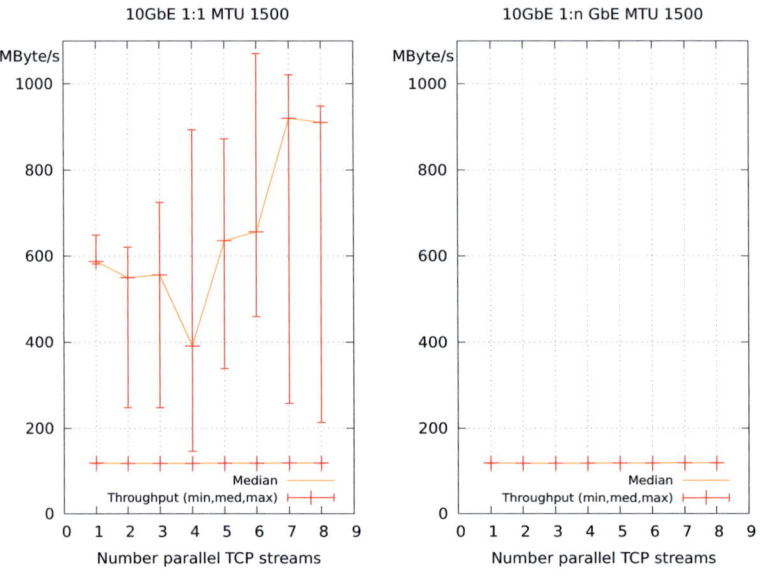

Figure 2: High fluctuations in 1:1 10 GbE connection compared to 1:N 10 GbE to 1 GbE links

e.g. for seven streams these figures were recorded (MByte/s): *29.8, 29.8, 29.8, 20.5, 18.4, 17.1, 17.0.* The same compilation for 10 GbE in a suboptimal case looks like this for seven streams *222 212 170 162 48.5 31.2* and in a more optimal run achieving far better total throughput: *228 215 202 164 161 146 139.* This differs pretty much from the experiments run with InfiniBand[23] (compare *Infiniband for Highspeed IP Networking*).

A pretty much different approach to cope with the rising number of packets in high speed networks got implemented by the network adaptor manu-

---

[23] For further reference see e.g. [OFED2011, Carter2007].

facturers by offloading certain repetitive tasks to the peripheral card itself. It releases the CPU from executing usual networking tasks, like computing the checksum and copying memory blocks [Leitao2009].

As other Ethernet configuration almost all offload features could be (de)-activated using the aforementioned `ethtool` utility. Set parameters can be checked with `ethtool -k <if>`, resulting in a list like this:

```
Offload parameters for p2p1:
rx-checksumming: off
tx-checksumming: off
scatter-gather: off
tcp segmentation offload: off
udp fragmentation offload: off
generic segmentation offload: off
```

Large Receive Offload (LRO) is a technique that increases inbound through-put of high-traffic network connections by reducing CPU overhead. It works by aggregating on the adaptor itself, multiple incoming packets from a single stream into a larger buffer before they are handed over to the net-work stack. This mechanism reduces the total number of packets that have to be processed, and removes all headers overhead [Menon2008]. A fur-ther option is to have multi-queuing on the receiving side when there are multiple applications using the network.

5.3 Application Layer

The networked application is the relevant part in for HPC and server oper-ators. The application performance is influenced by the lower layers of the network stack and its programming. Thus, the `dd` and `netcat` ex-periments were a rather artificial setup demonstrating the limits of single thread performance. As visible in Fig. 2 it thus does not necessarily ex-haust the 10 GbE connection capacity which is in line with the findings of [Microsoft2011]. Multiple TCP streams are required to actually utilize the bandwidth.

Usually a modern network application can run multi-threaded and make use of the CPU cores available like the kernel NFS server is doing. In a one-to-one connection over a single 10 GbE link, the load got distributed on the server side over the CPU cores available.

The experiments were using `dd` in direct IO on a single larger file to rule out any filesystem rescheduling and optimizations and make it more comparable to the `netcat` test runs. This resulted in link saturation but rendered the NFS client machine otherwise nearly unusable. With a rising amount of clients connecting to the same server, the load rises to the CPU limits as the high level application cannot control which thread answers which request, creating lots of cache misses and overhead. Thus, more available NFS server processes do not necessarily result in better performance in multi-client scenarios.

6 Conclusion

Most of today's servers are well suited to handle 10 Gbit/s traffic. From the very beginnings [Feng2003a, Feng2003b], when the machines were much less capable, the drivers less mature and a number of tweaks required most of the modern Linux distributions, modern machines provide a near to optimal setup already. Depending on the actual profile the machine is running on, the hardware could be optimized, especially for single thread scenarios platform and memory speed are relevant factors and improvements are directly measurable.

Many of the experiments and tests were run in direct machine to machine connections which are not likely to occur in many real-life scenarios. They definitely lack certain aspects and thus do not necessarily show the full picture. But they were meant to be setup fast and simple without requiring a full network infrastructure. Nevertheless, these experiments were able to show different behavior of Ethernet GbE and 10 GbE links, especially in parallel streams. While there was no difference at all how many connections ran over a Gigabit Ethernet line, the figures for 10 GbE were much more fluctuating.

The experiments demonstrated the difference between the line speed and connection tests of the `*perf` tools compared to the application level tests. The `*perfs` are good for establishing the network throughput and quality *on the way* between two endpoints in a given network, but other means of measurement are required to evaluate the end-to-end application level performance. The measurement setups and load scenarios used in the tests throughout this paper definitely could be refined. Especially in very unbalanced 10 GbE scenarios the measured average throughput depending on the last thread to end could result in figures well below the peak throughput in this experiment.

As it can be expected for the high speed connections above GbE, the MTU can be still a relevant factor, depending on the machine power and application as the ratio between standard MTU and jumbo frames is 1:6. Jumbo frames in large installations spanning different network segments with different MTU settings, might be burdening the intermediate router with packet fragmentation.

The upcoming IPv6 does not threaten the throughput in any sense as it processes IP packets as fast as IPv4 on modern kernels. The slightly decreased amount of payload resulting from the increased IPv6 header does not really influence the performance, especially not with larger MTUs.

The development of Ethernet does not stop at this point. 40 GbE adaptors become available and new generations of server hardware provide the necessary power and PCIe bandwidth to saturate such a link. The latest standard, 100 Gbit/s Ethernet, has not hit the server market yet, but already becomes available for high speed WAN connections like the FKZ to KIT link [Hoeft2011].

Bibliography

[Abdeljaouad2010] I. Abdeljaouad, H. Rachidi, S. Fernandes, and A. Karmouch. Performance analysis of modern tcp variants: A comparison of cubic, compound and new reno. In *25th Biennial Symposium on Communications (QBSC), 2010*, pages 80–83, 2010.

[Aggarwal2000] A. Aggarwal, S. Savage, and T. Anderson. Understanding the performance of tcp pacing. In *Nineteenth Annual Joint Conference of the IEEE Computer and Communications Societies*, volume 3, pages 1157–1165, 2000.

[Ahuja2006] Sanjay P. Ahuja and Krishna Dendukuri. An empirical evaluation of ipv6 in linux and windows environments. *Annual review of communications*, 59, 2006.

[Auernhammer2007] F. Auernhammer, A. Doering, M. Gabrani, and P. Sagmeister. Extension of an infiniband host channel adapter model and performance analysis. In *Baltic Conference on Advanced Topics in Telecommunication, Riga*, pages 55–70, 2007.

[Baiocchi2007] Angelo P. Castellani Andrea Baiocchi and Francesco Vacirca. Yeah-tcp: Yet another highspeed tcp. In *Proceedings on PFLDnet Workshop, 2007*, pages 37–42, 2007.

[Caini2009] C. Caini, R. Firrincieli, and D. Lacamera. Comparative performance evaluation of tcp variants on satellite environments. In *IEEE International Conference on Communications, 2009*, pages 1–5, 2009.

[Carter2007] Steven Carter, Makia Minich, and Nageswara S. V. Rao. Experimental evaluation of infiniband transport over local- and wide-area networks. In *Proceedings of the 2007 spring simulation multiconference - Volume 2*, SpringSim '07, pages 419–426, San Diego, CA, USA, 2007. Society for Computer Simulation International.

[Cerf2011] Vint Cerf, Van Jacobson, Nick Weaver, and Jim Gettys. Bufferbloat: What's wrong with the internet, a case study. *ACM Queue*, December 2011.

[Cohen1998] Reuven Cohen and Srinivas Ramanathan. Tuning TCP for High Performance in Hybrid Fiber Coaxial Broadband Access Networks. *IEEE/ACM Transactions on Networking*, 6, February 1998.

[Cohen2001] Reuven Cohen and Yaniv Hamo. Balanced packet discard in ATM networks. *Computer Communications*, 24(15–16), 2001.

[Dynowski2012] Marek Dynowski, Michael Janczyk, Janne Schulz, Dirk von Suchodoletz, and Sven Hermann. Das bwGRiD – High Performance Compute Cluster als flexible, verteilte Wissenschaftsinfrastruktur. In Paul Müller, Bernhard Neumair, Helmut Reiser, and Gabi Dreo Rodosek, editors, *5. DFN-Forum Kommunikationstechnologien – Verteilte Systeme im Wissenschaftsbereich*, pages 95–105. Gesellschaft für Informatik e.V. (GI), 2012.

[Feng2003a] Wu-chun Feng and Justin (Gus) Hurwitz. Initial end-to-end performance evaluation of 10-gigabit ethernet. In *11th Symposium on High-Performance Interconnects*, 2003.

[Feng2003b] Wu-chun Feng, Justin (Gus) Hurwitz, Harvey Newman, Sylvain Ravot, R. Les Cottrell, Olivier Martin, Fabrizio Coccetti, Cheng Jin, Xiaoliang (David) Wei, and Steven Low. Optimizing 10-gigabit ethernet for networks of workstations, clusters, and grids: A case study. In *Proceedings of the 2003 ACM/IEEE conference on Supercomputing*, SC '03, pages 50–59, New York, NY, USA, 2003. ACM.

[Foong2003] Annie P. Foong, Thomas R. Huff, Herbert H. Hum, Jaidev P. Patwardhan, and Greg J. Regnier. Tcp performance re-visited. In *IEEE International Symposium on Performance Analysis of Systems and Software (ISPASS'03)*, pages 70–79, 2003.

[Gerla2001] M. Gerla, M.Y. Sanadidi, Ren Wang, A. Zanella, C. Casetti, and S. Mascolo. Tcp westwood: congestion window control using bandwidth estimation. In *IEEE Global Telecommunications Conference GLOBECOM '01*, volume 3, pages 1698–1702, 2001.

[Gettys2011] Jim Gettys and Kathleen Nichols. Bufferbloat: Dark buffers in the internet. *Queue – Virtualization*, 9, November 2011.

[Ha2008] Sangtae Ha, Injong Rhee, and Lisong Xu. Cubic: a new tcp-friendly high-speed tcp variant. *SIGOPS Oper. Syst. Rev.*, 42:64–74, July 2008.

[Hoeft2011] Bruno Hoeft, Robert Stoy, Frank Schröder, Aurelie Reymund, Ralf Niederberger, Olaf Mextorf, and Sabine Werner. 100g ethernet in the wild – first experiences. *Journal of Physics: Conference Series*, 331 part 5, 2011.

[Kolano2010] Paul Z. Kolano and Robert B. Ciotti. High performance multi-node file copies and checksums for clustered file systems. In *Proceedings of LISA '10: 24th Large Installation System Administration Conference, San Jose*, pages 15–28, 2010.

[Leitao2009] Breno Henrique Leitao. Tuning 10gb network cards on linux – a basic introduction to concepts used to tune fast network cards. In *Linux Symposium, 2009, Montreal, Canada*, pages 169–184, 2009.

[Menon2008] Aravind Menon and Willy Zwaenepoel. Optimizing tcp receive performance, 2008.

[Microsoft2011] Microsoft Corp. Windows 8 SMB 2.2 File Sharing Performance, 2011. http://msdn.microsoft.com/en-us/library/windows/hardware/hh457617.aspx.

[Mo1999] J. Mo, R.J. La, V. Anantharam, and J. Walrand. Analysis and comparison of tcp reno and vegas. In *Eighteenth Annual Joint Conference of the IEEE Computer and Communications Societies*, volume 3, pages 1556–1563, 1999.

[Mohamed2006] M.S. Buhari S.S. Mohamed and H. Saleem. Performance comparison of packet transmission over ipv6 network on different platforms. *IEE Proceedings-Communications*, 153(3):425–433, June 2006.

[Montero2006] R.S. Montero, E. Huedo, and I.M. Llorente. Benchmarking of high throughput computing applications on grids. *Parallel Computing*, 32(4):267–279, 2006.

[Munir2007] Kashif Munir, Michael Welzl, and Dragana Damjanovic. Linux beats windows! – or the worrying evolution of tcp in common operating systems. In *PFLDnet Workshop, 2007*, pages 43–48, 2007.

[Narayan2009] Shaneel Narayan, Deryn Graham, and Robert H. Barbour. Generic factors influencing optimal lan size for commonly used operating systems maximized for network performance. *IJCSNS International Journal of Computer Science and Network Security*, 9:63–72, June 2009.

[OFED2011] OpenFabrics Alliance (OFA). OpenFabrics Enterprise Distribution (OFED) – Overview, 2011.

[Olsson2005] Robert Olsson. pktgen the linux packet generator. In *Proceedings of the Linux Symposium, Ottawa*, pages 11–23, 2005.

[Schneider2007] Fabian Schneider, Jörg Wallerich, and Anja Feldmann. Packet capture in 10-gigabit ethernet environments using contemporary commodity hardware. In Steve Uhlig, Konstantina Papagiannaki, and Olivier Bonaventure, editors, *Passive and Active Network Measurement*, volume 4427 of *Lecture Notes in Computer Science*, pages 207–217. Springer Berlin / Heidelberg, 2007. 10.1007/978-3-540-71617-4_21.

[Wu2010] Yixin Wu, Suman Kumar, and Seung-Jong Park. Measurement and performance issues of transport protocols over 10 gbps high-speed optical networks. *Computer Networks*, 54(3):475–488, 2010.

Acknowledgements

We would like to thank a couple of people who helped to organize this research and experiment setup, just to mention a few: Reza Rooholamini and Martin Hintelmann for creating the opportunity to jointly work for nearly three month at DELL Research Labs Parmer South in Austin and Gerhard Schneider and the University of Freiburg to support this trip.

bwIDM: Anbindung nicht-webbasierter IT-Infrastrukturen an eine SAML/Shibboleth-Föderation

Richard Zahoransky,[*] Saher Semaan[†]

Universität Freiburg

Zusammenfassung: Diese Arbeit beschreibt eine Proof-of-Concept Implementation einer Föderation aus existierenden webbasierten und nicht-webbasierter Diensten. Die Dienste der Föderation werden durch SAML / ECP gegenseitig zugänglich gemacht, ohne eine zentrale Nutzerdatenbank vorhalten zu müssen. Die einzelnen Föderationskomponenten vertrauen untereinander durch Zertifikate und Metadaten. Eine PAM-ECP-Implementierung wird gezeigt, die es ermöglicht, nicht-webbasierte Dienste mittels Shibboleth / ECP der Föderation anzuschließen. Die resultierenden Fragen des Datenschutzes, der Datenweitergabe und Sicherheit werden diskutiert.

1 Einleitung

Die Nutzung von organisationsübergreifenden Diensten innerhalb einer Föderation verschiedener Institutionen ist für viele Forschungsdisziplinen in der heutigen Zeit unvermeidlich und sogar notwendig. Das hier vorgestellte Projekt bwIDM[1] hat das Ziel, verteilt angebotene Ressourcen und Dienste der Universitäten des Landes Baden-Württemberg aus einem lokalen Kontext heraus zugänglich zu machen. Universitätsmitglieder sollen in der Lage sein, verschiedenste, auch nicht web-webbasierte Dienste (z.B. Desktop-Anwendungen, Grid- oder Cloud-Dienste) innerhalb und außerhalb der ei-

---

[*] richard.zahoransky@rz.uni-freiburg.de
[†] semann@uni-freiburg.de
[1] bwIDM: Übergreifendes Identitätsmanagement, `http://www.bwidm.de/`, letzter Aufruf: 26.04.2012

genen Universität mit ihrem lokalen Benutzeraccount zu benutzen, als wären diese Ressourcen physisch vor Ort. Hierfür soll keine landesweite zentrale Nutzerdatenbank aufgebaut werden. Stattdessen sollen die Benutzerverzeichnisse lokal an den Universitäten bestehen bleiben und durch diese betreut und gepflegt werden. Teile dieser Arbeit wurden bereits in [Simon12] veröffentlicht.

2 Aufbau einer Föderation

Diese Arbeit konzentriert sich auf die verteilte Nutzerverwaltung und Bildung einer Föderation durch den SAML[2] Standard. Dieser beschreibt den Austausch von Nachrichten zur Autorisierung und Authentifizierung zwischen verschiedenen Organisationen, die sich gegenseitig vertrauen. Eine Implementierung dieses Standards ist durch Shibboleth[3] gegeben. SAML baut nicht auf zentrale Nutzerdatenbanken auf. Shibboleth ermöglicht es daher, lokale Identitätssysteme beizubehalten und für die Föderation nutzbar zu machen. Dies begünstigt die Datensparsamkeit, erhöht die Ausfallsicherheit und minimiert die Gefahr des Datendiebstahls. Dementgegen stehen organisatorische Hürden, die einmalig bewältigt werden müssen.

Innerhalb einer Föderation werden Dienste durch Service Provider (SP) geschützt. Die jeweiligen SP besitzen keine eigene Benutzerverwaltung. Stattdessen vertrauen sie auf die Aussagen von Identitätsprovidern (Identity Provider: IdP) und gewähren entsprechend Zugang zu ihrem Dienst. Zertifikate, die zwischen IdP und SP ausgetauscht werden, stellen sicher, dass die Kommunikation zwischen SP und IdP vertrauenswürdig ist. IdPs setzen auf bestehende Benutzerverzeichnisse auf. Sie sind dafür zuständig, Benutzer zu authentifizieren und liefern dem SP auf Anfrage weitere Attribute über den Benutzer. Möchte ein Teilnehmer der Föderation die Dienste eines SP wahrnehmen und sich authentifizieren, benötigt er einen gültigen Account bei seinem lokalen IdP (siehe Bild 1). Nachdem der Benutzer authentifiziert wurde, kann der SP optional auf Grund von weiteren Attribu-

---

[2] Security Assertion Markup Language (SAML) http://www.oasis-open.org/standards, letzter Aufruf 26.04.2012
[3] What's Shibboleth? http://www.shibboleth.net/about/index.html, letzter Aufruf 26.04.2012

ten des Benutzers den Dienst für diesen speziellen Benutzer freigeben oder nicht.

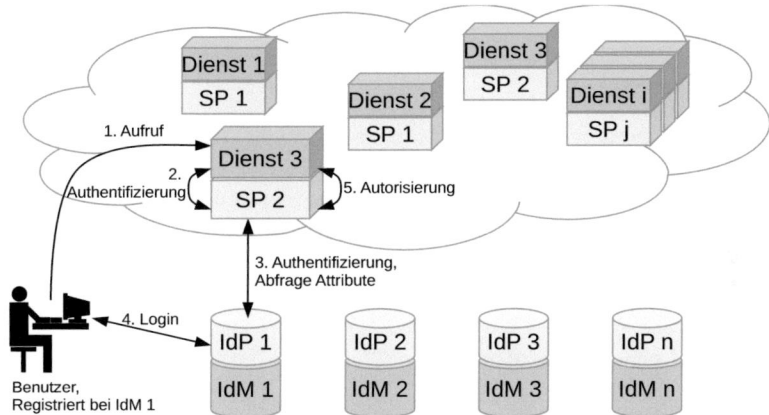

Bild 1: Ein Benutzer meldet sich für einen Dienst innerhalb einer Föderation an einem SP. Der SP leitet den Anfragenden an seinen lokalen IdP weiter. Dort meldet sich der Benutzer an, worauf der IdP die Authentifizierung an den SP weiterreicht.

Möchte eine Institution der Föderation beitreten, muss sie einen SAML2 fähigen IdP einrichten und die dazugehörigen Metadaten erzeugen. Diese beschreiben und beweisen die Identität des Ausstellers. Metadaten enthalten ebenfalls Informationen über die unterstützen Protokolle und Kontaktdaten eines Ansprechpartners für den Problemfall. Um sichere Verbindungen zu ermöglichen, beinhalten die Metadaten zusätzlich die CA-Zertifikate[4] für den jeweiligen Host. Sowohl IdP als auch SP machen sich über Metadaten bekannt.

Um die Verteilung der Metadaten zu erleichtern, lassen sich Discovery-Services (DS) innerhalb einer Föderation einsetzen. Dieser Dienst erfüllt zwei Aufgaben: Erstens aggregiert er die Metadaten der Teilnehmer und

---

[4] Im Rahmen dieses Projekts werden die Zertifikate durch DFN-PKI bereitgestellt, siehe `https://www.pki.dfn.de`, letzter Aufruf: 26.04.2012.

verteilt diese. Zweitens nutzt der DS die Informationen aus den Metadaten, um Authentifizierungsanfragen von Personen verschiedener Institutionen an den korrekten IdP weiterzuleiten.

3 Funktion

SAML im allgemeinen und die Implementierung durch Shibboleth zielen im Wesentlichen auf die Bereitstellung von Web-Anwendungen durch einen Web-Browser. Der SAML^5 Standard bietet mit dem Enhanced Client or Proxy (ECP) Profil eine Unterstützung für nicht web-basierte Dienste an. Nachfolgend werden beide Varianten beschrieben:

3.1 Aufruf eines Webdienstes

Das Bild 2 zeigt grafisch die Funktionsweise von SAML bzw. Shibboleth durch die Verwendung eines Browsers. Greift ein Benutzer auf eine durch Shibboleth geschützte Ressource zu, prüft das Shibboleth-Modul (der SP) die Existenz eines gültigen Session-Cookies. Existiert kein solches Cookie, setzt der SP sein eigenes Cookie und leitet den Browser auf die Webseite des Heimat-IdP oder auf die Webseite des DS. Landet der Benutzer auf der Seite des DS, wählt er von dort den IdP seiner Organisation aus (nicht im Bild dargestellt). Der Benutzer gibt daraufhin sein Passwort direkt auf der Webseite des IdP ein. SP oder DS benötigen kein Wissen über das Passwort. Nach der Passworteingabe ist der Benutzer authentifiziert und der IdP sendet seine Antwort in einer SAML-Assertion zusammen mit dem vom SP generierten Session-Cookie über den Browser zurück an den SP. Die digital unterschriebene SAML-Assertion repräsentiert die Authentifizierung des Nutzers am IdP. Ein letzter Redirect führt den Browser zurück zu dem SP. Das vom Browser vorgezeigte Session-Cookie ist dem SP diesmal bekannt und der Benutzer ist somit gegenüber dem SP authentifiziert. Der SP kann nun entsprechend seinen Regeln die Autorisierung durchführen.

---

^{5} Ab der Version 2.0

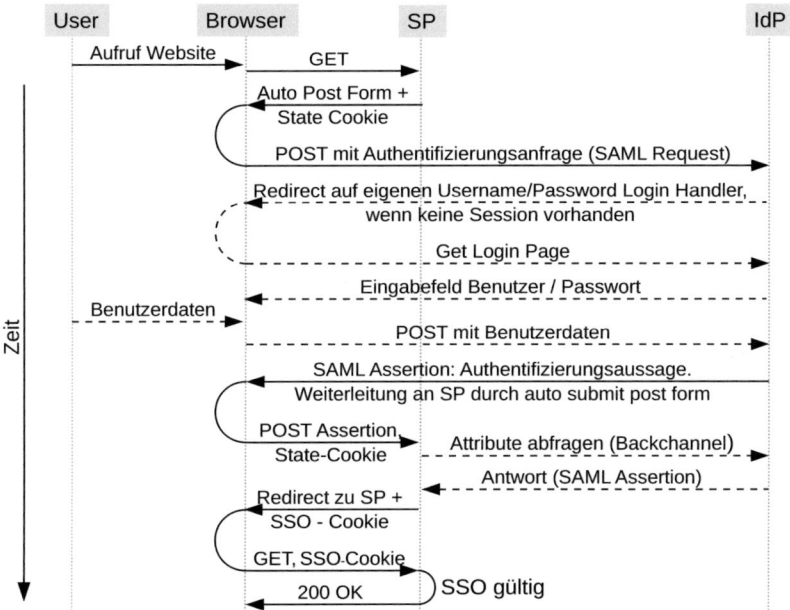

Bild 2: Single-Sign-On Anmeldung mit SAML2 [SWITCH-demo].

3.2 Enhanced Client or Proxy

Enhanced Client or Proxy (ECP) ist ein Unterprofil des SAML-Standards[6], um Anwendungen, die außerhalb eines Browsers arbeiten, in eine Föderation einzubinden. Da ein nicht-webbasierter Dienst nicht zwingend Browser-Redirects nutzen oder HTML-Seite anzeigen kann, muss dieser auf andere Weise die Authentifizierung durchführen [Koehler12]. Ein Dienst, der das ECP-Profil unterstützt, kann mit SP und IdP kommunizieren und direkt SAML-Assertions verarbeiten. Um einen Dienst ECP-fähig zu ma-

---

[6] SAML V2.0 Enhanced Client or Proxy Profile Version 2.0, `http://www.oasis-open.org/committees/download.php/43310/sstc-saml-ecp-v2.0-wd04.pdf`, letzer Aufruf: 26.04.2012

chen, sind Änderungen und Anpassungen notwendig, sowohl Server- als auch Clientseitig.

Möchte ein Benutzer auf einen ECP-fähigen Dienst zugreifen, verlangt der Dienst vom SP eine Authentifizierungsanfrage für den Heimat-IdP des Benutzers. Die Antwort vom SP ist eine SAML-Nachricht mit der entsprechenden, unterschriebenen Anfrage an den IdP als Inhalt. Der Dienst leitet die SAML-Nachricht an den entsprechenden IdP. Daraufhin prüft der IdP die Identität des Benutzers, beispielsweise über eine Passwortabfrage. Für eine erfolgreiche Authentifizierung muss der ECP-fähige Dienst diese Passwortabfrage an den Benutzer weiterleiten und die Eingabe zurück an den IdP senden. Ist die Identität durch den IdP geprüft, sendet dieser sein Ergebnis wieder als SAML-Nachricht zurück an den Dienst. Die Nachricht leitet der Dienst an den SP. Der SP prüft den Inhalt und teilt dem Dienst mit, ob sich der Benutzer erfolgreich authentifiziert hat, beziehungsweise gibt den entsprechenden Service frei.

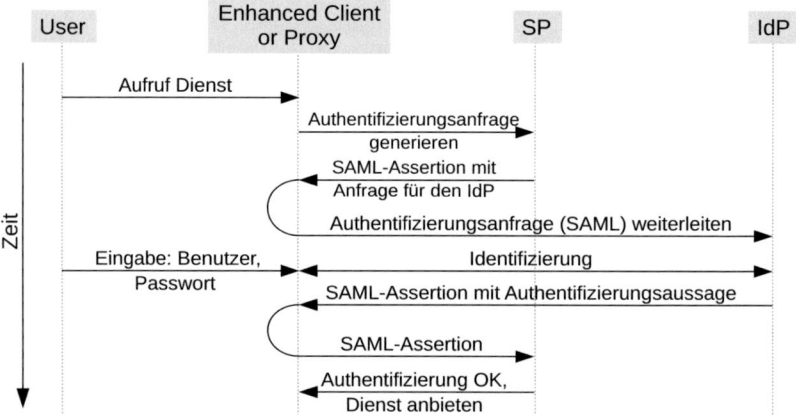

Bild 3: Vereinfachte Arbeitsweise von ECP. Ein nicht webbasierter Dienst kann durch das ECP-Profil föderationsfähig gemacht werden [SAML2].

4 Datenschutz und Sicherheit

SAML nutzt Zertifikate zur Überprüfung von Identitäten, gewährleistet Vertraulichkeit durch Verschlüsselung und stellt sicher, dass die Überprüfung des Passworts direkt bei der Heimatorganisation erfolgt. Somit gewährleistet Shibboleth mit dem SAML-Protokoll, dass

- die Prüfung des Passworts am IdP und nicht am SP erfolgt
- die Passwörter nicht im Klartext zum IdP übertragen werden
- Man-in-the-middle-Angriffe durch Nutzung von SSL/TLS erschwert sind [Gross03]
- der Nutzer der Datenweitergabe von Attributen durch den IdP aktiv zustimmen muss.

Der zuletzt genannte Punkt ist (in Deutschland) ein wichtiges Kriterium des Datenschutzes[7]. Die dem IdP angeschlossenen Datenbanken halten in vielen Fällen weitere Eigenschaften zu den Benutzeraccounts bereit. Die Weitergabe dieser Attribute an eine fremde Institution fällt unter das Datenschutzgesetz[8] und muss vom Accountinhaber ausdrücklich für jeden Dienst erlaubt werden. Konkret bedeutet dies, dass der IdP nach der Abfrage des Benutzerpassworts prüfen muss, ob die Authentifizierungsanfrage von einem SP stammt, dem der Nutzer bereits seine Einwilligung zur Datenabfrage gegeben hat. Sollte dies nicht zutreffen, darf der IdP die Attribute erst nach dem Einverständnis des Benutzers an den SP senden. Eine Implementierung dieser Funktionalität ist durch uApprove[9] bereits gegeben. uApprove setzt auf den IdP auf und zeigt dem Benutzer eine zusätzliche Webseite während dem Login-Vorgang, auf der er informiert wird, welche Attribute der SP abfragen möchte. Der Nutzer kann dem Vorgang aktiv zustimmen oder den Login-Prozess beenden. Das Bild 4 zeigt die Abfrage der Erlaubnis zur Datenweitergabe.

uApprove funktioniert nur für Webdienste, da andere Dienste nicht zwingend in der Lage sind, HTML-Seiten darzustellen. In diesem Fall kann die

---

[7] Bundesdatenschutzgesetz (BDSG), §§ 4 ff., Online verfügbar: `http://www.gesetze-im-internet.de/bdsg_1990/`, letzter Aufruf: 26.04.2012

[8] Verwaltungs- und Benutzungsordnung (VB) Universität Freiburg, § 5

[9] uApprove von SWITCH, `http://www.switch.ch/aai/support/tools/uApprove.html`, letzter Aufruf: 26.04.2012

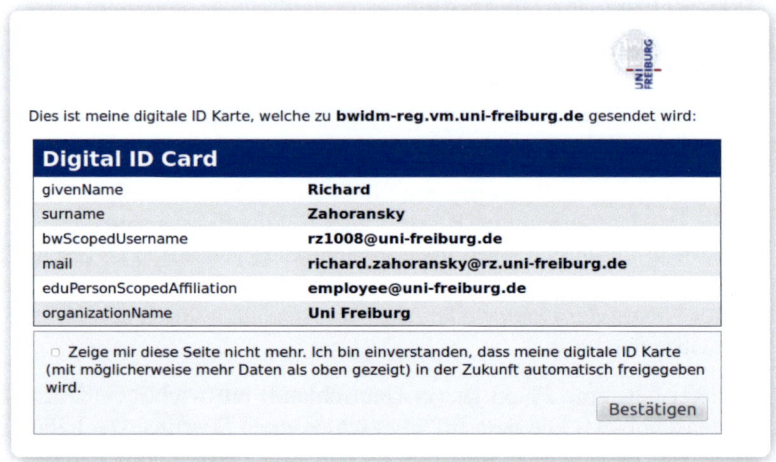

Bild 4: uApprove zeigt dem Benutzer, welche Attribute der SP vom IdP verlangt, und holt die Berechtigung des Benutzers ein (Browser-Screenshot).

Weitergabe der Attribute nicht durch den Benutzer überprüft und unterbunden werden.

Einem Dienst, der über ECP an die Föderation angebunden werden soll, stehen damit zwei Probleme gegenüber:

1. Wie geschildert, kann ein Benutzer eines ECP-fähigen Dienstes der Abfrage von Attributen währende des Login-Prozess nicht zustimmen.
2. Je nach Konzeption des Dienstes muss dem Server, der den Dienst bereitstellt, das Föderationspasswort zugänglich sein.

Auf beide genannte Punkte wird im Folgenden anhand eines implementierten, ECP-fähigen SSH-Servers näher eingegangen. Diese prototypische Implementierung steht exemplarisch für weitere, ECP-fähige Dienste.

Ein ECP-fähiger Dienst erhält dann eine hohe Benutzerakzeptanz, wenn sich dessen Bedienung durch die zusätzliche ECP-fähigkeit nicht ändert

[Amberg03]. Für das hier gezeigte Proof-of-Concept ist das der Fall. Der SSH-Client bedarf keiner Modifikation und verhält sich für den Anwender wie gewohnt. Auf der Server-Seite wurde ein Pluggable Authentication Module (PAM) [Morgan97] entwickelt, das die Authentifizierung durch ECP am SP und IdP durchführt. Das bedeutet, dass nur der SSH-Server ECP-fähig ist und nur dieser die Authentifizierung mit dem SP und IdP abwickeln kann. Damit der Server die Authentifizierung im Namen des Benutzers durchführen kann, benötigt dieser das vom Benutzer gelieferte Passwort, wie es in Bild 5 beschrieben ist. Hierdurch erhält der ECP-fähige Server Zugang zu dem Benutzeraccount:

- Der ECP-fähige Dienst nimmt das Benutzerpasswort selbst entgegen und hat somit unkontrollierten Zugriff auf den Benutzeraccount.
- Der Dienst ist in der Lage, den IdP nach Attributen abzufragen, ohne die Herausgabe dieser Attribute vom Benutzer erlauben zu lassen.

Diese beiden Punkte entsprechen weder dem SAML-Standard noch dem Datenschutzgesetz. Die demonstrierte Beispielimplementierung bietet den Föderationsmitglieder mehrere Möglichkeiten, den SSH-Server zu nutzen. Somit lassen sich die beiden genannten Probleme umgehen. Eine vorgeschaltete Login-Seite stellt sicher, dass der Benutzer sein Föderationspasswort dem SSH-Server nicht preisgeben muss, und gewährleistet, dass der Benutzer der Weitergabe seiner Attribute zustimmen muss. Im Folgenden werden verschiedene Ansätze zur Ermöglichung eines ECP-fähigen SSH-Dienstes diskutiert. Darauf aufbauend wird die momentane Implementierung des Proof-of-Concepts eingehender beschrieben. Die Tabelle 1 zeigt eine Übersicht der hier diskutierten, möglichen Varianten eines ECP-fähigen SSH-Dienstes an.

4.1 Anonymer Zugang

Mitgliedern der Föderation könnte es ermöglicht werden, sich mit ihrem Nutzernamen und ihrem Benutzerpasswort der Heimatorganisation direkt am ECP fähigen SSH-Server anzumelden. Das Benutzerpasswort muss dem SSH-Server anvertraut werden, damit dieser den Heimat-IdP fragen kann,

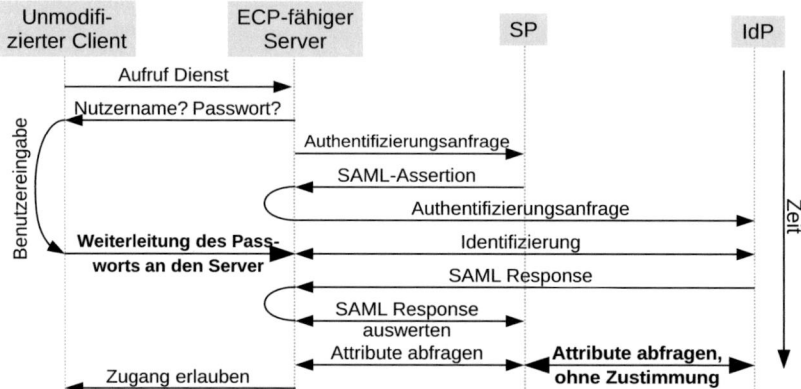

Bild 5: Kommunikationsschema eines ECP-fähigen Dienstes. Da der Client nicht ECP-fähig ist, kann nur der Server die Authentifizierung mit der Föderation durchführen. Hierfür muss dem Server das Passwort des Benutzers verfügbar sein. Dies entspricht nicht dem SAML2-Standard. Die Weitergabe der Attribute ohne Zustimmung des Benutzers entspricht nicht dem Datenschutzgesetz.

	Eigenes Home-Dir	Passwort verborgen	Abfragen d. Attribute	alternativer Login
Anonymer Zugang	-	-	-	-
Sofortiger Login	x	-	-	-
Anmelden m. Prüfung	x	-	x (ohne Zustimmung)	-
Register Seite	x	x	x	x

Tabelle 1: Übersicht der vorgestellten Login-Möglichkeiten

ob der Benutzer ein Account innerhalb der Föderation besitzt. Ist die Antwort vom IdP positiv, wird der Zugriff auf ein dienstlokales Gastkonto ohne persistentem Heimatverzeichnis gewährt. Dieser Ansatz bedingt keine lokale Datenhaltung. Da der SSH-Server keine Attribute abfragen muss, ist diese Variante konform mit dem Datenschutz. Die Autorisierung des Dienstes kann allerdings nur sehr grob erfolgen.

4.2 Sofortiger Zugang mit Heimatverzeichnis und eindeutigem Namen

Zusätzlich zur oben beschrieben Methode ist es möglich, eine eindeutige Zuweisung der Benutzer durch eine randomisierte, aber persistente Identität (PersistentID) zu ermöglichen. Solch eine persistentID wird vom Heimat-IdP für jeden Benutzer generiert und an die SP geliefert. Sowohl dieser Ansatz als auch der Anonyme Zugang sind mit den gleichen Nachteilen behaftet. Durch eine dienstlokale Datenbank ist es allerdings möglich, den Benutzern ein persistentes Heimatverzeichnis zuzuordnen. Auch wenn sich der Nachname eines Nutzers ändern sollte, bleibt die PersistentID erhalten.

4.3 Anmelden mit Prüfung der Attribute

Die beschriebenen Methoden lassen sich so erweitern, dass der SSH-Server zusätzlich die Attribute der Benutzer beim IdP erfragt. Somit ließe sich stets die Zugangsberechtigung prüfen - allerdings wäre die Abfrage der Attribute ohne Zustimmung und die Herausgabe durch den IdP ein Verstoß gegen den Datenschutz.

4.4 Zugang über Registrierungsseite

Um sowohl den Datenschutz zu beachten und nicht auf die Herausgabe des Föderationspassworts zu bestehen, funktioniert die Implementierung des Proof-of-Concepts nach folgendem Schema: Vor dem ersten Nutzen des SSH-Server muss der Nutzer mit seinem Browser auf eine Registrierungsseite navigieren. Somit lässt sich sicherstellen, dass ein Nutzer, der den SSH-Zugang erwünscht, der Datenweitergabe aktiv zustimmt. Daraufhin erstellt die Seite einen Eintrag in einer dienstlokalen Datenbank. Dem SSH-Server ist nach dieser Prozedur der Benutzer bekannt. Die Registrierungsseite zeigt dem Benutzer ein einmalig gültiges Passwort an, das für den SSH-Login verwendbar ist. Nach jedem Login wird das Passwort neu gesetzt. In zukünftigen Versionen bietet die Seite eine Option, dass der Benutzer sein öffentlichen Schlüssel hinterlegen kann. Somit entfällt die Eingabe des Einmal-Passworts. Eine Weitergabe des Passworts an den SP ist nicht mehr nötig. Die Zustimmung des Benutzers zur Weitergabe von Attributen kann eingeholt werden und die Heimatverzeichnisse auf dem SSH-Server sind persistent. Benutzer können sich de-registrieren, falls sie ihr Konto auf dem SSH-Server löschen möchten. Die hinterlegten Attribute und Daten werden dann vollständig gelöscht. Im Folgenden wird die detaillierte Funktionsweise geschildert.

5 Funktionsweise SSH-Login

Der Proof-of-Concept besteht aus einem selbst entwickeltem PAM-Modul, einer PostgreSQL-Nutzerdatenbank und mehreren PHP-Modulen, entwickelt von der Universität Karlsruhe (KIT) und der Universität Konstanz. In diesem Abschnitt wird auf die SSH Proof-of-Concept Implementierung näher eingegangen.

5.1 Registrierung über Webseite

Ein potentieller Nutzer des SSH-Servers öffnet zur erstmaligen Freischaltung des Diensts die Registrierungsseite mit seinem Browser. Die Seite ist durch Shibboleth geschützt. Nur Föderationsmitglieder haben darauf Zugriff. Das Benutzerpasswort wird durch Browserweiterleitung direkt am IdP eingegeben und ist dem SP nicht zugänglich. Wie im Bild 6 (Schritt 4) gezeigt, stimmt der Benutzer aktiv der Weitergabe seiner Attribute zu oder beendet alternativ die Sitzung.

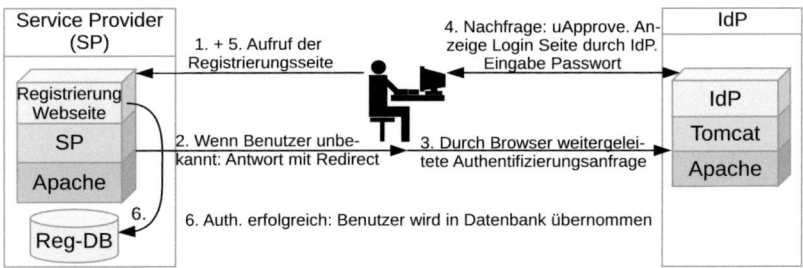

Bild 6: Notwendige Registrierung, um den ECP-fähigen SSH-Server zu nutzen. Die Registrierungsseite ist durch Shibboleth mit uApprove geschützt. Der Benutzer muss der Weitergabe seiner Attribute aktiv zustimmen. Der Browserredirect garantiert, dass der SP keinen Zugriff auf das Benutzerpasswort bekommt.

5.2 Registrierungsseite

Nach der Zustimmung wird der Browser zurück auf die Registrierungsseite geleitet. Da der Benutzer nun eine gültige SAML-Session besitzt, zeigt die Webseite die vom IdP gelieferten Attribute an. Mit einem Klick auf einen „registrieren"-Knopf werden die gelieferten Attribute gespeichert. Zusätzlich wird zu jedem Account eine User-ID, Username und temporäres Passwort (One-Time-Passwort: OTP) generiert und hinterlegt. Das temporäre Passwort wird im Browser angezeigt. Die Registrierung ist damit abgeschlossen. Der Benutzer hat mit den angezeigten Daten nun Zugriff auf den SSH-Server, wie bereits in Abschnitt 4.4 erwähnt. In einer zukünftigen Version der Registrierungsseite wird es möglich sein, dass der Benutzer direkt seinen öffentlichen Schlüssel hinterlegt.

5.3 Einloggen auf den SSH-Server

Das im Rahmen des bwIDM-Projekts entwickelte PAM-Modul untersucht jeden SSH-Login-Versuch. Stammt der einloggende Benutzer aus der Föderation, prüft das Modul die Eingabe des temporären Passworts. Alternativ kann sich der Benutzer über seinen privaten Schlüssel einloggen. Stimmt das temporäre Passwort oder der Schlüssel, erfolgt eine Abfrage der Attri-

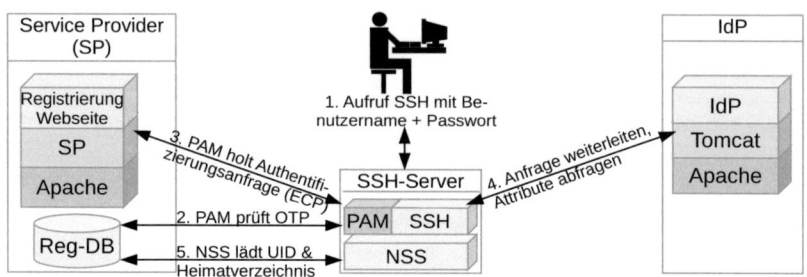

Bild 7: PAM bearbeitet den SSH-Loginversuch und prüft die Gültigkeit des Benutzereintrags per ECP am IdP. Hierfür kann der Benutzer sein OTP oder seinen Public Key nutzen. Nutzt der Benutzer sein persönliches Kennwort, bekäme der SSH-Server ungeschützten Zugriff auf dieses.

bute am Heimat-IdP des Benutzers. Da der SP dem IdP bekannt ist, entspricht der IdP der Anfrage und liefert die Attribute aus. Nur wenn dort noch ein aktiver Account besteht, wird dem Login-Versuch stattgegeben. Falls das temporäre Passwort zum Einloggen verwendet wurde, wird ein neues generiert. Durch die Verwendung dieser alternativen Loginvarianten benötigt der SSH-Server keinen Zugriff auf das persönliche Passwort. Zusätzlich kann sich der Benutzer auch mit seinem Benutzerpasswort der Heimatorganisation anmelden - nimmt dann allerdings in Kauf, dass das Passwort am SSH-Server einsehbar ist. Die Zuweisung von Föderationsaccounts zu lokalen Benutzernamen übernimmt der Name Service Switch (NSS) von Linux und nutzt hierfür die von der Registrierungsseite befüllte PostgreSQL-Datenbank. Dem System ist somit das Heimatverzeichnis, die UID und GID bekannt.

5.4 Ausscheiden eines Mitgliedes aus der Föderation

Scheidet ein Mitglied aus der Föderation aus, ist es sinnvoll, auch dessen hinterlegte Daten zu löschen. Die Registrierungsseite bietet dem Benutzer die Möglichkeit, seine gespeicherten Daten einzusehen und zu löschen.
Da die Nutzerdaten bei jedem Login geprüft werden, kann auf Statusän-

derungen eines Benutzers reagiert werden, ohne dass es einer manuellen, lokalen Datenbankpflege benötigt. Das PAM-Modul prüft bei jedem Login eines authentifizierten Nutzers dessen Attribute. Dabei wird geprüft, ob dem Nutzer immer noch die nötigen Rechte innerhalb der Föderation zugewiesen sind und der Benutzer immer noch Teil der Föderation ist. Zugang wird gewährt, wenn sowohl die Zugangsdaten als auch die zugewiesene Attribute gültig sind. Ändern sich die Attribute, werden diese Änderungen in der dienst-lokalen Datenbank übernommen. Scheidet ein Teilnehmer aus der Föderation aus, verweigert auch der SSH-Server den Zugang.

6 Fazit

In dieser Arbeit wurde ein Überblick der SAML-Föderation gegeben. Es wurde gezeigt, dass SAML und Shibboleth konform mit den herrschenden Datenschutzbestimmungen arbeiten. Da sich manche Dienste nicht web-fähig machen lassen, besteht die Notwendigkeit, eine Authentifizierung ohne die Anzeige von HTML-Seiten und HTTP-Redirects durchzuführen. Das in SAML integrierte ECP-Profil bietet diese Funktionalität. Anhand eines exemplarischen, ECP-fähigen SSH-Dienstes wurde gezeigt, dass nicht webfähige Dienste über ECP in eine Föderation integrierbar sind. Eine im Rahmen des bwIDM-Projekts entwickelte Registrierungsseite ermöglicht einem Benutzer, seine Datenfreigabe einzusehen und der Datenweitergabe zuzustimmen. Ebenfalls ist dem Nutzer die Möglichkeit gegeben, alternative Techniken für den Login zu nutzen. Die Weitergabe des Föderationspassworts an den Dienst ist nicht nötig. So bleiben die Datenschutzbestimmungen berücksichtigt, und ein ECP-fähiger Dienst darf konform mit den geltenden Bestimmungen auf die Attribute eines Benutzers zugreifen.

Literaturverzeichnis

[Amberg03] Michael Amberg, Markus Hirschmeier und Deniz Schobert. Dart - Ein Ansatz zur Analyse und Evaluierung der Benutzerakzeptanz. In *Wirtschaftinformatik Proceedings 2003*.

[Gross03] T. Gross. Security analysis of the SAML single sign-on browser/artifact profile. In *Computer Security Applications Conference, 2003. Proceedings. 19th Annual*, pages 298 – 307, Dezember 2003.

[Koehler12] J. Köhler, S. Labitzke, M. Simon, M. Nussbaumer und H. Hartenstein. FACIUS: An Easy-to-Deploy SAML-based Approach to Federate Non Web-Based Services. In *IEEE International Conference on Trust, Security and Privacy in Computing and Login-Node Communications (TrustCom-2012)*, Liverpool, UK, Juni 2012.

[Morgan97] Andrew G. Morgan. Pluggable Authentication Modules for Linux: An implementation of a user-authentication API. *Linux J.*, 1997(44es), Dezember 1997.

[SAML2] OASIS. Profiles for the OASIS Security Assertion Markup Language (SAML) V2.0. Technical report, OASIS Standard, März 2005.

[SWITCH-demo] SWITCH. Expert AAI Demo. Online verfügbar: http://www.switch.ch/aai/demo/2/expert.html, Letzter Aufruf 25.04.2012.

[Simon12] Michael Simon, Marcel Waldvogel, Sven Schober, Saher Semaan und Martin Nussbaumer. bwIDM: Föderieren auch nichtwebbasierender Dienste auf Basis von SAML. In *DFN Forum Kommunikationstechnologien*, volume 5 of *Lecture Notes in Informatics (LNI - Proceedings, GI-Edition)*, pages 119–128, Germany, Regensburg, Mai 2012.

Das bwGRiD Wissenschaftsportal

Christian Mosch,[*] Bastian Boegel,[†] Helmut Lang[‡]

Universität Ulm

Zusammenfassung: Das bwGRiD Wissenschaftsportal [Mosch2011] bietet Wissenschaftlern im Land Baden-Württemberg einen vereinfachten kommandozeilenfreien Zugang zum bwGRiD [Dynowski2012] und dessen Applikationen. Neben umfangreichen Funktionen zum standortübergreifenden Job- und Datenmanagement stellt das Portal auch einfache webbasierte Benutzerschnittstellen (Portlets) [Kussmaul2005] zu ausgewählten Programmen der Themenbereiche Chemie, Mikrosystemtechnik, Medizin, Ingenieurswissenschaften, Workflowmanagement und Bioinformatik zur Verfügung. Anhand der grafischen Benutzerschnittstelle zu den Chemieapplikationen Gaussian [Frisch2009] und NWChem [Valiev2010] werden im Rahmen dieses Beitrags einige didaktische Konzepte zur Einbindung von Portlets in die Lehre erläutert. Um eine effiziente und schnelle Integration weiterer Applikationen in das Portal zu ermöglichen, wurde eine Klonfunktionalität entwickelt, welche am Beispiel des Dacapo-Portlets vorgestellt wird. Sowohl neue als auch erfahrene Nutzer profitieren von der Unterstützung durch einen Avatar, der die Anwender in Schritten durch Aufgaben leiten, zu einzelnen Portalelementen gezielte Hilfestellungen geben und allgemeine Fragen beantworten kann. Die Basis für das Portal bildet die in einer Kooperation mit Kollegen am Karlsruher Institut für Technologie (KIT) entwickelte Java-Bibliothek Gatlet [Bozic2011], welche die Schnittstelle zwischen Portal und Grid bereitstellt.

1 Einleitung und Übersicht

Das bwGRiD [Dynowski2012] ist ein Verbund von Hochleistungsrechnern, der im Rahmen einer Kooperation zwischen neun Universitäten, Fachhochschulen und Forschungseinrichtungen in Baden-Württemberg an mehreren Standorten verteilt betrieben wird. Dabei soll die außerordentliche Rechenleistung des bwGRiDs den Wissenschaftlerinnen und Wissenschaftlern im Land möglichst einfach und effizient zur Verfügung gestellt werden. Es hat

---

[*] christian.mosch@uni-ulm.de
[†] bastian.boegel@uni-ulm.de
[‡] helmut.lang@uni-ulm.de

sich jedoch herausgestellt, dass der kommandozeilenbasierte Zugang mittels der Grid-Middleware Globus [Foster2006] und die Nutzung von Software über die Kommandozeile für Nutzer mit wenig Computererfahrung eine große Hürde sein kann. Daher ist ein wesentlicher Fokus der Entwicklungen im bwGRiD eine Vereinfachung des Zugangs zum Grid. Das Absenken dieser Hürde war einer der Kernaspekte des bwGRiD Portalprojektes [Mosch2011], welches im Arbeitspaket 5 der ergänzenden Maßnahmen[1] fortgeführt wird.

Um dieses Ziel zu verwirklichen, muss folglich die obligatorische Verwendung der Kommandozeile als Benutzerschnittstelle vermieden werden. Wesentliche Softwarepakete sollen durch eine grafische Benutzeroberfläche erreichbar sein. Darüber hinaus muss sichergestellt werden, dass die Benutzerschnittstellen bei Änderungen in der Softwarestruktur am Grid, zum Beispiel wenn sich der Name der Binärdatei einer Software ändert, möglichst zeitnah und für alle Nutzer transparent angepasst werden können. Auch sollen Nutzer verschiedener Betriebssysteme von unserem Angebot in vollem Umfang profitieren. Ein portal- und browserbasierter Ansatz kann diese Forderungen unmittelbar erfüllen und wurde deshalb auch ausgewählt.

Aufgrund der hohen Komplexität der Vorgänge, welche bei der Abbildung von Gridmechanismen mit Zertifikaten und bei der Einbindung wissenschaftlicher Applikationen auftreten können, ist ein javabasiertes Portalsystem eine sinnvolle Ausgangsbasis für das Projekt. Dies wird auch dadurch gestützt, dass viele Bibliotheken und Hilfsprogramme in diesem Umfeld in Java programmiert sind, zum Beispiel [Foster2006, Nieuwpoort2007, Hook2005, Herraez2007, ChemAxon2011]. Außerdem bieten Portalsysteme in der Regel bereits ohne weiteren Programmieraufwand wichtige Servicefunktionen, wie beispielsweise eine Nutzerverwaltung und das Management von Portlets [Kussmaul2005]. Ausgehend von einer Empfehlung des D-Grids[2] und nach weiterer eigener Evaluation wurde beim Start des Projektes das GridSphere Portal [Novotny2004] als Basis für die Entwicklung unseres eigenen Portalsystems gewählt. Neben der unmittelbaren Unterstützung von Grid-Basisfunktionen waren dabei auch

---

[1] http://www.bw-grid.de/bwservices/bwgrid-ergaenzende-massnahmen (Zugriff 2012-05-21)

[2] http://iwrwww1.fzk.de/dgrid-neu/index.php?id=81 (Zugriff 2012-05-14)

das Zusammenspiel mit Portlets gemäß JSR168 Standard^3 [Abdelnur2003] und die freie Verfügbarkeit im Rahmen von „Open Source" ausschlaggebend. Leider wurde die Weiterentwicklung von GridSphere während der Projektlaufzeit eingestellt. Dadurch fehlt zum Beispiel die Unterstützung für den JSR286 Standard^4 [Hepper2008] und es gibt keine Sicherheitsupdates mehr. Daher wurde ein Umstieg auf ein anderes Portalsystem unvermeidbar. Nach einer ausführlichen Evaluation der am Markt verfügbaren „Open Source" Portalsysteme mit JSR286 Unterstützung^5, haben wir uns vor kurzem dazu entschlossen, alle Basisfunktionen und wesentliche Applikationsportlets zu dem Portalframework Liferay [Sezov2011] zu portieren. Neben den oben genannten Kriterien hat Liferay eine um Größenordnungen aktivere *Community* als vergleichbare Projekte und bietet außerdem auch kommerziellen Support. Bei der Portierung soll noch stärker auf eine portalunabhängige Umsetzung geachtet werden. Alle über den Standard JSR286 hinausgehenden, für die Portlets unbedingt notwendigen Funktionen, zum Beispiel die Abfrage der Daten des aktuellen Nutzers mit seinen Berechtigungen oder die Interaktion mit dem Grid, werden dabei von der von uns entwickelte Bibliothek Gatlet [Bozic2011] bereitgestellt.

Gatlet wird auch im bisherigen GridSphere-basierten Portal bereits intensiv verwendet und stellt wichtige Funktionen für den Zugriff auf das Grid in einfacher Weise zur Verfügung. Einerseits erleichtert sich dadurch die Portierung der Applikationsportlets erheblich, andererseits ermöglichen die Gatletmethoden den Portletprogrammierern eine effiziente und schnelle Implementierung der Interaktion ihrer Portlets mit dem Grid. Gatlet stellt jedoch nicht nur die Schnittstelle zum Grid bereit. Es verfügt darüber hinaus auch über eine automatische Accountverwaltung, eine Ressourcendatenbank, einen Ressourcenmonitor, einen Jobmonitor, einen Dateibrowser, ein Metasubmit-System, ein E-Mail-System und viele weitere hilfreiche Funktionen. Zusätzlich stehen den Entwicklern mittels einer Tag-

---

^{3} Der JSR (*Java Specification Request*) 168 Standard beschreibt, wie Portlets beschaffen sein müssen, damit sie gemeinsam reibungslos in einem Portal genutzt werden können.

^{4} Der JSR 286 Standard ist eine Erweiterung des JSR 168 Standards.

^{5} Siehe zum Beispiel `http://holisticsecurity.wordpress.com/2011/06/14/which-portal-solution-should-i-use` und `http://fleksray.org/vergleich-enterprise-portale.html` (Zugriff 2012-05-16).

library[6] [PelegriLlopart2002] und „Cascading Style Sheet (CSS) Definitionen" [Bos1998] Möglichkeiten zur Verfügung, um zu einem einheitlichen „Look-and-Feel" zu gelangen. Das Gesamtpaket dieser Entwicklungsumgebung wird von uns in regelmäßigen Abständen an die Portletentwickler in Form der sogenannten Portaltemplates[7] verteilt (siehe Abbildung 1).

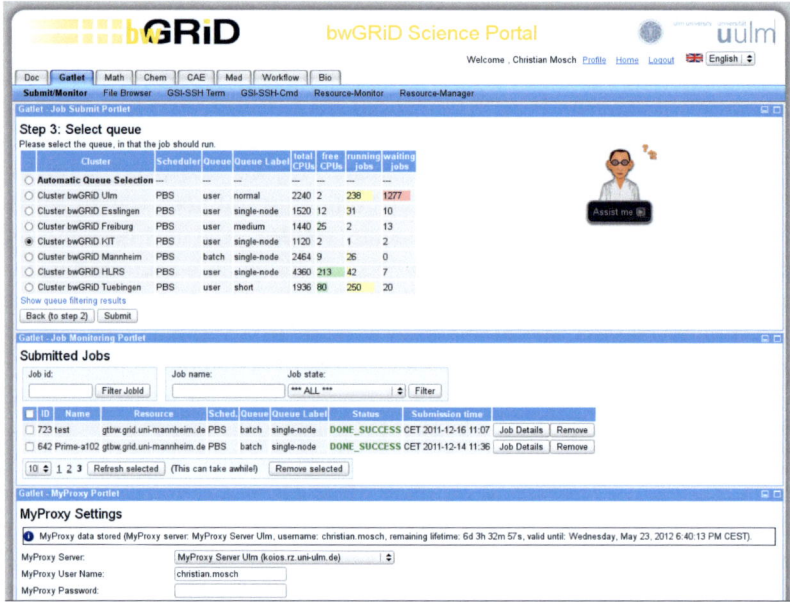

Abbildung 1: Beispiel für einige Komponenten der Portaltemplates: Avatar, Queueauswahl des Jobsubmit Portlets, Jobmonitor und MyProxy Portlet.

Aufbauend auf diesen Templates entwickeln die Portletentwickler webbasierte Schnittstellen zu bestimmten Softwarepaketen der Themenbereiche Mikrosystemtechnik (Freiburg), Medizin (Mannheim/Heidelberg), Ingenieurswissenschaften (Karlsruhe), Workflowmanagement (Stuttgart), Bioinformatik (Tübingen) und Chemie (Ulm). Die Portlets sollen dabei die

---

[6] Mittels der Taglibrary werden den Portlets genormte Funktionen zur Verfügung gestellt. Meist enthalten Tagkomponenten auch Webelemente.

[7] http://www.bw-grid.de/portal/download (Zugriff 2012-05-20)

Nutzer bei der Interaktion mit dem Grid bestmöglich unterstützen. Das bedeutet zum Beispiel, dass soweit möglich die Parameter für das Queueingsystem automatisch gesetzt oder dass zumindest sinnvolle Standardwerte mit klaren Hilfstexten zu den möglichen Wertebereichen angeboten werden. Darüber hinaus sollten die applikationsspezifischen Portlets die Nutzer bei der Verwendung der Softwarepakete unterstützen, etwa bei der Erzeugung von Eingabedaten oder beim Auswerten der Ergebnisse.

Ohne ein leistungsfähiges Hilfesystem wäre die Benutzerschnittstelle des Portals weniger komfortabel und effizient. Daher wurde zur Unterstützung und Leitung des Nutzers ein Avatar entwickelt und in das Portal integriert. Er bietet umfangreiche Hilfestellungen zu interaktiven Elementen des Portals an, kann den Nutzer Schritt für Schritt durch verschiedene Aufgaben führen und besitzt die Fähigkeit, auf frei formulierte Fragen zu antworten. Sowohl Anfänger als auch erfahrene Nutzer profitieren von der Unterstützung durch den Avatar, da dieser den Nutzern die Kontrolle über den Ort und den Umfang der Hilfestellung lässt. Das Avatarsystem steht dabei als Framework zur Verfügung, welches von den einzelnen Anwendungskomponenten verwendet werden kann.

Da die meisten Funktionen des Portals im Gatlet-Framework verankert sind und somit Gatlet die wesentliche Komponente für die Portlets ist, wird im Kapitel 2 eine Übersicht über die Struktur des Portals und die Funktionen von Gatlet gegeben. Eine Möglichkeit für eine effiziente und schnelle Integration weiterer Applikationen in das Portal wird in Kapitel 3 anhand der Klonfunktionalität des Dacapo-Portlets vorgestellt. Am Beispiel der grafischen Benutzerschnittstelle zu den Chemieapplikationen NW-Chem und Gaussian werden im Kapitel 4 einige didaktische Konzepte zur Einbindung von Portlets in die Lehre erläutert. Der aus Sicht des Nutzers unmittelbar und zu jeder Zeit hilfsbereite Avatar wird mit seinen im gesamten Portal wirkenden Möglichkeiten im Kapitel 5 präsentiert. Abschließend werden im Kapitel 6 die weiteren Pläne bezüglich des Portals diskutiert.

2 Gatlet und die Portaltemplates

Alle im bwGRiD entwickelten Applikationsportlets basieren auf den von Ulm zur Verfügung gestellten Portaltemplates. Neben der rein funktionellen Seite der Portaltemplates, die weiter unten beschrieben wird, besitzen die Templates auch mehrere logistische Funktionen. Zum einen fassen sie alle für die Entwicklung und den Betrieb erforderlichen Komponenten, wie zum Beispiel den Apache Tomcat Webserver [Vukotic2011], GridSphere [Novotny2004], JavaGAT [Nieuwpoort2007] (*Grid Application Toolkit*), Gatlet [Bozic2011] und mehrere Basis-, Service- und Beispielportlets zu einem Paket mit automatischer Installation zusammen. Dies reduziert für die Applikationsentwickler erheblich den Aufwand bei der Installation und sorgt dafür, dass die Entwickler schneller produktiv werden können. Zum anderen sorgt ein einheitliches Templatesystem dafür, dass alle Entwickler auf der gleichen Basis arbeiten und so die Interoperabilität und Homogenität der individuell erstellten, aber im gemeinsamen Portal bereitgestellten Portlets einfacher sichergestellt werden kann.

Die zentrale Komponente des Portals ist Gatlet, welches mit Hilfe von JavaGAT auf die Globus-Server des bwGRiDs zugreift. Abbildung 2 zeigt eine Übersicht der verschiedenen Komponenten des Portals. In den folgenden Absätzen wird beschrieben, wie die Komponenten des Diagramms bei den verschiedenen Abläufen im Portal zusammenspielen.

Beim ersten Zugriff auf das Portal authentifiziert sich der Benutzer via HTTPS (Hypertext Transfer Protocol Secure) mittels seines im Browser gespeicherten Grid Nutzerzertifikats, ausgestellt von dem Deutschen Forschungsnetz (DFN)[8]. Danach kann der Nutzer auf alle Seiten des Portals zugreifen, jedoch noch nicht auf das Grid und auch nicht auf die Portlets, die ohne Gridzugriff nicht funktionieren können. Im nächsten Schritt lädt der Nutzer mittels des von uns für den Firefox entwickelten Grid Proxy Managers [Boegel2011] (siehe Abbildung 3) ein in der Regel sieben Tage gültiges und mit einem Passwort geschütztes Proxyzertifikat[9] auf einen MyProxy Server[10] [Fleury2006]. Im letzten Schritt wird dann im Portal mittels des MyProxy Portlets (siehe Abbildung 1) aus dem Proxyzertifikat am MyProxy Server ein kurzlebiges Portal Proxyzertifikat abgeleitet. Nun hat der Nutzer den vollen Zugriff auf seine Accounts an allen Gridstandorten.

---

[8] `https://www.pki.dfn.de/grid` (Zugriff 2012-05-18)

[9] Ein Proxyzertifikat ist ein Zertifikat mit kurzer Laufzeit, welches von dem ursprünglichen Nutzerzertifikat abgeleitet worden ist.

[10] Unser MyProxy Server ist über das Internet direkt erreichbar. Das Übertragen und Speichern der Proxyzertifikate erfolgt ausschließlich authentifiziert und verschlüsselt.

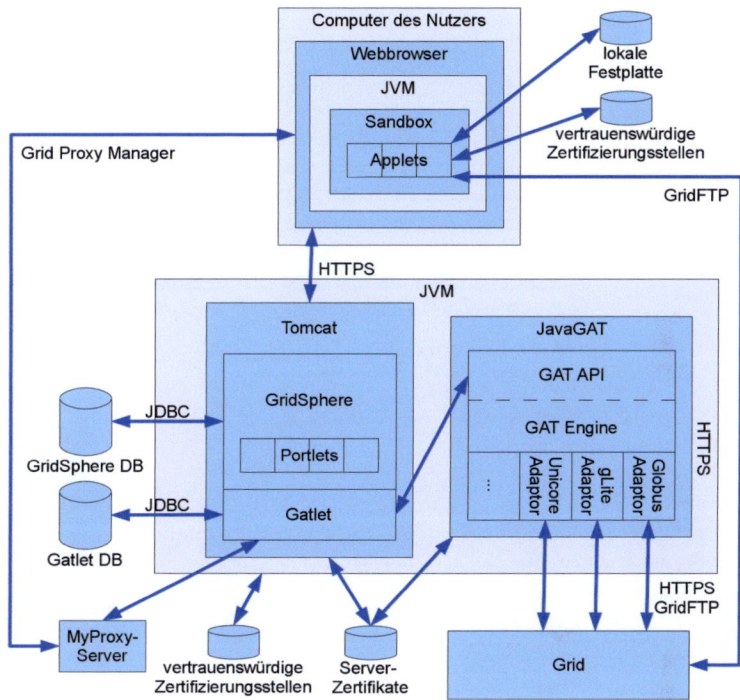

Abbildung 2: Architektur des Portals mit Gatlet [Bozic2011] und JavaGAT [Nieuwpoort2007] (für Details siehe Text).

Auf dem Portalserver läuft der Applikationsserver Apache Tomcat. Das Portalsystem GridSphere wird als Servlet unter der Regie des Applikationsservers betrieben. Die JSR168 konformen Portlets wiederum laufen unter Kontrolle des GridSphere Portals. Hier sind nicht nur die applikationsspezifischen Portlets angesiedelt, sondern auch alle von Gatlet zur Verfügung gestellten Service Portlets, wie zum Beispiel das MyProxy, das Jobsubmit und

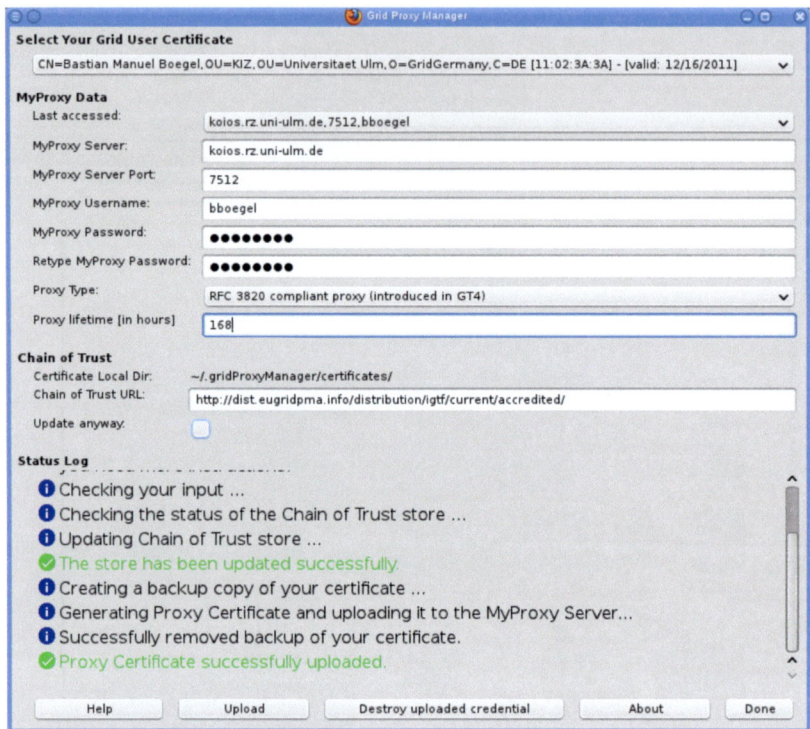

Abbildung 3: Das Firefox Plugin „Grid Proxy Manager" [Boegel2011] ersetzt den mühsamen Weg über den Kommandozeilenbefehl *grid-proxy-init*, der erst nach einer aufwändigen Globus-Installation zur Verfügung steht.

das Jobmonitor Portlet (siehe Abbildung 1). Gatlet stellt noch viele weitere solche Portlets zur Verfügung. Einige davon werden weiter unten noch vorgestellt. Wenn jetzt ein Nutzer mittels des Jobsubmit Portlets die Eingabedaten für einen neuen Job vorbereitet hat und er den Job anschließend submittieren will, dann übergibt das Jobsubmit Portlet das dabei erstellte Jobobjekt an die Gatlet Jobservice Methode *submitScriptJob*. Diese Methode reicht dann alle notwendigen Daten inklusive des Portal-Proxyzertifikats an die GAT API (*application programming interface*) weiter. Die API verwendet einen Adaptor[11], in unserem Fall den Globus Adaptor, um mit dem entsprechenden Standort des Grids zu kommunizieren und den Job dort zu submittieren. Anschließend kann man mittels des Jobmonitor Portlets den Job überwachen, nach Jobende auf die Ergebnisdaten zugreifen und den Job abschließend löschen.

GAT selbst stellt zwar mittels eines Adaptors die Verbindung zur Middleware her, kann aber weder Ressourcen noch Benutzer noch Jobs verwalten. Daher war die Entwicklung von „Gatlet" als Schnittstelle zwischen Portal und Middleware notwendig (siehe Abbildung 2). Gatlet verwaltet Benutzer, Ressourcen sowie Jobs und stellt diese in Form von Services dem Portal bzw. den Portlets zur Verfügung. Ein weiterer Vorteil von Gatlet ist, dass es eine Abstraktionsschicht zum Grid bildet. Das heißt, die Portletentwickler verwenden nur Gatlet und nicht das darunterliegende GAT. Dies ermöglicht es zum Beispiel, GAT später gegen eine andere Implementierung auszutauschen, ohne dass in den Portlets etwas geändert werden muss. Außerdem setzt Gatlet die vom jeweiligen Adaptor benötigten Parameter automatisch. Zur Protokollierung und Speicherung von Nutzer-, Job- und Transaktionsdaten sind sowohl an GridSphere als auch an Gatlet eigene Datenbanken per JDBC (*Java Database Connectivity*) angebunden.

Ein weiteres zentrales Portlet ist der *Dateibrowser* (siehe Abbildung 4). Er besitzt eine Vielzahl an Funktionen. Man kann Dateien und Verzeichnisse zwischen verschiedenen Standorten kopieren bzw. synchronisieren, ganze Verzeichnisbäume packen oder Archivdateien entpacken sowie Verzeichnisse und Dateien erzeugen, löschen und umbenennen. Es ist sogar möglich, Dateiinhalte direkt per Doppelklick anzeigen zu lassen. Mit der *Up-/Download*-Funktion kann man Dateien vom eigenen Rechner auf den aktuell ausgewählten Gridstandort hochladen bzw. Dateien, zum Beispiel Ergebnisse, von dem Gridstandort auf den eigenen Rechner herunterladen. Die Dateiübertragung wird dabei nicht über das Portal abgewickelt. Die Daten werden direkt zwischen dem eigenen Rechner und dem gewünschten

---

[11] Ein Adaptor ist im Wesentlichen eine Implementierung der Interface-Routinen für eine bestimmte Middleware.

Gridstandort übertragen (siehe direkte GridFTP Verbindung in der Abbildung 2).

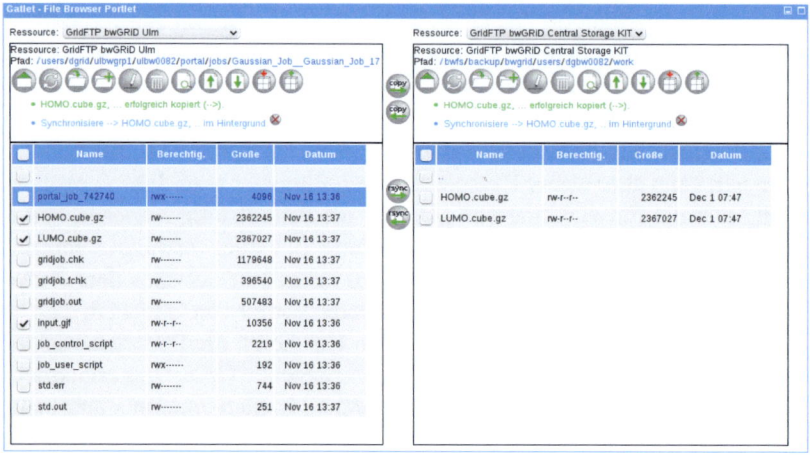

Abbildung 4: Der Dateibrowser, das Portlet zur Dateiverwaltung.

Mit dem GSI-SSH-Portlet[12] (siehe Abbildung 5) wurde eine Möglichkeit geschaffen, sich über das Portal direkt per Kommandozeile an den verschiedenen Standorten einzuloggen. Dadurch bietet das Portal auch Benutzern mit Kommandozeilenerfahrung einen einfachen Weg, ohne lokale Globus Installation von jedem Ort der Welt aus auf das bwGRiD zuzugreifen. Dies ist etwa dann sehr praktisch, wenn man sich auf einer Konferenz befindet, das DFN Gridzertifikat jedoch nur auf dem Rechner zuhause ist und man trotzdem die eigenen Jobs am Grid kontrollieren möchte.

Benutzer, die sich nicht mit den speziellen Eigenschaften der Ressourcen an den verschiedenen Standorten auskennen, werden von einem *Metasubmit-System* bei der automatischen Nutzung des Grids unterstützt. Nach Aktivierung sucht das System nach geeigneten Ressourcen und

---

[12] GSI-SSH (*Grid Security Infrastructure – Secure Shell*) ist eine modifizierte Version von OpenSSH, die zusätzlich Grid Sicherheitsmechanismen (Zertifikate) für die Nutzerauthentifizierung verwendet.

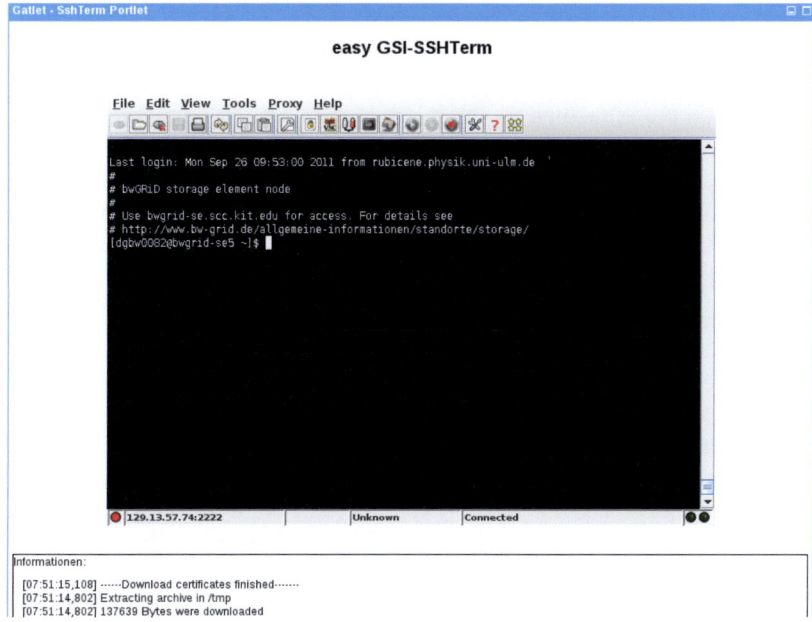

Abbildung 5: GSI-SSHTerm: Kommandozeilenzugriff ohne Globusinstallation.

Queues, wählt eine aus und submittiert den Job dort. Dabei werden nur Queues berücksichtigt, die den Anforderungen des Jobs entsprechen. Zum Beispiel müssen die Queues die benötigte Software, die geforderte Zahl der Rechenknoten und die maximale Joblaufzeit erfüllen können.

Eine eigene *Taglibrary* zur Bereitstellung genormter Portletkomponenten unterstützt die Anwendungsentwickler bei der Etablierung eines einheitlichen *Look-and-Feels*. Die entsprechenden Tags werden sowohl von den Kernportlets als auch von den verschiedenen Anwendungsportlets genutzt. Zum Beispiel dient das *QueueResourcesTableTag* zur Anzeige der Queues und wird in allen Portlets verwendet, die Jobs abschicken können. Das entsprechende Tag ist im Jobsubmit Portlet in Abbildung 1 zu sehen. Ein weiteres Beispiel ist das *BaseStorageResourceTag*, das dazu dient, den

Inhalt von Verzeichnissen anzuzeigen. Die Datei- und Verzeichnisfunktionen werden dabei direkt im Tag verarbeitet. Der Portletentwickler kann einfach das Tag in seinem Portlet verwenden und erhält damit automatisch die gesamte Funktionalität des Tags. Zwei dieser Tags nebeneinander sind in der Abbildung 4 zu sehen. Ein weiterer Vorteil der Taglibrary ist, dass Änderungen an einem Tag automatisch allen Applikationen zur Verfügung stehen. Wenn also eine neue Tabellenspalte zu einem Tag mit Tabelle hinzugefügt wird, so wird diese Änderung automatisch ohne Eingriff der Portletentwickler in allen Portlets sichtbar.

Die Eigenschaften der Ressourcen am bwGRiD ändern sich von Zeit zu Zeit, wenn unter anderem eine Software an einem Standort installiert oder die maximale Queuelaufzeit angepasst wird. Der *Grid-Ressourcen-Importer* vereinfacht die Aktualisierung der Ressourcen der Test- und Produktivportale, indem er alle für das Portal benötigten Ressourcen-Daten aus einer XML-Datei lädt. Neben vielen weiteren Daten enthält die Datei Informationen zu den Site-, Cluster-, Globus-, Login-, GridFTP-, MyProxy-, Software- und Queue-Ressourcen. Die Datei wird regelmäßig aktualisiert und liegt den Portaltemplates in der jeweils aktuellen Fassung bei. Sie kann bei Bedarf auch separat verteilt werden. Beim Import werden bereits importierte Ressourcen aktualisiert. Der Importmechanismus erspart dem Administrator eines Portals, also auch den Portletentwicklern mit Testportalen, das individuelle Einrichten bzw. Aktualisieren der einzelnen Ressourcen (siehe Abbildung 6).

Gatlet fragt regelmäßig den Status der Queues der Grid-Ressourcen ab und überwacht so deren Verfügbarkeit. Dies ermöglicht, nicht verfügbare Grid-Ressourcen im Portal temporär zu deaktivieren, falls an der Grid-Ressource Wartungsarbeiten durchführt werden. Diese Ressourcen werden dem Benutzer also gar nicht für den Submit vorgeschlagen. Sollte die Ressource wieder erreichbar sein, wird sie automatisch wieder aktiviert.

Mit dem umfangreichen Angebot an Basisportlets und Gatletdiensten stehen sowohl den Nutzern als auch den Programmieren viele hilfreiche Werkzeuge zur Verfügung. Es wird jedoch aufgrund der Komplexität der Aufgabenstellung, insbesondere von Seiten der wissenschaftlichen Applikationen, aber auch durch die Heterogenität und Eigenentwicklung des

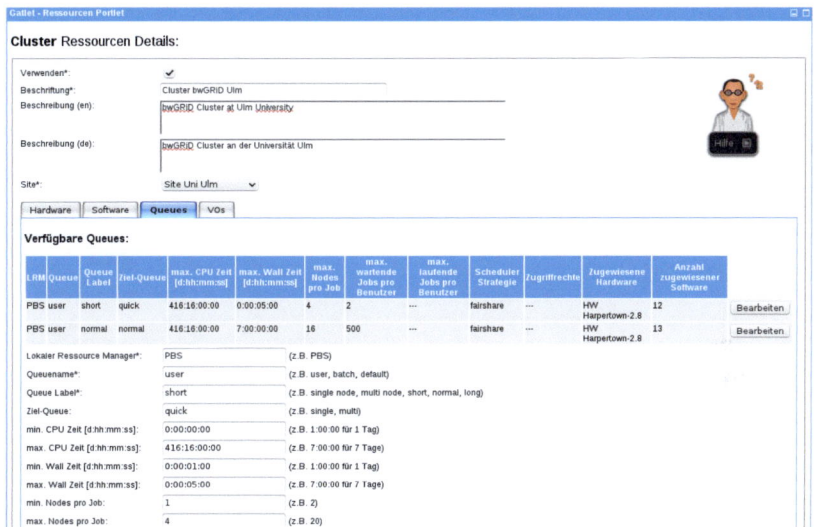

Abbildung 6: *Grid-Ressourcen-Importer*: Dialog zum Einrichten von Ressourcen nach Import der XML-Datei.

Grids, immer wieder zu einem nicht unerheblichen Anpassungsbedarf kommen. Eine solche Anpassung wurde bereits in der Einleitung erwähnt, die Portierung des Portals zu Liferay. Aber auch die Applikationsportlets müssen kontinuierlich weiter entwickelt und an den Bedarf der Wissenschaftler angepasst werden. Zwei sehr weit fortgeschrittene Portlets (das Dacapo-Portlet und der Chemieeditor) werden in den nächsten Kapiteln vorgestellt.

3 Das Dacapo-Portlet mit Klonfunktionalität

Die Quantenchemieapplikation Dacapo [Hammer1999] wird von vielen Nutzern im bwGRiD verwendet. Unter den Nutzern ist auch ein erheblicher Anteil, der sich im Umgang mit der Kommandozeile schwer tut und der daher die Möglichkeit eines webbasierten Zugriffs auf die Applikation sehr begrüßt. Aus diesem Umfeld heraus ist das Dacapo Portlet (siehe Abbildung 7) entstanden, welches die wichtigsten Bedürfnisse der *Community* deckt und sich auch für Experten eignet.

Abbildung 7: Hauptseite des Dacapo Portlets mit Bereichen für Programmeingabedaten und Jobparameter.

Die Hauptseite des Portlets gliedert sich in einen Bereich für die Eingabedaten des Programms, einen für die Jobparameter und einen für übergeordnete Schaltflächen. Für alle Elemente der Seite kann der Avatar Hilfestellungen geben. Insbesondere bei den Eingabedaten ist es besonders hilfreich, dass er auch ein ausführlich kommentiertes Beispiel anbieten kann. Der Inhalt aller Eingabefelder wird vor dem Submittieren überprüft. Wenn man beispielsweise mehr Kerne anfordert als das Grid bieten kann, erhält man einen Hinweis mit der Bitte um Korrektur. Innerhalb einer Session merken sich alle Eingabefelder des Portlets ihren Inhalt, auch wenn man an eine andere Stelle im Portal wechselt oder die Seite neu lädt. Dies ist sehr praktisch, wenn man viele ähnliche Jobs submittieren möchte, bei denen sich nur wenige Parameter individuell ändern. Neben der automatischen Queueauswahl und der manuellen Wahl der Queue besteht auch die Möglichkeit, nach dem ersten submittierten Job alle weiteren Jobs automatisch zum gleichen Cluster zu senden.

Die neuesten Erweiterungen des Portlets sind eine Möglichkeit zur Auswahl einer bestimmten Softwareversion, die Option zum Versand von E-Mails beim Ende des Jobs und ein umfangreiches Management großer *Restartdateien*. Man kann wählen, ob eine *Restartdatei* beim Jobende geschrieben oder beim Start gelesen werden soll. Letzteres setzt natürlich voraus, dass man vorher eine *Restartdatei* erzeugt hat. Das Management der in der Regel relativ großen *Restartdatei* wird vom Portal übernommen. Je nach Standort werden dafür bei Bedarf automatisch *Workspaces*, d.h. temporäre Speicherbereiche, angelegt bzw. verlängert. Der Benutzer wird dabei durch ein Info-Fenster über die Haltbarkeit der von ihm erzeugten Daten informiert.

Das Dacapo Portlet ist eines der am weitesten fortgeschrittenen Portlets, welches aufgrund seiner vielen und ausgereiften Servicefunktionen auch als Template für andere Portlets dienen kann. Um dies so einfach wie möglich zu gestalten, haben wir eine Klonfunktionalität entwickelt. Mit ihrer Hilfe kann man in wenigen Minuten aus dem Dacapo Portlet ein neues, vollwertiges Portlet mit allen notwendigen Dateien erzeugen und muss dann nur noch wenige Anpassungen bezüglich der neuen Software vornehmen. Dies betrifft zum Beispiel den Aufbau des Queueingsystemskriptes. Die Klonfunktionalität ist besonders gut geeignet für Software, welche eine ähnliche Eingabe- und Ausgabestruktur wie das Ausgangsportlet besitzt. Wenn hier jedoch deutliche Abweichungen zu erwarten sind, weil etwa das Benutzerinterface mit weiteren Eingabefeldern versehen werden muss, dann ist der Aufwand bis zu einem neuen funktionsfähigem Portlet deutlich größer. Allerdings ist die Stärke des Klonsystems, dass alle Klone wieder klonbar sind und sich auf diesem Weg mit der Zeit ein großer Fundus an möglichen Ausgangsportlets aufbauen kann.

4 Der Chemieeditor für NWChem und Gaussian

Der Chemieeditor ist eines der aufwändigsten Portlets des Portals. Bei ihm stehen neben der Vereinfachung des Gridzugangs auch deutlich weitreichendere Ziele im Vordergrund. Zum einen verfolgt das Portlet ein didaktisches Konzept, um Nutzern die grundlegende Struktur der Eingabeformate der unterstützten Chemieprogramme näher zu bringen. Zum anderen besitzt es eine Teamworkfunktion, mit deren Hilfe Dozenten Kurse vorbereiten und den Kursteilnehmern Molekülstrukturen zur Verfügung stellen können.

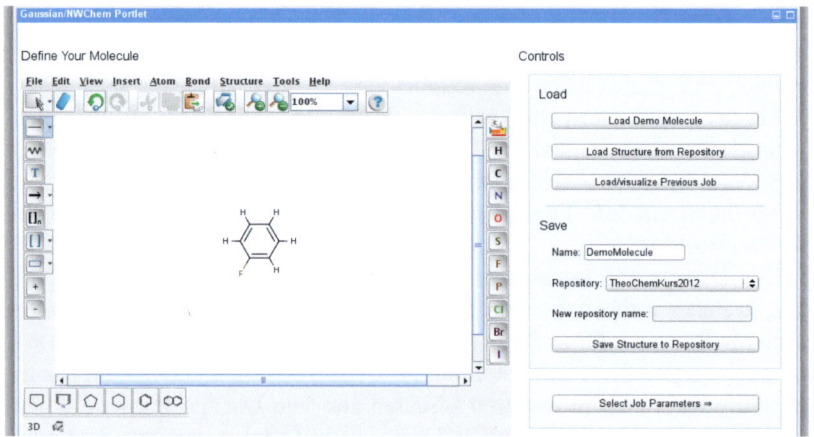

Abbildung 8: Der Moleküleditor ist der Ausgangspunkt für alle Chemiejobs.

Der Ausgangspunkt aller Arbeiten mit diesem Portlet ist der auf Marvin [ChemAxon2011] basierende Moleküleditor (siehe Abbildung 8). Mit seiner Hilfe kann man unabhängig vom später gewählten Chemieprogramm Molekülstrukturen erstellen. Auf der zweiten Seite des Portlets kann man dann zwischen den Chemieprogrammen NWChem und Gaussian wählen und zusätzlich wesentliche quantenchemische Parameter beeinflussen, wie z. B. den Basissatz, die Methode oder den Jobtyp. Wenn man dann zur dritten Seite des Portlets wechselt, wird aus den Moleküldaten und den quantenchemischen Parametern automatisch eine für das gewählte Programm korrekte Eingabedatei erzeugt. Diese wird auf der Seite angezeigt und kann direkt editiert werden. Durch Variation der quantenchemischen Parameter und Moleküldaten kann man nun unmittelbar deren Einfluss auf die Eingabedateien sehen und so deren grundlegende Struktur erlernen. Nutzer, die

über die elementaren Parameter des Portlets hinaus Änderungen vornehmen wollen, können im letzten Schritt vor dem Abschicken des Jobs die
Eingabedatei direkt bearbeiten. Ist der Nutzer mit der Eingabedatei zufrie-
den, kann der Quantenchemiejob submittiert werden. Dabei berücksichtigt
das Portlet automatisch die lizenzrechtlichen Zugriffsrechte des Nutzers auf
die kommerzielle Software Gaussian.

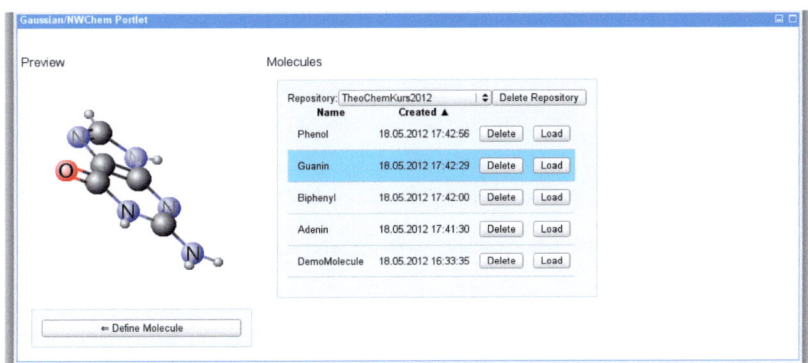

Abbildung 9: Laden eines Moleküls aus dem Repository.

In der Abbildung 8 ist noch eine weitere wesentliche Funktion des Portlets zu sehen. Im Bereich *Save* kann ein Dozent Moleküldaten in einem
öffentlichen *Repository* speichern. Der Name für das *Repository* kann frei
gewählt werden. Die Kursteilnehmer können dann später über den Bereich
Load auf diese Moleküldaten zugreifen (siehe Abbildung 9). Somit bietet
das Portlet eine Teamworkfunktion, die eine effiziente Vorbereitung von
Lehrveranstaltungen erlaubt.

Auch bei der grafischen Auswertung der Ergebnisse erhält der Nutzer
Unterstützung durch das Portlet. So können zum Beispiel die atomaren Po-
sitionen von Relaxationsrechnungen oder die molekularen Orbitale mittels
des Programms Jmol [Herraez2007] untersucht werden (siehe Abbildung
10).

Viele der Innovationen des Chemieeditors machen das Portlet zu einem
hervorragenden Werkzeug, um neue Nutzer an die Quantenchemie im Grid

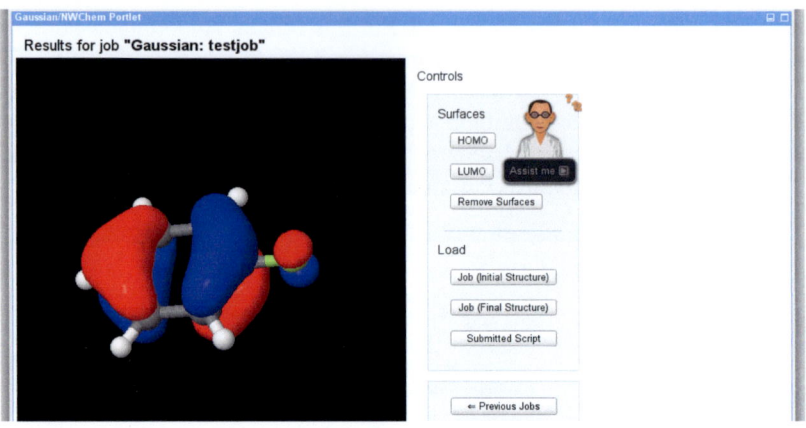

Abbildung 10: Auswerten der Ergebnisse mittels Jmol.

heranzuführen. Auch ist es für die Zukunft des Portlets wichtig, dass neben den notwendigen Korrekturen und Anpassungen an neue Webtechnologien und Veränderungen im Gridumfeld auch von Dozenten benötigte Erweiterungen berücksichtigt werden. So wäre eine Unterstützung weiterer Chemieprogramme von großem Vorteil. Auch muss bei der Teamworkfunktion mit Erweiterungsbedarf gerechnet werden.

5 Der Avatar

Wissenschafler, die das Grid für eigene Berechnungen oder in der Lehre verwenden wollen, möchten in der Regel möglichst schnell zu verwertbaren Ergebnissen gelangen. Daraus resultiert ein gewisser Unwille, sich mit grundlegenden Konzepten des Gridcomputings oder des Portals vertiefend auseinanderzusetzen. Beispielsweise interessiert den typischen Nutzer des Portals nicht, warum er ein Proxyzertifikat braucht und wie dieses Zertifikat zur Verbesserung der Sicherheit beiträgt. Deswegen ist eines der Ziele des Hilfesystems, dem Anwender möglichst schnell ein effizientes Arbeiten mit dem Portal zu ermöglichen. Dabei wird der Nutzer durch klare Handlungsanweisungen zu konkreten Zielen geführt. Die zugrundeliegenden komplexen Konzepte werden in diesem Fall nicht näher erläutert, da diese für das Erreichen des Ziels irrelevant sind.

Wie diese Aufgabenstellung mit dem hier beschriebenen avatarbasiertem Hilfesystem gelöst wurde, zeigt das Beispiel in den folgenden Absätzen. Angenommen ein Nutzer möchte mit dem in Kapitel 3 beschriebenem Portlet einen Dacapo-Job submittieren. Nachdem er sich im Portal eingeloggt hat und zur entsprechenden Seite für Dacapo gelangt ist, wird ihm allerdings vom Dacapo-Portlet nur eine Warnung angezeigt, dass kein „aktives Credential" gefunden wurde. Einem typischen Chemiker, der zum ersten mal mit dem Grid arbeiten möchte, ist der Begriff „Credential" normalerweise nicht geläufig. Daher weiß er nicht, was er in dieser Situation tun soll, und ist zunächst frustriert.

Eine konventionelle Herangehensweise an dieses Problem wäre es jetzt, einen Hilfebereich im Portal anzubieten, in dem das Konzept eines Proxyzertifikats beschrieben wird und der erläutert, wie man an ein solches gelangt. Dabei ergeben sich aber einige für diese Art von Hilfestellung typische Probleme. Zum Beispiel erhöht sich die kognitive Belastung des Nutzers [Chandler1991] und es kann eine „Lost in Hyperspace"-Situation entstehen [Theng1998].

Beim vorliegenden System wird der Avatar als kleines Icon dargestellt (siehe Abbildung 7) und steht immer zur Verfügung. Benötigt der Nutzer Hilfe, wie in der Situation aus dem Beispiel, aktiviert er den Avatar durch einen Klick auf „Hilfe". Der Avatar bietet dann verschiedene Möglichkeiten zur Unterstützung an. Eine der Optionen startet abhängig vom aktuellen Kontext eine Schritt-für-Schritt Anleitung. Auf der Seite des Dacapo-Portlets werden nun alle Elemente markiert und nummeriert, die zur Erzeugung eines Proxyzertifikates und dem anschließenden Erstellen und Submittieren eines Dacapo-Jobs benötigt werden. Dabei gibt der Avatar klare Anweisungen, welche Eingaben in welches Feld gemacht werden müssen (siehe Abbildung 11).

Während dieser Schritt-für-Schritt-Anleitungen werden vom Avatar lediglich die Eingabefelder besucht, die für die Erfüllung der Aufgabe essentiell sind. Dies spiegelt die Zielsetzung wieder, den Benutzer möglichst

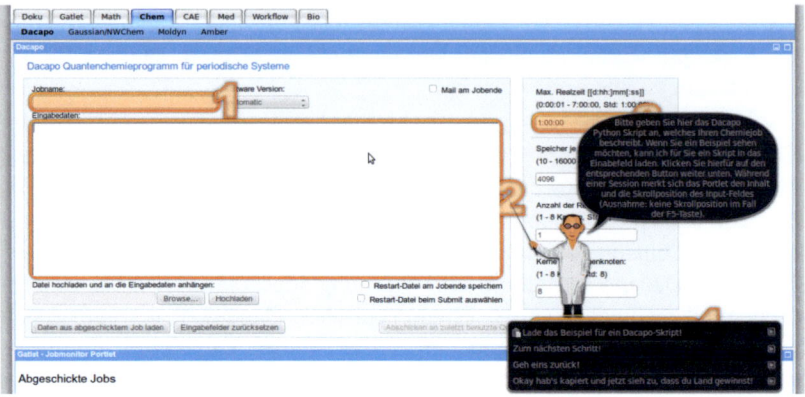

Abbildung 11: *Schritt-für-Schritt-Anleitung*: Der Avatar erläutert Schritte zur Erstellung eines Dacapo-Jobs.

schnell zu einem ersten Erfolgserlebnis – einem im Grid laufenden Job – zu führen. Die Vorteile dieses Ansatzes konnten in einer Nutzerevaluation gezeigt werden. Die benötigte Zeit zum Submittieren eines Dacapo-Jobs wurde unter Verwendung des Avatars von 22 Minuten bei konventioneller Hilfe auf Basis von HTML Texten auf 12 Minuten reduziert.

Ausgehend von dem Wissen, welches der Nutzer durch die Schritt-für-Schritt-Anleitungen erworben hat, kann er die Parameter seiner Berechnungen an eigene Bedürfnisse anpassen. Die dazu benötigte Hilfe zu weiteren Elementen der Benutzerschnittstelle bietet der Avatar über die Option „Hilf mir mit einem Element auf dieser Seite". Wird diese gewählt, werden alle Elemente, zu denen der Avatar weitere Informationen besitzt, markiert. Klickt der Nutzer auf eine dieser Markierungen wird der entsprechende Text angezeigt.

Ein zusätzlicher Anwendungsfall, den das System abdeckt, richtet sich an interessierte Benutzer, die beispielsweise doch gerne näheres zu Proxyzertifikaten wissen möchten. Dazu bietet der Avatar die Möglichkeit zur Eingabe von Fließtextfragen. Antworten auf solche Fragen können die bereits erläuterten Schritt-für-Schritt Anleitungen, einfache Antworten in einer Sprechblase oder komplexere Antworten sein. Bei komplexen Antworten wird eine Art Präsentation gestartet, bei der beliebige HTML-Inhalte gezeigt werden und der Avatar Bemerkungen zu einzelnen Bereichen der dargestellten Inhalte machen kann.

Die Funktionalität des Avatars bietet sowohl neuen als auch erfahrenen Nutzern eine wertvolle Unterstützung. Durch seinen modularen Aufbau und seine Integration in das Portletkonzept eignet er sich hervorragend zur Integration in die Applikationsportlets an den verschiedenen Standorten.

6 Zusammenfassung und Ausblick

Das bwGRiD Wissenschaftsportal bietet den Nutzern umfangreiche Möglichkeiten zum Job- und Datenmanagement und wird bereits landesweit eingesetzt. Zusammen mit der Klonfunktionalität sind die bis ins Detail ausgearbeiteten Funktionen des Dacapo-Portlets der Ausgangspunkt für eine neue Generation von Portlets, die für die Nutzer einfach und effizient zu bedienen sind und die vom Portletprogrammierer zügig erstellt werde können. Die neuen Didaktik- und Teamworkkonzepte im Chemieeditor Portlet bieten zusätzliches Potential, um weitere Nutzer zu akquirieren. Entsprechende Anfragen liegen uns von Dozenten mehrerer Universitäten im Land vor. Der Avatar rundet das Gesamtkonzept mit seinen verschiedenen Möglichkeiten zur Unterstützung des Nutzers ab.

Aktuelle Entwicklungen im Bereich der Portale, Java und Webtechnologien sowie der Zugangsverfahren zu den Clustern erfordern Anpassungen, die zur Zeit im Rahmen der ergänzenden Maßnahmen[13] vorgenommen werden. Dabei wäre zum einen die Portierung zum Liferay-Portalsystem zu nennen, die etwas aufwändiger ist, als dies ursprünglich geplant war. Weiter soll für zukünftige Clustersysteme neben dem zertifikatbasierten Zugang auch ein neues einfacheres Verfahren auf Basis des bwIDM Systems[14] implementiert werden. Ein erstes Konzept hierfür wird zur Zeit in Zusammenarbeit mit den Kollegen von Arbeitspaket 1 der ergänzenden Maßnahmen erstellt. Der Wechsel vieler Linux-Distributionen weg von Oracle Java zu

---

[13] `http://www.bw-grid.de/bwservices/bwgrid-ergaenzende-massnahmen` (Zugriff 2012-05-21)

[14] `http://www.bw-grid.de/bwservices/bwidm` (Zugriff 2012-05-21)

anderen Java-Varianten führt insbesondere bei der Interaktion mit Zertifikaten, aber auch an anderen Stellen zu Problemen. Hier muss eine Lösung gesucht werden, wobei durch den Wechsel zu bwIDM vermutlich einige der Probleme wegfallen. Langfristig sollten auch neuere Webtechnologien, etwa der Trend zu HTML5, in die zukünftige Entwicklung des Portals einfließen.

Literaturverzeichnis

[Abdelnur2003] Alejandro Abdelnur und Stefan Hepper. JSR 168: Portlet Specification. URL http://www.jcp.org/en/jsr/detail?id=168 (Zugriff 2012-05-21), Oktober 2003.

[Boegel2011] Bastian Boegel und Christian Mosch. Grid Proxy Manager 1.7. URL http://addons.mozilla.org/de/firefox/addon/grid-proxy-manager/ (Zugriff 2012-05-18), 2011.

[Bos1998] Bert Bos, Håkon Wium Lie, Chris Lilley und Ian Jacobs. Cascading Style Sheets, level 2: CSS2 Specification. URL http://www.w3.org/TR/2008/REC-CSS2-20080411/ (Zugriff 2012-05-20), Mai 1998.

[Bozic2011] Stefan Bozic. Gatlet – a Grid Portal Framework. ISGC International Symposium on Grids and Clouds, Taipei, Taiwan, 2011. URL http://event.twgrid.org/isgc2011/slides/MiddlewareandInteroperability/2/ISGC2011_Presentation_Gatlet.pdf (Zugriff 2012-05-16).

[Chandler1991] Paul Chandler und John Sweller. Cognitive Load Theory and the Format of Instruction. *Cognition and Instruction*, 8(4):293–332, 1991.

[ChemAxon2011] Marvin – a collection of tools to draw and visualize chemistry. ChemAxon Kft. Záhony u. 7, Building HX 1031 Budapest, Hungary, 2011. URL http://www.chemaxon.com/products/marvin (Zugriff 2012-05-19).

[Dynowski2012] M. Dynowski, M. Janczyk, J. Chr. Schulz, D. von Suchodoletz und S. Hermann. Das bwGRiD – High Performan-
ce Compute Cluster als flexible, verteilte Wissenschaftsinfrastruktur. In P. Müller, B. Neumair, H. Reiser und G. Dreo Rodosek, Herausgeber, 5. *DFN-Forum Kommunikationstechnologien – Verteilte Systeme im Wissenschaftsbereich*, pages 95 –
105. Gesellschaft für Informatik e.V. (GI), 2012. Siehe auch
http://www.bw-grid.de (Zugriff 2012-05-14).

[Fleury2006] Terry Fleury, Jim Basney und Von Welch. Single Sign-On
for Java Web Start Applications Using MyProxy. In *Proceedings of the ACM Workshop on Secure Web Services (associated with the 13th ACM Conference on Computer and Communications Security)*, November 2006. URL http://grid.
ncsa.illinois.edu/myproxy/ (Zugriff 2012-05-18).

[Foster2006] Ian Foster. Globus Toolkit Version 4: Software for Service-
Oriented Systems. *J. Comput. Sci. and Technol.*, 21(4):513–
520, 2006. URL http://www.globus.org/alliance/
publications/papers/IFIP-2006.pdf (Zugriff 2012-05-
15).

[Frisch2009] M. J. Frisch, G. W. Trucks, H. B. Schlegel, G. E. Scuse-
ria, M. A. Robb, J. R. Cheeseman, G. Scalmani, V. Baro-
ne, B. Mennucci, G. A. Petersson, H. Nakatsuji, M. Caricato,
X. Li, H. P. Hratchian, A. F. Izmaylov, J. Bloino, G. Zheng,
J. L. Sonnenberg, M. Hada, M. Ehara, K. Toyota, R. Fuku-
da, J. Hasegawa, M. Ishida, T. Nakajima, Y. Honda, O. Ki-
tao, H. Nakai, T. Vreven, J. A. Montgomery, Jr., J. E. Peralta,
F. Ogliaro, M. Bearpark, J. J. Heyd, E. Brothers, K. N. Ku-
din, V. N. Staroverov, R. Kobayashi, J. Normand, K. Ragha-
vachari, A. Rendell, J. C. Burant, S. S. Iyengar, J. Tomasi,
M. Cossi, N. Rega, J. M. Millam, M. Klene, J. E. Knox, J. B.
Cross, V. Bakken, C. Adamo, J. Jaramillo, R. Gomperts, R. E.
Stratmann, O. Yazyev, A. J. Austin, R. Cammi, C. Pomelli,
J. W. Ochterski, R. L. Martin, K. Morokuma, V. G. Zakrzewski,

G. A. Voth, P. Salvador, J. J. Dannenberg, S. Dapprich, A. D. Daniels, Ö. Farkas, J. B. Foresman, J. V. Ortiz, J. Cioslowski und D. J. Fox. Gaussian 09 Revision B.1. Gaussian Inc. Wallingford CT 2009, URL http://www.gaussian.com (Zugriff 2012-05-15).

[Hammer1999] B. Hammer, L. B. Hansen und J. K. Nørskov. Improved adsorption energetics within density-functional theory using revised Perdew-Burke-Ernzerhof functionals. *Phys. Rev. B*, 59(11):7413–7421, 1999. Rep. Sci. Res. Inst. 4, 56 2002; URL http://www.camp.dtu.dk/software and https://wiki.fysik.dtu.dk/dacapo (Zugriff 2012-05-14).

[Hepper2008] Stefan Hepper. JSR 286: Portlet Specification 2.0. URL http://www.jcp.org/en/jsr/detail?id=286 (Zugriff 2012-05-21), Juni 2008.

[Herraez2007] Angel Herráez. *How to use Jmol to study and present molecular structures*. Lulu Enterprises: Morrisville, NC, USA, 2007. ISBN 978-1847992598, URL http://jmol.sourceforge.net (Zugriff 2012-05-18).

[Hook2005] David Hook. *Beginning Cryptography with Java*. Wrox; 1st edition, 2005. ISBN 978-0764596339, URL http://www.bouncycastle.org (Zugriff 2012-05-17).

[Kussmaul2005] Timo Kussmaul. Die Java-Portlet-Spezifikation. *JavaSPEKTRUM, SIGS-DATACOM Verlag, Vol. 3*, pages 39 – 43, 2005. URL http://www.sigs.de/publications/js/2005/03/kussmaul_JS_03_05.pdf (Zugriff 2012-05-15).

[Mosch2011] Christian Mosch, Bastian Boegel, Helmut Lang, Kieron Taylor, Marek Dynowski, Jürgen Hesser, Siarhei Yakushevich, Alexander Zyl, Elisabeth Syrjakow, Yuriy Yudin, Tatyana Krasikova, Denis Nurmukhametov, Stephan Storch und Kevin Körner. Abschlussbericht für das bwGRiD Portalprojekt 2010 – 2011. Ministerium für Wissenschaft, Forschung und Kunst, Baden-Württemberg, 2011. Siehe auch `http://www.bw-grid.de/portal` (Zugriff 2012-05-14).

[Nieuwpoort2007] Rob V. van Nieuwpoort, Thilo Kielmann und Henri E. Bal. User-Friendly and Reliable Grid Computing Based on Imperfect Middleware. In *Proceedings of the ACM/IEEE Conference on Supercomputing (SC'07)*, November 2007. URL `http://www.cs.vu.nl/ibis/papers/nieuwpoort_sc_2007.pdf` und `http://gforge.cs.vu.nl/gf/project/javagat` (Zugriff 2012-05-17).

[Novotny2004] J. Novotny, M. Russell und O. Wehrens. GridSphere: an advanced portal framework. In *Euromicro Conference, Proceedings. 30th*, pages 412–419, August 2004. URL `http://java-source.net/open-source/portals/gridsphere` (Zugriff 2012-05-14).

[PelegriLlopart2002] Eduardo Pelegri-Llopart und Anil Vijendran. JSR 52: A Standard Tag Library for JavaServer Pages. URL `http://www.jcp.org/en/jsr/detail?id=52` (Zugriff 2012-05-20), Juli 2002.

[Sezov2011] Richard Sezov. *Liferay in Action*. Manning, 2011. ISBN 978-1935182825, URL `http://www.liferay.com` (Zugriff 2012-05-19).

[Theng1998] Yin Leng Theng und Harold Thimbleby. Addressing Design and Usability Issues in Hypertext and on the World Wide Web by Re-Examining the "Lost in Hyperspace"Problem. *Journal of Universal Computer Science*, 4(11):839–855, 1998.

[Valiev2010] M. Valiev, E.J. Bylaska, N. Govind, K. Kowalski, T.P. Straatsma, H.J.J. van Dam, D. Wang, J. Nieplocha, E. Apra, T.L. Windus und W.A. de Jong. NWChem: a comprehensive and scalable open-source solution for large scale molecular simulations. *Comput. Phys. Commun.*, 181:1477, 2010. URL `http://www.nwchem-sw.org` (Zugriff 2012-05-15).

[Vukotic2011] Aleksa Vukotic. *Apache Tomcat 7*. Apress, 2011. ISBN 978-1430237235, URL `http://tomcat.apache.org` (Zugriff 2012-05-18).

Danksagungen

An erster Stelle möchten wir dem Ministerium für Wissenschaft, Forschung und Kunst Baden-Württemberg für die finanzielle Förderung und Herrn Castellaz, Frau Illison und Herrn Peters für die hervorragende Unterstützung des Projektes danken. Ebenso geht großer Dank an Herrn Prof. Dr. Großmann des Kommunikations- und Informationszentrums der Universität Ulm für die Initiierung und Begleitung des Projektes.

Weiter möchten wir den Kolleginnen und Kollegen am Karlsruher Institut für Technologie (KIT) und an der Universität Ulm sowie den Mitarbeiterinnen und Mitarbeitern des gesamten bwGRiD Projektes für ihre Unterstützung danken. Großer Dank geht auch an alle Kolleginnen und Kollegen des bwGRiD Portalprojektes, die die applikationsspezifischen Portlets entwickelt haben. Für Details zu den Portlets und den Entwicklern sei hier auf den Abschlussbericht des Portalprojektes beim Ministerium verwiesen.

Wesentliche Teile von Gatlet und den Portaltemplates stammen von Bastian Boegel (Ulm) und Stefan Bozic (KIT). Der Avatar wurde von Helmut Lang (Ulm) entwickelt. Neben den Autoren des Artikels hat auch Christian Spann (Ulm) entscheidend zum Dacapo-Portlet beigetragen. Der ursprüngliche Entwurf des Chemieeditor Portlets von Dr. Kieron Taylor und Dr. David Benoit (Ulm) wurde später durch die Autoren erheblich erweitert. Abschließend möchten wir Ceriel Jacobs von der Freien Universität Amsterdam für die Unterstützung bezüglich des GAT-Frameworks danken.

Flexible Cluster Node Provisioning in a Distributed Environment

Sebastian Schmelzer,* Dirk von Suchodoletz,†
Michael Janczyk,‡ Gerhard Schneider§

Lehrstuhl für Kommunikationssysteme, Universität Freiburg

Zusammenfassung: Für große Rechnerzahlen, wie beispielsweise im bw-GRiD, werden zur Reduktion des Administrationsaufwandes und zur schnellen Bereitstellung neuer Maschinen effiziente Managementlösungen gesucht. Viele Cluster- und Grid-Installationen setzen bereits auf einen lokalen Netzwerkboot. Dieser ist jedoch oft einer Reihe von Einschränkungen unterworfen, die sich mit dem vorgeschlagenen System für den Grid-Betrieb vorteilhafter und flexibler lösen lassen. So bietet ein zentraler Konfigurations- und Steuerdienst in der Verbindung mit einem sehr flexiblen Bootloader Möglichkeiten, die weit über die Fähigkeiten eines rein PXE basierten Ansatzes hinausgehen. Eine Nutzung könnte das bedarfsgerechte Starten unterschiedlicher Systeme auf Cluster-Knoten, gesteuert durch das zentrale Management, sein. Ebenso bietet es die Möglichkeit, den Rollout-Prozess sowie den Austausch von (Spezial-)Systemen zwischen den Institutionen zu vereinheitlichen und zu vereinfachen. Als Basis wird hierzu eine abstrakte Boot-Middleware Open-SLX eingesetzt, die seit einigen Jahren in Freiburg entwickelt wird.

1 Einleitung und Idee

Das bwGRiD steht für Ziele wie Resource-On-Demand, schnelles Deployment, flexible Anpassung an bestimmte Nutzerwünsche sowie die Virtualisierung von Ressourcen bei gleichzeitiger geographischer Verteilung über die Landesuniversitäten [Dynowski2012]. Zur Realisierung des Projekts

---

* sebastian.schmelzer@rz.uni-freiburg.de
† dirk.von.suchodoletz@rz.uni-freiburg.de
‡ michael.janczyk@rz.uni-freiburg.de
§ gerhard.schneider@rz.uni-freiburg.de

werden die lokalen HPC-Cluster für die Nutzer transparent über das 10 GB/s Netz BelWü[1] zu einem Verbund zusammengeschlossen, um sicherzustellen, dass verfügbare Computing-Ressourcen für die akademische Forschung standortunabhängig und hochverfügbar bereitstehen. Geprägt wird diese Infrastruktur durch gemeinsame Standards beim Zugriff auf die Ressourcen, bei der Authentifizierung und bei der Verteilung der Jobs. Zu Projektbeginn wurde eine einheitliche Hardwareausstattung gemeinsam beschafft, um die Vorteile eines solchen Vorgehens zu evaluieren und eine einfache Verteilung von Betriebssystem-Installationen zu erlauben.

Durch die unterschiedlichen Anforderungen der Standorte, die voneinander abweichenden Jobprofile und den beständigen Ausbau der Infrastruktur entwickelt sich eine Hardwarelandschaft automatisch auseinander, da die Partner eine gewisse Unabhängigkeit genießen und Erfahrungen mit unterschiedlichen Konfigurationen gesammelt werden sollen. Trotzdem ist es wünschenswert, eine gemeinsame Grundinstallation beizubehalten, die auf jeder eingesetzten Hardware läuft. Hierbei sollten zudem die Anpassungen an die jeweiligen Gegebenheiten an wenigen, gut dokumentierten Stellen erfolgen.

Aus einem ursprünglich einheitlichen Ansatz, der sich um eine Skript-Sammlung mit vielen lokalen, statischen Anpassungen dreht, ist eine unübersichtliche Situation entstanden, die einerseits eine Auseinanderentwicklung des Basissystems nicht verhinderte und andererseits eine zentrale Pflege zunehmend schwierig macht. Die derzeitige Situation erschwert es zudem, einen Parallelbetrieb verschiedener Varianten des Grundsystems zu erlauben, um beispielsweise auf spezielle Jobprofile oder Anwenderwünsche einzugehen oder einfache Tests für aktualisierte und zukünftige Grundsystemversionen durchzuführen. So bleibt die Konfiguration der einzelnen Cluster-Segmente trotz aktueller Entwicklungen im Bereich des Software-Deployments immer noch aufwändig und bindet Personal. Damit vergeht oft wertvolle Zeit, bis neu beschaffte Maschinen tatsächlich den bwGRiD-Anwendern bereitgestellt werden können, was bei der typischerweise hohen Anzahl an neuen Rechenknoten eine nicht unerhebliche Ressourcenverschwendung bedeuten kann. Deshalb empfiehlt es sich, einen koordi-

---

[1] Landeshochschulnetz Baden-Württemberg, http://www.belwue.de

nierten, übergreifenden Ansatz für einen flexibles netzbasiertes Deployment zu entwickeln.

Dieser Artikel diskutiert nach der Darstellung des Status Quo im bw-GRiD ein verteiltes Remote-Boot-Konzept, welches seit einiger Zeit am Rechenzentrum der Universität Freiburg in verschiedenen Einsatzszenarien erprobt wird [Schmelzer2011a, Schmelzer2011b]. Das Konzept nutzt hierzu verschiedene Varianten des jahrelang erprobten und eingesetzten LAN-Boots und kombiniert diese mit einem zustandslosen Betrieb der Rechnerknoten, die bei jedem Hochfahren dynamisch anhand genau definierter Prozeduren konfiguriert werden. Schnelle Datennetze wie das BelWü erlauben dabei sogar eine Bereitstellung von Grundsystemen über Standorte hinweg, um auf diesem Wege einfache Tests zu ermöglichen. Damit kann das vorgestellte System sowohl lokal an einer Einrichtung als auch als zentraler Dienst, der von mehreren Einrichtungen gemeinsam eingesetzt wird, realisiert werden. Eine Nutzung in verteilten Rollen, die den einzelnen Administratoren erlaubt, verschiedene lokale oder entfernte Basis-Systeme anzubieten, ist dabei leicht umsetzbar.

2 Grundlagen des Remote-Boots

Festplattenlose beziehungsweise Stateless-Boots über das Netzwerk werden im Linux-Bereich und insbesondere im HPC-Umfeld schon sehr lange praktiziert [McQuillan2000, Katz2002]. Die eigentliche Betriebssysteminstallation liegt hierbei auf einem Server und wird mehreren Clients beziehungsweise den Cluster-Nodes zur Verfügung gestellt. Hierbei nutzt der Client die BIOS Erweiterung PXE,[2] um aus dem Netzwerk einen Kernel sowie ein *initramfs*-Container zu beziehen und diese zu starten. Zusätzlich zu dem Vorgehen, wie es bei einem lokalen Bootvorgang üblich wäre, muss in der im *initramfs* enthaltenen *init*-Script die Einrichtung der Netzwerkkarte und anschließend das Einbinden des Root-Filesystems über das Netzwerk erfolgen. Dessen Bereitstellung erfolgt über Netzwerkdateisysteme oder -Block-Devices, wie beispielsweise NFS oder NBD. Dabei genügt bereits eine Bandbreite von 1 GBit/s auf Clientseite. Auf der Serverseite

---

[2] Preboot Execution Environment, siehe beispielsweise [Intel2000].

empfiehlt sich eine 10 GBit/s Anbindung, um mehrere hundert Knoten mit einem Remote-System zu versorgen. Für den Start eines Linux-Systems werden etwa 50 – 80 MByte übertragen. Einmal in Betrieb genommen, verursachen die Clients eine sehr geringe Netzlast, da Programme und Bibliotheken, wenn sie einmal angefordert wurden, im Cache des Betriebssystemkerns erhalten bleiben.

Da alle Clients auf ein gemeinsames Rootdateisystem zugreifen, wird dieses schreibgeschützt exportiert. Ansonsten würden die Änderungen eines Clients mit allen anderen Rechner interferieren. Auf Grund dessen wird über das nur lesbare Dateisystem eine beschreibbare Schicht unter Zuhilfenahme eines Union File Systems gelegt, die die Änderungen auf dem Dateisystem im Arbeitsspeicher ablegt. So kann das laufende Betriebssystem wie auf einem schreibbaren Root-Filesystem agieren.

Große Vorteile des Remote-Boots sind zum einen Tests eines Systems vor der eigentlichen Übernahme in die Produktivnutzung, das Ausprobieren verschiedener Software- und Systemumgebungen sowie der unkomplizierte, schnelle und flexible Einsatz, ohne eine bestehende Infrastruktur zu beeinträchtigen. So kann eine neue Systemumgebung ohne großen Mehraufwand gestartet und getestet werden. Zum anderen wird das „zustandslose" System bei Neustart der Rechner wieder auf den Urzustand zurückgesetzt. Diese Systeme sind somit gegen versehentliche oder böswillige Manipulation weniger anfällig, da sie einfach wiederhergestellt werden können.

3 Status Quo: Remote-Boot im bwGRiD

Die bisherige Remote-Boot-Konfiguration im bwGRiD wurde für die anfänglich homogene Hardware-Ausstattung erstellt und macht unter Umständen bei einer nachträglichen Beschaffung neuer, zum bisherigen Maschinentyp heterogener Rechenknoten eine Anpassung der Konfigurationsskripten notwendig. Diese Software-Sammlung wird am Höchstleistungsrechenzentrum Stuttgart (HLRS) entwickelt und gepflegt. Sie wurde jedoch bisher an mehreren Standorten lokal verändert und erweitert. Durch die lokalen Anpassungen wird die Entwicklung erschwert, da diese Änderungen nicht an die Entwickler zurückfließen und unter Umständen wieder lokal angepasst werden müssen. Die Skriptsammlung dient lediglich dazu, ein

Betriebssystem für den Remote-Boot vorzubereiten. Es besteht weder die Möglichkeit der Konfiguration dieses Systems noch der Koordination einer einheitlichen Softwareumgebung, wie sie in Grids, insbesondere dem bwGRiD, gefordert wird. Eine modulare Weiterentwicklung des Remote-Boot-Systems ist derzeit nicht möglich.

Neue Client-Systeme werden über aufeinanderfolgende Skriptaufrufe erstellt und folgen grob einem Schema, das mit anderen Remote-Boot-Lösungen vergleichbar ist. Zunächst muss ein Referenzsystem angelegt und konfiguriert werden. Das Betriebssystem ist auf Scientific-Linux 5, ein RedHat-Enterprise-Linux-Derivat, beschränkt. Derzeit wird im bwGRiD die Version 5.5 eingesetzt. Ein minimales gemeinsames Softwarespektrum wird mit Hilfe eines Installationsskripts eingepflegt, durch welches die meisten Softwaregruppen in das Betriebssystem installiert werden. Anschließend werden alle nicht benötigten Dienste deaktiviert. Die Konfiguration der Clients kann im Referenzsystem erfolgen. Einige Standorte nutzen dazu jedoch die Management-Software CFEngine.[3] Nach der Konfiguration des Systems wird es mit Hilfe eines weiteren Skripts und `rsync` in ein Unterverzeichnis auf dem Server übertragen. Dabei werden weitere Anpassungen vorgenommen. Es werden beispielsweise einige Dateien unterhalb von `/etc` durch Links ersetzt. Die eigentlichen Dateien werden beim Boot des Systems in ein *tempfs* kopiert, auf das die Links verweisen. So können diese Dateien trotz einem schreibgeschützt eingebundenen Dateisystem beschrieben werden. Außerdem wird ein *initramfs*-Container erstellt, der die Netzwerkkartentreiber beinhaltet, die beim Booten für das Einbinden des Root-Filesystems benötigt werden. Netzwerk und *ramfs* werden durch ein zusätzliches Runlevel-Skript konfiguriert, das direkt nach Ende des *initramfs* gestartet wird. Die wenigen Skripte erlauben eine schnelle und geschickte Möglichkeit, Remote-Boot-Systeme zu generieren. Die Einfachheit erleichtert die Pflege und die Fehlersuche, sie macht die Lösung aber auch starr und bietet nur minimale Konfigurationsmöglichkeiten.

---

[3] Webseite der Management-Software CFEngine, `http://cfengine.com`.

4 Anforderungen an ein Site-übergreifendes Boot-Framework

Die meisten Grid- und Cluster-Installationen gehen in der Regel von einer weitestgehend einheitliche Hardwarekonfiguration aus. Dies ist jedoch auf Dauer nicht immer durchführbar. Ein Remote-Boot-System muss deshalb flexibel ausgelegt sein, um unterschiedlichste Hardware unterstützen und neue Komponenten integrieren zu können. Das wird seitens einer entsprechenden Remote-Boot-Umgebung durch die dynamische Hardwareeinrichtung beim Start der Clients und der Konfiguration einer breiten Palette von Netzwerkkartenmodulen für den Start erreicht.

Generisches Basis-System & lokale Erweiterungen Weiterhin soll das Basis-Betriebssystem sowie der Softwarebestand über die im Verbund vertretenen Institutionen einheitlich sein.[4] Zur Abbildung lokaler Anforderungen und Konfigurationen können stattdessen modulare Erweiterungen eingesetzt werden. Bereits jetzt wird das Softwarepaket `modules`[5] eingesetzt, um diverse Versionen einer Software in einem System parallel anbieten zu können. Dieses kann auch weiterhin genutzt werden, um temporäre wie lokale Änderungen auf der Shell-Ebene durchzuführen. Diese Konfigurationsmöglichkeit reicht unter Umständen jedoch nicht aus. So soll es außerdem möglich sein, spezielle Job-Umgebungen anzubieten, um eventuelle Unzulänglichkeiten der Standardumgebung ausgleichen zu können. Eigene Umgebungen für veraltete Bibliotheken, aber auch für spezielle Hardware wie GPUs und Anwendungsfelder wie interaktive Jobs und Visualisierung können erforderlich sein. Darüber hinaus ist es möglich, neue Umgebungen zu testen und Updates, die nicht im laufenden Betrieb durchgeführt werden können, anzubieten.[6]

---

[4] Vergleiche hierzu beispielsweise [Dynowski2012].

[5] Das Modules-Paket manipuliert bei Bedarf die Shell-Umgebung. Insbesondere werden `$LD_LIBRARY_PATH` und `$PATH` für die zu betreibende Software angepasst. Projektseite: `http://modules.sourceforge.net`.

[6] Die Updates werden hierbei in das Vorlagensystem installiert und dieses als neue Umgebung zur Verfügung gestellt.

Kontinuierliche Systemupdates Cluster werden je nach Art der abgearbeiteten Jobs üblicherweise mehrere Monate ohne einen Neustart der Systeme betrieben. Für einen definierten Zustand über diesen Zeitraum sind atomare Kopiervorgänge bei Online-Updates essentiell. Es sollte sichergestellt sein, dass eine Datei oder ein Ordner nicht zwischenzeitlich fehlt oder eine ältere Version eingespielt wird. Die Konfiguration der Clients sollte in einem globalen Verzeichnis auf dem Server erfolgen und beim Update des Client-Systems automatisch in dieses übertragen werden. Die Systemumgebung muss für alle Clients auch nach einer Änderung auf dem Server homogen bleiben, ansonsten kann keine reibungslose Abarbeitung von Jobs gewährleistet werden.

Essentiell ist zudem die Möglichkeit, Clients einzeln konfigurieren zu können. Zusätzliche Hardware-Konfigurationen wie von GPUs benötigt und spezielle Umgebungen zur Visualisierung und für interaktiven Jobs können über eine gesonderte Client-Konfiguration erfolgen. Dies kann dynamisch beim Start des Systems oder statisch auf dem Server geschehen.

Effiziente Verteilung der Root-Filesysteme In WAN-Umgebungen existieren weitergehende Anforderungen an den Transport und die Sicherheit der Daten. Um Latenzen bei Dateizugriffen so gering wie möglich zu halten, werden schnelle Netzwerkdateisysteme beziehungsweise -Block-Devices, die den Anforderungen des Betriebs über Weitverkehrsnetze genügen, benötigt. Zum Ausgleich der Netzwerklatenz und der Bandbreitenschwankungen, die durch die gleichzeitige Nutzung mehrerer Dienste an den Hochschulen, wie dem derzeit im Aufbau befindlichen Landes-Hochschul-Datenspeicher,[7] entstehen können, wird ein Proxy-Server für den Remote-Boot-Service entwickelt. Vorteile solcher Proxies sind die einfachere Aktualisierbarkeit eines Systems und Redundanz des Services. Außerdem obliegt ein Proxy der Kontrolle eines lokalen Administrators, der für die lokale Sicherheit des Systems zuständig ist und einen autarken Betrieb der Remote-Boot-Services ermöglicht. Die globalen Update-Zyklen erhalten die Homogenität der Systemumgebungen.

---

[7] bwLSDF: Large-Scale Data Facility, http://www.bw-grid.de/bwservices/bwlsdf.

Sicherheit Um versehentliche beziehungsweise böswillige Veränderungen des Systems auf dem Transportweg über Weitverkehrsnetzwerke zu verhindern, sollen sich Absicherungsmechanismen in den Service integrieren lassen. Ein möglicher Ansatz hierfür ist die Verwendung eines durch eine PKI gesicherten Vertrauensankers auf der Clientseite, mit dessen Hilfe Integritätsüberprüfungen des Dateisystems ermöglicht werden. Als ein solcher Vertrauensanker könnte beispielsweise der Netzwerk-Bootloader *iPXE* [8] mit einem eingebetteten Zertifikat dienen. Ein weiterer Ansatz wäre die (vollständige) Verschlüsselung des Netzwerkblock-Geräts.

Neben der Absicherung der generischen Root-Dateisysteme sollte die Konfiguration der Clients geschützt werden. Diese beziehen die Nodes beim Boot über den zentralen webbasierten Konfigurationsdienst. Hier werden auch sicherheitskritische Einstellungen wie für die Anbindung an Authentifizierungsdienste oder Zertifikate ausgetauscht. Deswegen ist hierfür ein Austausch der Daten über eine gesicherte Verbindung vorgesehen.

5 Ausgangspunkt: OpenSLX, ein Remote-Boot-Service der Universität Freiburg

Das an der Universität Freiburg entwickelte Komponentenset zum Betrieb eines Remote-Boot-Service (OpenSLX) wird dort seit einigen Jahren für den Betrieb netzwerkbootender Lehrpools eingesetzt [vSuchodoletz2007]. Zudem wird es für den Betrieb der Cluster Nodes des Black Forest Grids[9] genutzt. Neben dem Standardbetrieb wurde das ursprüngliche System am Rechenzentrum in Freiburg für Einsatz über Weitverkehrsnetze erweitert [Schmelzer2011b, Schmelzer2009]. Das Open-Source-Softwarepaket OpenSLX stellt dabei ein allgemeines Framework für die Einrichtung, Konfiguration und Verwaltung eines Remote-Boot-Dienstes bereit.[10] OpenSLX vereinheitlicht hierzu die verschiedenen und teilweise unvollständigen An-

---

[8] *iPXE* Homepage, http://ipxe.org.

[9] Das BFG, http://www.bfg.uni-freiburg.de, besteht aus einer interdisziplinären Gruppe von Forschern, von zur Zeit etwa 20 Instituten der Universität Freiburg sowie von verschiedenen externen Einrichtungen.

[10] Siehe hierzu die Projektseiten: http://openslx.org sowie http://lab.openslx.org.

sätze der einzelnen Linux-Distributionen unter einer gemeinsamen Abstraktionsschicht. Darin enthalten ist eine Trennung des gemeinsamen Root-Filesystems einer Client-Gruppe von der individuellen Konfiguration einzelner Maschinen. Dies realistiert OpenSLX durch eine Sammlung von Skripten, die viele Standard-Distributionen, unter anderem auch RedHat und Scientific Linux, für den Stateless-Betrieb vorbereitet.

Darüber hinaus implementiert es eine Boot-Middleware, die für den Benutzer des laufenden Rechenknotens optimalerweise unsichtbar bleibt, so dass dieser keine speziellen Anpassungen an seiner Software vornehmen muss. Die Anpassungen und Änderungen finden im Hintergrund, hauptsächlich während des Starts der Maschine statt. Dieser wurde dabei so optimiert, dass er bestenfalls weniger Zeit als ein Betriebssystemstart von einer Festplatte braucht. Zur Realisierung der Abstraktion von verschiedenen Distributionen und Versionen unterscheidet OpenSLX zwischen vier Stadien (Abbildung 1).

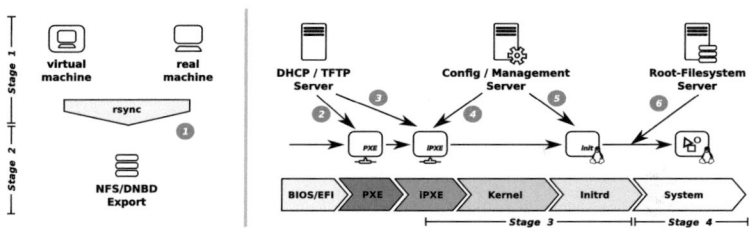

Abbildung 1: Übersicht OpenSLX: Vom Referenzsystem bis zum gebooteten Client in vier Stadien.

Diese Stadien umfassen sowohl die Einrichtungsschritte auf dem Boot-Server als auch auf den individuellen Clients. *Stage 1* bezeichnet die primäre Einrichtung einer Linux-Distribution durch das Abbild einer Referenzinstallation von einem eigens hierfür eingerichteten Vorlagensystem, welches ein dedizierter Rechner oder eine virtuelle Maschine sein kann. Diese Abbildung erfolgt mittels in OpenSLX enthaltener Skripte (die im Hintergrund rsync nutzen) in ein Unterverzeichnis auf dem Boot-Server

(1). Diese Grundinstallation kann durch lokale Anpassungen seitens des Administrators oder durch Zusatzkomponenten erweitert werden. Im anschließenden *Stage 2* werden hieraus Root-Dateisystem-Exporte erzeugt, die auf verschiedene Weise bereitgestellt werden. Dabei kann es sich um ein via NFS angebotenes Unterverzeichnis oder einen per Blockdevice bereitgestellten SquashFS-Container[11] handeln. Das Ganze ist so angelegt, dass sich von einem Server eine Reihe solcher Installationen verwalten und anbieten lässt. Neben der Bereitstellung der Dateisysteme ist der Boot-Server auch für die Erzeugung angepasster *initramfs*-Container zuständig.

Während *Stage 1* und *2* die Vorbereitung des Betriebssystems auf dem Server beschreiben, stehen die darauf folgenden *Stages* für die Stufen des Bootvorgangs des individuellen Clients. Der Client bootet wie in einem vergleichbaren Remote-Boot-Setup zunächst über PXE (2). Jedoch wird in dem hier vorgestellten Ansatz nicht direkt das eigentliche System gebootet, sondern zunächst die freie PXE Implementierung *iPXE* geladen (3). *iPXE* ist in der Lage, Konfigurationsdaten nicht nur über TFTP zu beziehen, sondern unterstützt zusätzliche Netzwerkprotokolle wie beispielsweise HTTP oder FTP. Dieser Umweg ermöglicht eine dynamische Entscheidung zum Zeitpunkt des Bootvorgangs, welches System zu starten ist, da die Konfiguration von *iPXE* direkt durch eine Schnittstelle der webbasierten zentralen Verwaltung erzeugt wird (4).

Anschließend werden Kernel und der *initramfs*-Container des zu bootenden Systems geladen und gestartet. Ab diesem Punkt wird vom sogenannten *Stage 3* gesprochen. Der *initramfs*-Container ist ein komprimiertes *CPIO*-Paket,[12] welches neben dem Init-Skript und einigen Kernel-Modulen für ein erstes Hardware-Setup eine auf BusyBox[13] basierende minimale Systemumgebung enthält. Am Ende des Bootvorgangs des Linux-Kernels entpackt dieser den Inhalt des *initramfs*-Archivs in ein im Arbeitsspeicher liegendes Filesystem und startet die darin enthaltene *init*. Im folgenden findet zunächst die Einrichtung der Netzwerk-Hardware sowie das Einbinden

---

[11] Komprimierter Filesystem-Container, vergleiche hierzu `http://squashfs.sourceforge.net`.

[12] Hierbei handelt es sich um ein einfaches Datei-Archiv-Format.

[13] Kompaktes Paket diverser Core-Utilities, `http://busybox.net`.

des Root-Dateisystems statt. Darauf folgend wird das individuelle Setup des einzelnen Clients durch die von OpenSLX erzeugten Skripten durchgeführt, welche bei Bedarf mit dem zentralen Konfigurationsdienst kommunizieren (5). Im letzten *Stage* übergibt das OpenSLX-Init an das jeweils angepasste Runlevel-System der Distribution [Schmelzer2009], wobei es mit sehr verschiedenen Ansätzen, angefangen vom klassischen `Sys-V-Init` mit seinen optimierten Fassungen, `Upstart` bis hin zum `SystemD` umgehen kann.

6 Erweiterungen für den Grid-Betrieb

Ausgehend von dem erprobten, bestehenden Setup für den Remote-Boot an der Universität Freiburg, gilt es, die Erfahrungen, die mit der Forschung im Bereich WAN-Boot[14] sowie mit den aktuellen Entwicklungen von verteilten Netzwerk-Blockdevices gesammelt wurden, in einem neuen, attraktiven Dienst zusammenzuführen, bei dessen Entwicklung auch die Anforderungen des Grid-Betriebs betrachtet werden. Hierzu müssen eine Reihe von Komponenten mit einem bestimmten Featureset zusammenspielen, um das geplante System zu realisieren.

6.1 Dynamisches Boot-Framework

Um eine dynamische Entscheidung über das zu bootende System zu ermöglichen, wird im hier beschriebenen Ansatz auf die freie PXE Implementierung *iPXE* zurückgegriffen, welche im Funktionsumfang dahingehend erweitert wurde, dass neben TFTP auch andere Protokolle, wie beispielsweise HTTP, zum Empfang von Menü- und Konfigurationsdaten genutzt werden können. Das Bootmenü und damit die Bootentscheidung können somit bei jedem Startvorgang dynamisch erzeugt werden. Dies ermöglicht es auf Seiten des Web-Interfaces weiteren Kriterien, wie IP-Adresse, Uhrzeit oder der Auslastung des Clusters für die Bootentscheidung zu Hilfe zu nehmen. Ein weiterer Vorteil des Verfahrens ist, dass damit jeder Start eines Cluster-Nodes (sowie welches System gestartet wurde) an zentraler Stelle protokolliert werden kann.

---

[14] Vergleiche hierzu die Überlegungen in [Schmelzer2011a].

6.2 Zentraler Konfigurationsdienst

Neben der Verwaltung der ihm bekannten Clients und der Regeln, welche Systeme nach welchen Bedingungen gestartet werden sollen, ist die Aufgabe des zentralen Konfigurations- und Management-Dienstes (Abbildung 1: *Config/Management Server*) die Verwaltung von Client- bzw. Gruppenspezifischen Einstellungen und Erweiterungen. Der Dienst bietet zum einen ein Web-Interface zur Administration durch den Anwender, zum anderen stellt er die entsprechenden Schnittstellen zur Verfügung, auf die die Skripte während des Bootprozesses auf dem Client zurückgreifen. Das Konzept hat sich bereits in prototypischer Form bewährt (siehe [Schmelzer2009]) und wird im Moment in die nächste Generation von OpenSLX integriert. Zu einem späteren Zeitpunkt soll dieser auch die Erzeugung der *initramfs*-Archive steuern, die zur Zeit noch von einem Skript aus der klassischen OpenSLX Umgebung erzeugt werden.

Ziel ist es, eine logische Trennung von Maschinenkonfiguration und Bereitstellung der Root-Filesysteme für die verschiedenen Linux-Varianten zu erreichen. Dies wird durch die Abstraktion von Standardaufgaben mit der Hilfe von Plugins ermöglicht. So sollen beispielsweise Aufgaben wie die Konfiguration der User-Authentifizierung, das Einbinden von lokalen Netz-Laufwerken, die Anbindung an einen zentralen Logging-Dienst oder vergleichbare Dienste steuerbar sein. Auch bietet eine einheitliche API für Erweiterungen die Möglichkeit, auch in Zukunft das System einfach an neue Erfordernisse anzupassen. So wäre beispielsweise eine Anbindung an den bwLSDF für das Verarbeiten großer Datenmengen denkbar (siehe auch [Garcia2011]).

Daraus folgen zwei elementare Vorteile: Zum einen ermöglicht es dem Anwender, das Dateisystem-Abbild generisch zu halten, zum anderen lässt sich somit die Konfiguration für die Einbindung in die lokale Infrastruktur einfach auf andere Grundsysteme transferieren.

6.3 Assistierte Image-Erstellung

Eine weitere webbasierte Komponente zur Erleichterung der Administration stellt das Interface für die Erstellung, Verwaltung und Verteilung der

Root-Filesysteme dar (*RootFS Server*). Die wichtigsten Funktionen werden die Möglichkeit, Grund-Systeme von anderen Institutionen zu importieren, und die assistierte Erstellung neuer Systeme sein. Dieses soll dem Wunsch nach Vereinheitlichung der Grund-Systeme Rechnung tragen und den Administrationsaufwand verringern.

Die Erstellung neuer Grund-Systeme soll so erleichtert werden, dass auch Administratoren von anderen Forschungsgruppen in der Lage sind, speziell auf ihr Anwendungsgebiet angepasste Systeme zu erzeugen. Der Arbeitsablauf soll den Anwender dabei unterstützen, ein bereits eingerichtetes Referenzsystem in ein neues Grund-System zu überführen, und hierbei beispielsweise auf fehlende Abhängigkeiten oder ähnliches hinweisen. Der Import selbst wird durch einen zusätzlichen Dienst im Hintergrund abgewickelt, dessen Status sich über das Web-Interface jederzeit verfolgen lässt.

6.4 Site-übergreifender Austausch von Grund-Systemen

Neben dem parallelen Betrieb mehrerer Systeme an einem Standort, beispielsweise um die nächste Generation der zugrundeliegenden Distribution zu testen, bietet das vorgeschlagene Framework die Möglichkeit, auch Basis-Systeme anderer Institutionen zu nutzen. Dies hat den Vorteil, dass sich die einzelnen Einrichtungen auf bestimmte Anwendungsbereiche spezialisieren und die Systeme daraufhin optimieren können. Für die Gewährleistung eines reibungslosen Austauschs von Systemen bedarf es eines dafür geeigneten Netzwerkspeichers. Elementar ist hierbei die Möglichkeit, ein entferntes System im lokalen Netz dynamisch zwischenzuspeichern (Caching) als auch eine Versionskontrolle der bereitgestellten Images. Hierfür befindet sich ein spezielles Distributed Network Block Device in Entwicklung und Erprobung.

Der bereits vorgestellte *RootFS Server* bildet den administrativen Überbau für den Austausch und die Verwaltung der Systeme. Eine schematische Darstellung eines institutionenübergreifenden Setups zeigt die Abbildung 2.

Distributed Network Block Device 3 Traditionell kommt für die Verteilung des Root-Filesystems über das Netz bootender Cluster-Knoten NFS

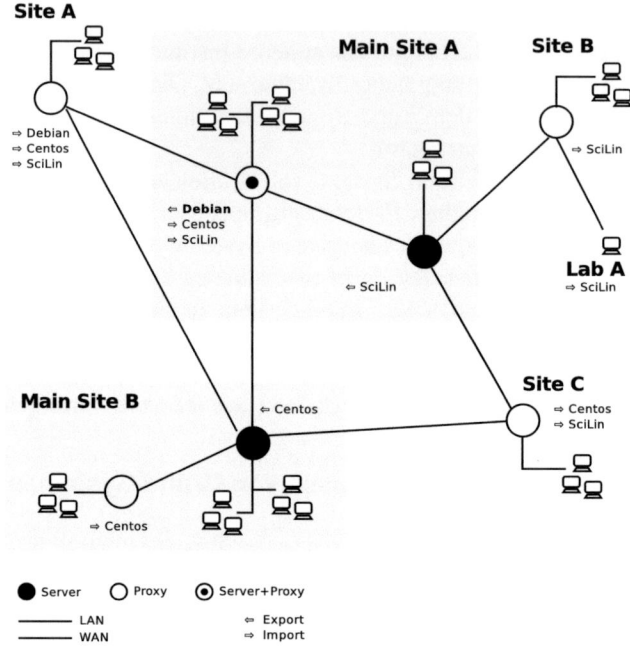

Abbildung 2: Site-übergreifender Austausch von Grund-Systemen

zum Einsatz. Dieses ist leicht zu administrieren und hat sich über Jahre bewährt. Mit den bisherigen Versionen gestaltete sich die Redundanz über verschiedene Server hinweg als schwierig. Dieses ändert sich mit der Version 4.1, welches Parallel NFS (pNFS) spezifiziert [Hildebrand2005, Hildebrand2007]. Jedoch produziert NFS einen gewissen Netzwerk-Grundtraffic und bietet eine suboptimale Performance über Weitverkehrsnetze. Ein NFS-Proxy lässt sich bisher nicht einfach realisieren. Vielversprechender sind hierbei die Versuche mit Network Block Devices. Hierbei wird mittels Squashfs ein komprimiertes Filesystem-Image erzeugt, welches dann über das Netzwerk verteilt wird. Da NBDs nur auf Blockebene arbeiten, besitzen sie wesentlich weniger Overhead und profitieren vom Block-Cache des Linux-Kernels. In Frage kommen hierfür das bereits im Kernel enthaltene NBD sowie das an der Universität Freiburg entwickelte Distributed Network Block Device (DNBD). Das DNBD in der aktuellen Version 3^{15} ist eine vollständige Neuentwicklung, dessen Hauptziel es ist, die Vorteile des NBD und seiner Vorgänger zu vereinen. Die maximale Auslastung der zur Verfügung stehenden Bandbreite wird durch eine starke Parallelisierung und die Auslagerung der I/O intensiven Operationen in den Linux Kernel erreicht. Mit der Verwendung von redundanten Servern und der Möglichkeit der Clients, selbstständig einen optimalen Server zu wechseln, wird die Ausfallsicherheit und Lastverteilung des Setups sichergestellt. Zudem bietet der DNBD3 einem einfachen Proxy-Dienst, der die schnelle Anbindung einer großen Anzahl Clients im lokalen Netz an externe Ressourcen ermöglicht.

7 Ausblick

Das Prinzip des Netzwerk-Boots hat sich seit Jahren bewährt und wird deshalb in vielen Cluster- und Grid-Infrastrukturen eingesetzt. Das bisherige Betriebsmodell des bwGRiD stößt an seine konzeptionellen Grenzen, die sich als zu einschränkend für zukünftige Entwicklungen des Projekts herausstellen könnten. Alternativkonzepte liegen bereits vor und sind an anderen Stellen, wie beispielsweise im BFG, bereits erfolgreich getestet worden. Damit existieren Prototypen, welche eine Grundlage für einen Testlauf im bwGRiD bilden können. Bisher existierten die verschiedenen Bereiche getrennt nebenander. Mit der zunehmenden Grid- und Compute-Joberfahrung am Rechenzentrum in Freiburg ließen sich jedoch Testläufe organisieren. Hierfür ist ist entsprechende Koordination von Administratoren und Anwendern wünschenswert, um eine sinnvolle Planung und Evaluation zu erlauben.

So bietet ein zentraler Konfigurations- und Steuerdienst in der Verbindung mit einem flexibleren Bootloader beziehungsweise Bootloader-Ersatz Möglichkeiten, die weit über die Fähigkeiten eines rein PXE-basierten An-

---

[15] Webseite des DNBD3 Kernel-Moduls, `http://lab.openslx.org/projects/dnbd3`.

satzes hinausgehen. Eine Nutzung könnte das bedarfsgerechte Starten unterschiedlicher Systeme auf Cluster-Knoten, gesteuert durch das zentrale Management, sein. Das vorgeschlagene Konzept erhebt keinen Ausschließlichkeitsanspruch, sondern sieht die Verteilung von Administrationsrollen vor, welche eine Koexistenz verschiedener Boot-Lösungen erlaubt.

Literaturverzeichnis

[Dynowski2012] M. Dynowski, M. Janczyk, J. Schulz, D. v. Suchodoletz und S. Hermann. Das bwGRiD – High Performance Compute Cluster als flexible, verteilte Wissenschaftsinfrastruktur. In Paul Müller, Bernhard Neumair, Helmut Reiser und Gabi Dreo Rodosek, Herausgeber, *5. DFN-Forum Kommunikationstechnologien – Verteilte Systeme im Wissenschaftsbereich*, pages 95–105. Gesellschaft für Informatik e.V. (GI), 2012.

[Garcia2011] A.O. Garcia, S. Bourov, A. Hammad, J. van Wezel, B. Neumair, A. Streit, V. Hartmann, T. Jejkal, P. Neuberger und R. Stotzka. The Large Scale Data Facility: Data Intensive Computing for Scientific Experiments. In *Parallel and Distributed Processing Workshops and Phd Forum (IPDPSW), 2011 IEEE International Symposium on*, pages 1467–1474, Mai 2011.

[Hildebrand2005] D. Hildebrand und P. Honeyman. Exporting Storage Systems in a Scalable Manner with pNFS. In *CITI Technical Report 05-01*, pages 106–111. University of Michigan, 2005.

[Hildebrand2007] D. Hildebrand und P. Honeyman. Direct-pNFS: scalable, transparent, and versatile access to parallel file systems. In *Proceedings of the 16th international symposium on High performance distributed computing*, HPDC '07, pages 199–208, New York, NY, USA, 2007. ACM.

[Intel2000] Intel Corp. Preboot Execution Environment (PXE) specification version 2.0, 2000. http://www.pix.net/software/pxeboot/archive/pxespec.pdf.

[Katz2002] M.J. Katz, P.M. Papadopoulos und G. Bruno. Leveraging standard core technologies to programmatically build Linux cluster appliances. In *Conference on Cluster Computing – Proceedings, 2002*, pages 47–53, 2002.

[McQuillan2000] J. McQuillan. The Linux Terminal Server Project: Thin clients and Linux. In *4th Annual Linux Showcase & Conference, Atlanta*, 2000.

[Schmelzer2009] S. Schmelzer und D. v. Suchodoletz. Network Linux Anywhere. *LinuxTag 2009*, Juni 2009. http://blog.openslx.org/wp-content/uploads/2009/07/networklinuxanywhere-paper.pdf.

[Schmelzer2011a] S. Schmelzer, D. v. Suchodoletz, G. Schneider, D. Weingaertner, L.C.E. d. Bona und C. Carvalho. Universal remote boot and administration service. In *Network Operations and Management Symposium (LANOMS), 2011 7th Latin American*, pages 1–6, 2011.

[Schmelzer2011b] S. Schmelzer, D. v. Suchodoletz und G. Schneider. Netzwerkboot uber Weitverkehrsnetze – Ansatz zur zentralen Steuerung und Verwaltung von Betriebssystemen uber das Internet. In Paul Müller, Bernhard Neumair und Gabi Dreo Rodosek, Herausgeber, *4. DFN-Forum Kommunikationstechnologien*, pages 37–46. Bonner Köllen Verlag, 2011.

[vSuchodoletz2007] D. v. Suchodoletz. Neue Konzepte für flexible Multimedia-Schulungsumgebungen. In *Neue Medien als strategische Schrittmacher an der Universität Freiburg*, pages 97–100. Universitätsverlag Freiburg, 2007.

Evaluation of Network Bonding Performance in Client/Server Scenarios

Konrad Meier,* Sebastian Schmelzer,† Dirk von Suchodoletz‡

University of Freiburg

Abstract: Fast data networks play a major role in high performance computing for node interconnects, network filesystems or blockdevices and distributed network applications. With the rising demand for compute power, larger amount of data is transferred and the existing Ethernet connection speeds become insufficient. Often it is costly to update the whole network infrastructure only to remove individual bottlenecks in the existing configuration. Ethernet bonding is a method to bind several independent Ethernet links to a single, virtual one and therefor provides a good compromise in order to add network bandwidth on critical links. This paper dicusses the actual state of Linux Ethernet network bonding in the field of high performance networking, storage and client root filesystem provisioning. It compares the different bonding modes regarding performance, throughput and balanc of traffic flows and presents recommendations for certain network configurations.

1 Introduction

Ethernet is one of the most popular networking technologies of today and available in nearly every network device ranging from the traditional application in servers and desktops to the domain of appliances and home networking. The standard itself is rather old and dates back to the end of the 1970ies [Brock2003]. Since then, a race could be observed: New Ethernet standards were introduced often well ahead of the actual capabilities of the average hardware available. Over time the hardware caught up, but the

---

* konrad.meier@rz.uni-freiburg.de
† sebastian.schmelzer@rz.uni-freiburg.de
‡ dirk.von.suchodoletz@rz.uni-freiburg.de

bandwidth demands exceeded the installed network equipment. Sometimes an upgrade to the next generation is a good option, but more often newer network components are highly expensive or not yet available. Not only the network adapters in the core servers are to be upgraded, but also a number of components, e.g. the core switches and routers. Therefore, hardware manufacturers in cooperation with operating system vendors introduced in the 1990s the possibility to combine two more physical Ethernet links to one logical channel. This technique takes into account the fact that administrators and users would be happy with just doubling or tripling the network capacity without jumping directly to the next Ethernet generation. At the beginning, a special hardware was required or at least identical Ethernet interface cards. Many manufacturer offered their own implementations, e.g *Etherchannel* by Cisco, *Port Aggregation* by Hewlett-Packard or *Trunking* by Sun Microsystems. At the beginning many of those techniques were proprietary implementations mainly to aggregate multiple links between switches. Today, combining multiple links is known as *Ethernet bonding*, *link aggregation* or in other environments called *teaming*, *port aggregation* or *trunking*.

As Linux is the predominantly applied operating system for high performance computing (HPC) we will focus solely on the Linux implementation throughout this paper. A recent overview and practical application on Linux bonding can be found in [Rankin2011]. The articles [Aust2006, Hsueh2006] give a wider overview on Linux bonding. The discussion of bonding as a typical means for network performance improvement in cluster application can be found e.g. in [Watanabe2008].

This paper is structured as follows: Section 2 introduces the different bonding modes, their requirements and operating modes. In section 3 we explain the two major test setups we use for our experiments. These tests evaluate the different bonding modes and compare a single link with next generation Ethernet technology. Section 4 summarizes the findings and discusses their practical impact.

2 Bonding Requirements and Operating Modes

The idea of bonding is to join a number of interfaces usually of the same link speed to create a virtual interface aggregating the link speeds. In order to achieve a high availability multiple links also create a redundant setup. Several bonding modes are predefined and can be set via the kernel module loading parameter *mode*.[1] Every bonding consists of a virtual bonding interface and a number of attached slave interfaces. An example configuration for Debian-Linux is given in the appendix. The various bonding modes achieve different objectives. For example, a redundant connection to the server is achieved best by mode 1 (active backup), but the other modes also have a fault tolerance although it is not their primary feature. A common objective is to aggregate multiple links to increase the maximum throughput; this can be achieved by mode 0 (balance-rr), 2 (balance-xor), 5 (balance-tlb) or mode 6 (balance-alb). Though all provide a somewhat increased throughput they do not fit all scenarios: Set to mode 0 two gigabit links combined to one virtual link almost double the data rate of a single connection. Optimizing power consumption could be another objective like discussed in [Koibuchi2009].

In this paper we focus on bonding modes that provide load balancing and thus increase the maximum throughput on the server side. The following modes are evaluated in this paper:

- Mode 0 (balance-rr)

- Mode 2 (balance-xor) and Mode 4 (IEEE 802.3ad)

- Mode 5 (alance-tlb) and Mode 6 (balance-alb)

The bonding modes can be sorted into three different groups. The first group contains *packet orientated* transmitting policies, which only includes mode 0 (balance-rr). The second group bases on XOR policies for link selection and consists of mode 2 and 4. Mode 5 and 6 belong to the last group which is based on a connection orientated policy.

---

[1] For detailed information see: http://www.kernel.org/doc/Documentation/networking/bonding.txt

Mode	Algorithm	Description
0	balance-rr	Round-robin policy: This mode simply transmits packets in a sequential order from the first available slave through the last. With this mechanism it provides both load balancing and fault tolerance.
1	active-backup	Active-backup policy. Only one slave in the bond is actually transmitting packets. The other one is used if the first slave fails.
2	balance-xor	XOR policy: This mode selects a slave device based on XOR transmission policy. This mode enables load balancing and fault tolerance.
3	broadcast	Broadcast policy: A simple broadcast policy which transmits all packets on all slave interfaces and thus offers fault tolerance.
4	802.3ad	Dynamic link aggregation: IEEE standard conforming 802.3ad dynamic link aggregation. This mode utilizes all slaves in the active aggregator according to the 802.3ad specification.
5	balance-tlb	Adaptive transmit load balancing: The outgoing traffic is distributed according to the current load (computed relative to the speed) on each slave. This mode also provides fault tolerance.
6	balance-alb	Adaptive load balancing: It combines balance-tlb with receive load balancing (rlb) for IPV4 traffic. The receive load balancing is achieved by ARP negotiation. Like mode 5 this mode also provides fault tolerance.

Table 1: Supported Bonding Modes by the Linux Kernel

Mode 4 is an exception as it requires a switch that supports the IEEE 802.3ad standard. All other modes mostly work without specially configured switches. For the XOR based bonding modes the slave link is selected according to packet information from either layer 2 or layer 3 and 4. For example, link selection based on layer 2 information is calculated as follows:

```
link = ((([source MAC] XOR [destination MAC]) MOD count)
```

Besides configuring the bonding mode, a couple of options can be set using parameters during module load. The *arp_interval* defines the ARP link monitoring frequency in milliseconds. The default setting, value 0, disables the monitoring. For values greater zero the *arp_ip_target* is to be set, which specifies the IP addresses to use as ARP monitoring peers.[2] The *downdelay* is valid only for the miimon[3] link monitor and specifies the time (in milliseconds) to be waited before disabling a slave in case of a failure. The opposite value is the *updelay*, it defins the time to be waited before enabling a slave after the link recovered. If the 802.3ad mode is selected, *lacp_rate* set to 0 would request the partner to transmit LACPDUs every 30 seconds, with a value of 1 to transmit every second. *primary* is a string value of eth0, eth1, ... which specifies the primary slave for the virtual bonding interface.

3 Test Setup

HPC setups commonly require fast fileservers both for the root filesystem of the cluster nodes and for a readable and writable share to provide and receive user and job data. Fast fileservers usually require read-only exports to the clients, as all clients share a common filesystem when booting from the network. A block device with a suitable filesystem like SquashFS or NFS provide a solution. Read- and writeable shares are usually achieved by network filesystems like NFS or Lustre. [Hildebrand2007]
File servers typically require a high network throughput with a scalable number of connections. Two different setups cover the main requirements:

- NBD block device server provides a read-only filesystem for Linux network booted compute cluster nodes and desktop machines.

---

[2] An example to monitor multiple IP addresses would look like *arp_ip_target=172.16.1.254, 172.16.1.212*. One address is usually the router's.
[3] Media Independent Interface Link Monitoring

- NFSv3 server provides a fast read-write network filesystem for a large number of cluster nodes.

As a preliminary requirement: a fast Machine is necessary to saturate one link. Additional CPU load caused by the bonding method must also be considered.

3.1 Machine Hardware and Software Configuration

A test setup is required to compare the different bonding modes. The complete setup consists of one server one high bandwidth client and 61 clients. The hardware is given in table 2. To generate network traffic for a realistic

Server	CPU: Dual AMD Opteron 2.3 GHz 6134 RAM: 64 GByte DDR3 Network 1: Intel Ethernet X520 Server Adapter Network 2: 3 x Intel Ethernet I350-T4 quad-port gigabit Adapter
High Bandwidth Client	CPU: Dual Intel Xenon 2.3 GHz E5520 RAM: 24 GByte DDR3 RAM Network: Intel Ethernet X520 Server Adapter
Client	CPU Dual Core AMD or Intel RAM: 4 GByte RAM Network: Single Gigabit Ethernet link
Switch	Alcatel-Lucent OmniSwitch 6850E

Table 2: Hardware deployment for the experiments run

test scenario a network block device is installed. The software DNBD3 [4] is used as both the block device server and client. Through this block device a 6 GByte file is shared to the clients.

---

[4] DNBD3: Distributed Network Block Device 3: http://lab.ks.uni-freiburg.de/projects/ma-d nbd3 DNBD3 is a in-house special purpose development of at the University of Freiburg and is similar to the linux kernels NBD, Network Block Device http://nbd.sourceforge.net

The server uses the Linux Kernel 3.2 and the driver version 3.6.7 for the 10 GBit/s and version 3.2.10 for the 1 GBit/s cards. The high bandwidth client uses a 3.0 kernel with driver version 3.3.8 for the 10 GBit/s interface. The 61 clients use kernel 2.6.32 and driver version 2.1.0 for the 1 GBit/s link.

3.2 First Setup: High Bandwidth-Client

In this setup, a single 10 GBit/s link is tested against a bonding of 10 x 1 GBit/s with a 10 GBit/s Client. Figure 1a shows the first setup without

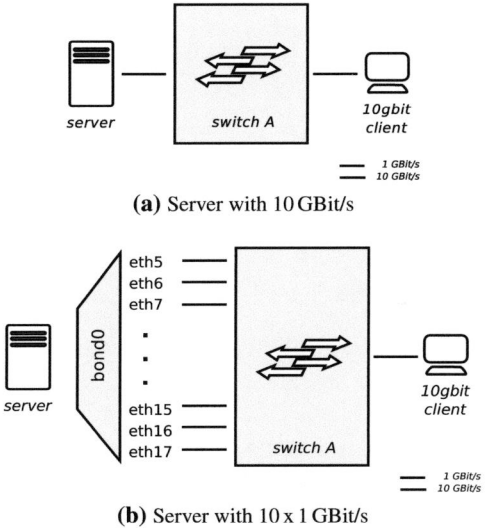

(a) Server with 10 GBit/s

(b) Server with 10 x 1 GBit/s

Figure 1: 10 GBit/s high bandwidth-client setup

bonding configured as a baseline reference setup. The server is directly connected to a switch via fibre optical cable. The client is connected to the same switch. The bonding setup is shown in figure 1b. In this experiment, the client remains untouched. The server is connected via 10 x 1 GBit/s links to the switch. In this setup, the influence of the bonding configuration on the throughput is measured for a single client.

Like described in the last section a block device server/client is used to generate traffic. The client reads the data from the block device via *dd* and writes it to */dev/null*. During the tests the resulting CPU load never exceeded the the CPU capacity of the client.

Test-Results

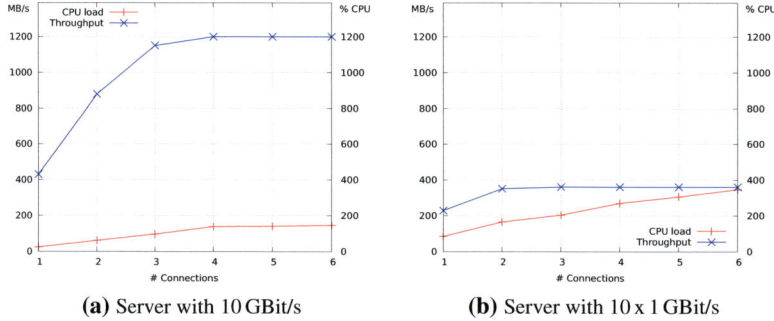

(a) Server with 10 GBit/s   (b) Server with 10 x 1 GBit/s

Figure 2: 10 GBit/s Client Results

Figure 2a shows the results of a client and server with a 10 Gbit/s interface. Since the throughput of a single connection is limited by the speed of a single CPU core. Multiple connections maximize the throughput. The speed limit is reached with the fourth connection, additional connections do not achieve a higher throughput. Below the speed limit CPU utilization increases linearly with the number of connections. Additional connections above the limit slightly increase CPU usage. In Figure 2b the results for the bonding setup are given. These results show a setup with bonding-mode 0 (balance-rr). The maximum speed limit is almost reached with the second connection and the third only increases the throughput to its maximum of

360 MByte/s. For a single client with a high bandwidth connection a bonding setup as shown gives more throughput than a single 1 GBit/s link, but compared to the 10 GBit/s setup the throughput is very limited. Also the CPU load in the bonding setup is clearly higher than the single 10 GBit/s setup. For a single connection the CPU load in the 10 GBit/s setup is 24 % compared to 84 % in the bonding setup.

3.3 Second Setup: Bonding with Large Number of Clients

A server setup with 10×1 GBit/s links is compared to a server setup with only one 10 GBit/s link. The difference between the first and second setup is the number of clients. Here we use up to 61 clients to evaluate the different bonding modes. Figure 3a shows the reference setup with a 10 GBit/s link connecting the server to the switch. Every client is connected to this switch via a single 1 GBit/s link. The bonding setup is shown in figure 3b. For the virtual bonding interface 10×1 GBit/s links are used to achieve an equivalent theoretical throughput. The traffic is aggregated by switch A and then forwarded to switch B where it is distributed to the clients. This way, the input of switch B is is equal speed and link type as the reference setup. The client setup and switch B remains the same.

Test-Results

Figure 4a shows the results for the setup with a 10 GBit/s link to the server. The number of clients ranges from 1 to 61. The Performance scales with every added client till the maximum throughput of the link to the server is reached.

In figure 4b the results of the first bonding setup are shown. In this setup, bonding mode 0 (balance-rr) is configured. The maximum throughput is 360 MB/s. Here, bonding of more than four 1 GBit/s links does not increase the throughput. The CPU load for a single client roughly doubles the load of the reference setup (55 % in figure 4b compared to 23 % in figure 4a. The results for XOR based bonding modes 2 and 4 are given in figure 4c and 4d. The maximum throughput for mode 4 is limited by the capabilities of the switch which supports up to 8 links. Throughput in XOR

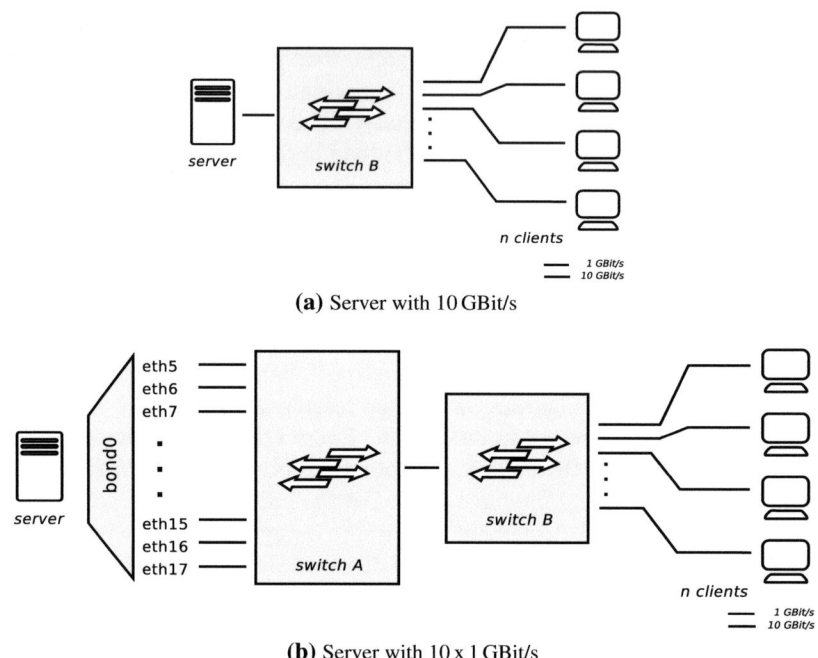

(a) Server with 10 GBit/s

(b) Server with 10 x 1 GBit/s

Figure 3: n 1 GBit/s Client Setups

based modes does not necessarily scale linearly with the number of clients. This manifests as plateau in the graph: Instead of assigning a free link to a connecting client, the throughput is divided between clients sharing one link. For example, in figure 4c the total throughput does not increase between 7 to 10 clients. One major drawback of the XOR based technique is the unfair distribution of bandwidth between the clients. Given 61 clients and bonding mode 2, one client receives 74,5 MByte/s, another client only 11,7 MByte/s. The slow client shares a single bonding slave with numerous other clients which are equally slow.

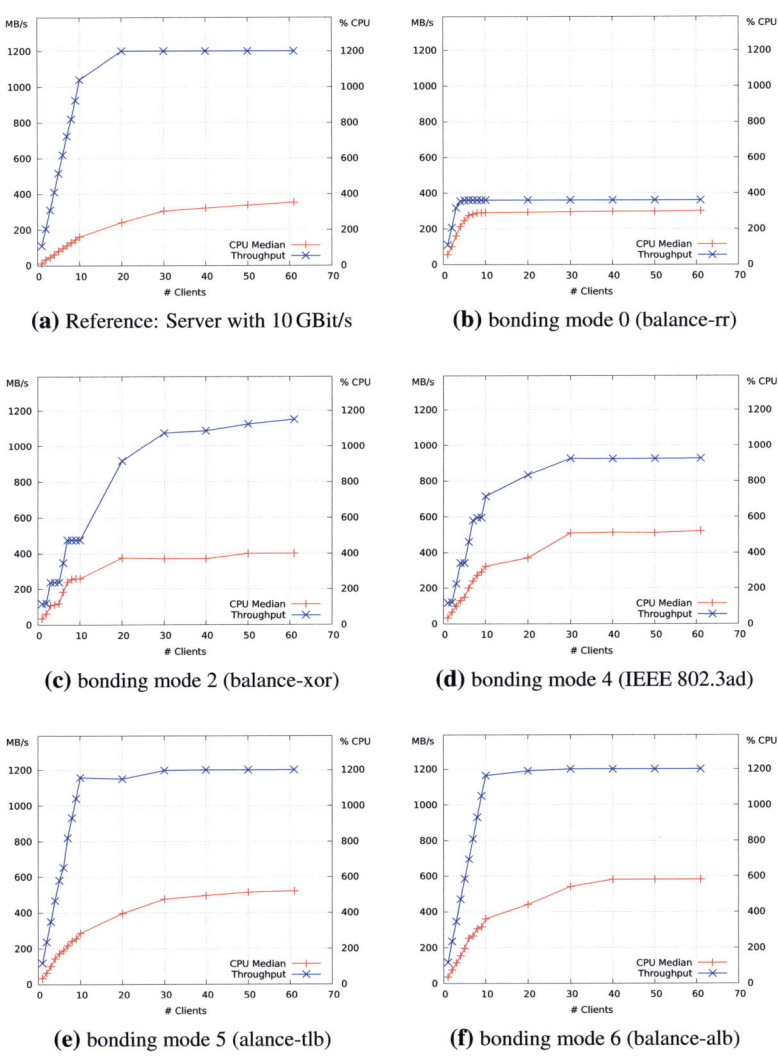

(a) Reference: Server with 10 GBit/s

(b) bonding mode 0 (balance-rr)

(c) bonding mode 2 (balance-xor)

(d) bonding mode 4 (IEEE 802.3ad)

(e) bonding mode 5 (alance-tlb)

(f) bonding mode 6 (balance-alb)

Figure 4: Results: Server with 10 x 1 GBit/s and n 1 GBit/s Client.

Bonding mode 5 and 6 scale very well as shown in figure 4e and 4f. The throughput increases linearly with the number of clients up to the maximum link speed. The throughput measurements are almost identical for both modes. The CPU load for mode 5 is slightly lower than mode 6. Both bonding modes, however, provide a significantly reduced CPU load compared to the single 10 GBit/s link.

4 Conclusion

Bonding is a sensible solution if the throughput in a high performance network only needs to be doubled or tripled. Often an update to the next level of Ethernet requires upgrading the network components, too, which to a certain degree is hereby avoidable. Especially in high performance computing the existing hardware can further be used if the network interconnections between nodes are the limiting factor. In addition to increasing bandwidth, includes a simple network link failover solution. In connection-oriented scenarios with a large number of clients a bonding of 10 x 1 Gbit/s interfaces offers a good alternative to a single 10 Gbit/s card. If bonding mode 5 or 6 is set, the throughput is identical to a single 10 Gbit/s interface. Nevertheless, if the ten server connections require the installation of a new switch, the upgrade to 10 Gbit/s is considerable. Especially for a lower number of aggregated links, there the required port is often already available on the installed network equipment. A larger number of connections requires a higher amount of energy which has to be considered as well as the expenses for the network equipment. The expenses for the server equipment used in the test setup is nearly the same for one 10 GBit/s or 12 x 1 GBit/s ports. Of course is the number of required PCIe slots for the the 10 x 1 GBit/s higher than a single 10 GBit/s card. The introduced test setup needed three PCIe x4 slots.

As bonding creates its own virtual interface, processing the Ethernet packets passing through, it adds extra load to the CPU depending on a predefined mode. For example, if setting mode 0, the additional CPU load is relatively high compared to other modes. In all other modes the additional CPU load is mensurable but is not a limiting factor.

When demands for throughput exceed a certain threshold (depending on factors such as ports, pre-existing cable and component infrastructure) switching to the next standard is inevitable. Especially with high bandwidth clients in the network, as shown in section 3.2, an upgrade is necessary; otherwise the client throughput is very limited.

A new alternative to bonding drivers called *team devices*[5] was included into the Linux kernel with the version 3.3. This feature is designed as a user-space program and is supposed to be a fast and simple implementation alternative to bonding. Currently, this alternative is still in development (04/2012).

Bibliography

[Aust2006] S. Aust, Jong-Ok Kim, P. Davis, A. Yamaguchi, and S. Obana. Evaluation of linux bonding features. In *International Conference on Communication Technology (ICCT)*, 2006.

[Brock2003] G.W. Brock. *The second information revolution.* Harvard Univ Pr, 2003.

[Hildebrand2007] Dean Hildebrand and Peter Honeyman. Direct-pnfs: scalable, transparent, and versatile access to parallel file systems. In *Proceedings of the 16th international symposium on High performance distributed computing*, HPDC '07, pages 199–208, New York, NY, USA, 2007. ACM.

[Hsueh2006] Chin-Wen Hsueh, Hsin-Hung Lin, and Guo-Chiuan Huang. Boosting ethernet using regular switching hubs. *Journal of Information Science and Engineering*, 22:721–734, 2006.

[Koibuchi2009] Michihiro Koibuchi, Tomohiro Otsuka, Hiroki Matsutani, and Hideharu Amano. An on/off link activation method for low-power ethernet in pc clusters. In *IEEE International Symposium on Parallel & Distributed Processing (IPDPS), 2009*, 2009.

---

[5] first announcement of the *team device*: http://git.kernel.org/?p=linux/kernel/git/torvalds/linux-2.6.git;a=commitdiff;h=3d249d4ca7d0ed6629a135ea1ea21c72286c0d80

[Rankin2011] Kyle Rankin. Hack and /- bond, ethernet bond. *Linux Journal*, 2011.

[Watanabe2008] T. Watanabe, M. Nakao, T. Hiroyasu, T. Otsuka, and M. Koibuchi. The impact of topoloy and link aggregation on pc cluster with ethernet. In *IEEE International Conference on Cluster Computing (Cluster2008)*, pages 280–285, 2008.